TREASURES OF
Oregon & Washington

The Columbia River Gorge

by William Faubion
and Judi Bailey

a part of the Morgan & Chase Treasure Series
www.treasuresof.com

MORGAN & CHASE PUBLISHING INC.

Morgan & Chase Publishing, Inc.
531 Parsons Drive, Medford, Oregon 97501
(888) 557-9328
www.treasuresof.com

Printed and bound by Taylor Specialty Books–Dallas TX
First edition 2008
ISBN: 978-1-933989-19-8

THE
TREASURE
SERIES

I gratefully acknowledge the contributions
of the many people involved in the writing and production of this book.
Their tireless dedication to this endeavour has been inspirational.
–Damon Neal, Publisher

The Morgan & Chase Publishing Home Team

Operations Department:
V.P. of Operations–Cindy Tilley Faubion
Travel Writer Liaison–Anne Boydston
Shipping & Receiving–Virginia Arias
Human Resources Coordinator–Heather Allen
Customer Service Relations–Elizabeth Taylor, Vikki West,
IT Engineer–Ray Ackerman
Receptionist–Samara Sharp

Production Department:
Office Manager–Sue Buda
Editor/Writer–Robyn Sutherland
House Writer–Prairie Smallwood
Proof Editor–Clarice Rodriguez
Photo Coordinator–Wendy L. Gay
Photo Editor–Mary Murdock
Graphic Design Team–C.S. Rowan, Jesse Gifford, Jacob Kristof

Administrative Department:
CFO–Emily Wilkie
Accounting Assistants–David Grundvig, Tiffany Myers
Website Designer–Molly Bermea
Website Software Developer–Ben Ford

Contributing Writers:
Mary Beth Lee, Mark Allen Deruiter, Andre' Osborne, Jeffery Clark, Mike Hartman, Pam Hamilton, Paul Cusenza,
Stephanie Dixon, Catherine Perez, Dusty Alexander, Glen Ahlquist, Jeanie Erwin, Jennifer Buckner, Karuna Glomb,
Kate Zdrojewski, Laura Young, Marek Alday, Mary Knepp, Nancy McClain, Patricia Smith, Paul Hadella,
Robert J. Benjamin, Sandy McLain, Sarah Brown, Timothy Smith, Todd Wels, Tamara Cornett

Special Recognition to:
Casey Faubion, April Higginbotham, Gregory Scott, Megan Glomb, Eric Molinsky, Marie Manson, William M. Evans, Gene Mitts

This book is dedicated to Oregon & Washington's
most amazing resource, the people who live there.

Foreword

Welcome to *Treasures of Oregon and Washington*. This book is a resource that can guide you to some of the most inviting places in Oregon and Washington, states filled with rich history and lush natural beauty. From the scenic Oregon sand dunes to the breathtaking Cascade Mountain Range, Oregon and Washington offer stunning views and phenomenal coastal vistas. While much of the natural splendor is untouched, Oregon and Washington's intelligent and pioneering people have created some of the finest galleries, shopping and cuisine to be found anywhere in the world.

While visiting Oregon and Washington, you should partake in the fascinating cultural heritage of both states. Take a moment to visit the interesting and moving events throughout both states. Everything from Native American pow wows, to pioneer fairs, to lumberjack festivals, to incredible play productions, the Pacific Northwest has it all. If you enjoy outdoor recreation Oregon and Washington are playgrounds made in Heaven. There are endless hiking trails just waiting to be explored with amazing waterfalls, profuse wildflowers, towering ferns and a vast array of gorgeous scenery. Oregon and Washington's unmatched natural features will have you reaching for your camera before you can even think of making an itinerary. It's also a place of great diversity, with an admirable collection of restaurants, art galleries, bed-and-breakfasts, and endless shopping opportunities.

In preparing *Treasures of Oregon and Washington*, we talked to literally thousands of business people about their products and their passions. We walked the Rogue Wilderness Trail as we reflected on the Pacific Northwest history. We visited community theatres and hundreds of attractions such as zoos, museums and an abundant array of breathtaking gardens. You are holding the result of our efforts in your hands. The *Treasures of Oregon and Washington* is a 285-page compilation of the best places in Oregon and Washington to eat, shop, play, explore, learn and relax. We had the privilege of seeing all the great people and places this book is about. All you have to do now is enjoy the result of our efforts.

—Cindy Tilley Faubion

Brad Owen
Lieutenant Governor

A Welcome Message from Lt. Governor Brad Owen

We who are blessed to live in Washington are extremely proud of our state. As you will see in Treasures of Washington and Oregon we have many opportunities to enjoy it. If you do not live here, perhaps this book will inspire you to visit. The wonders you will see within these pages is only a glimpse of our beautiful state.

Washington is a state of glorious mountain ranges, pristine waters, an archipelago of charming islands, awesome gorges, thousands of acres of protected wildlife preserves and recreational lands.

You may have already been up to the top of the world-famous Space Needle in Seattle or have had a chance to ride a boat across the waters of Puget Sound, Lake Chelan or on the mighty Columbia River. We are the home of snow-capped Mt. Rainier, one of the highest peaks in the country and the most heavily glaciated. And just a little to the south of Rainer is the very active Mount St. Helens, which erupted violently in 1980. The mountain continues to draw thousands of visitors every year who are anxious to see the aftermath of the volcano's destruction – and its dramatic recovery.

Beyond our natural beauty, Washington is home to some fantastic sports teams, enjoys a thriving arts and entertainment community, and offers many superb places to dine and lodge. We are also known around the world as the makers of large commercial aircraft, fine coffee and exquisite wine. Washington is also famous for its apples and potatoes and its abundant opportunities for outdoor recreation.

But most of all what you will find in Washington is a state of friendly, hospitable people who are committed to making you feel welcome. So, please, begin to learn about our great state in the book and then get out and explore our treasures in person!

With warm regards,

Brad Owen

Lt. Governor of Washington

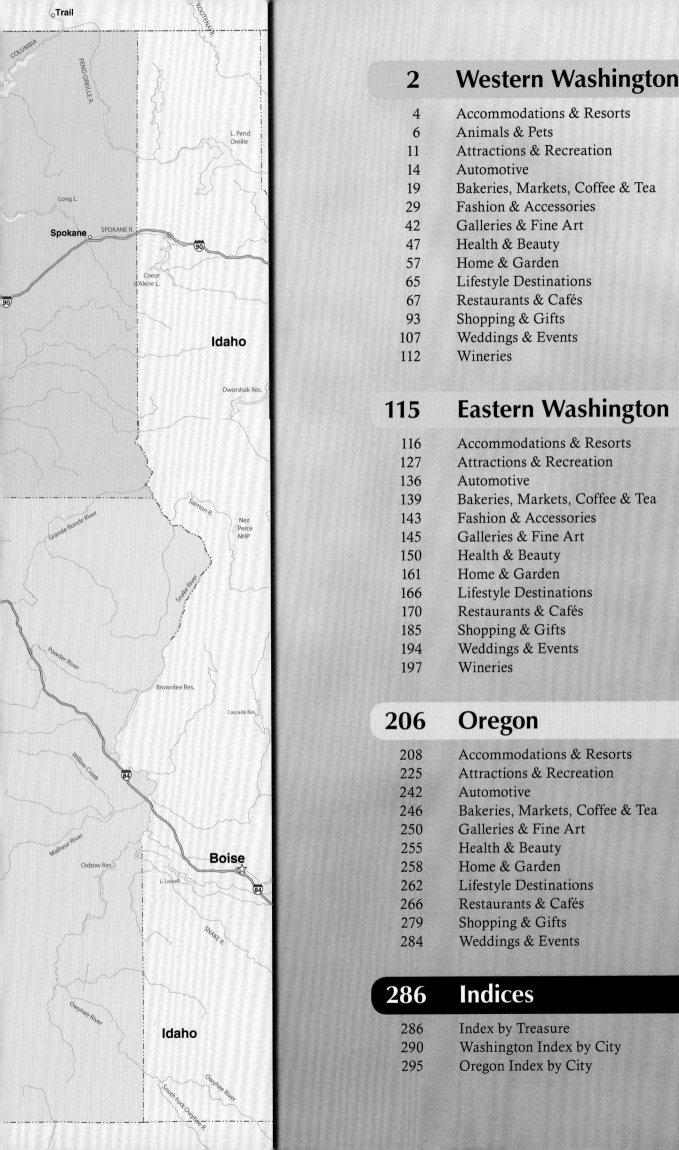

WESTERN
WASHINGTON

Top: Olympia Harbor
Left: Seattle
Right: Snoqualmie Falls
Bottom: Mount Rainier

WESTERN WASHINGTON

Accommodations
& Resorts

The Inn at El Gaucho

In Seattle, Paul Mackay is a legend in hospitality. Mackay's latest creation, the Inn at El Gaucho, has 18 junior suites and is located in the heart of Seattle's hip Belltown district. More than just a place to stay, the Inn at El Gaucho aims to wow you by anticipating your every need. Each suite comes equipped with a high-definition plasma television with digital cable, free long-distance phone service, high speed Internet and Wi-Fi. Services of the 24-hour concierge include delivering the morning paper to your door. Ask for the Full El Gaucho Treatment and the staff of the El Gaucho restaurant will serve you in your room. The Inn at El Gaucho sports a retro-swank 1950s decor with handmade Italian leather furnishings. Enjoy Pacific Coast Feather featherbeds and Anichini linens, towels and bathrobes. Choose from views of the hotel's atrium, Elliot Bay, the Olympic Mountains or the city lights of Belltown. Set the mood for a good time with your Bose Wave stereo system and enjoy beautiful Reidel stemware. If you want to crank it up a notch, check out El Gaucho's tailored packages, which offer such extras as fresh flowers, chocolate truffles, and champagne served to your room. Combining the amenities of a hotel with the service of a bed and breakfast, the Inn at El Gaucho is destined to become a Paul Mackay classic. Book your next Seattle stay at the Inn at El Gaucho for an unforgettable experience.

2505 1ˢᵗ Avenue, Seattle WA (206) 728-1133
http://inn.elgaucho.com

WESTERN WASHINGTON

Animals
& Pets

Downtown Dog Lounge

Mahatma Gandhi said, "The greatness of a nation and its moral progress can be judged by the way its animals are treated." Based on this yardstick, Seattle ranks high thanks to the Downtown Dog Lounge. At this urban dog retreat, an exceptional staff of trained professionals doggedly attends to your precious pups' every need. Downtown Dog Lounge is a salon that offers everything from overnight boarding to full service *spaw* and grooming services, including pawdicures, herbal baths and licensed massage. Dr. Clare Morris and her urban veterinary team are on staff at the Elliot Avenue facility and are just a phone call and a short trip away from the second location on Bell Street. Both facilities are equipped with live web cams so that you can check on your dog at any time. Pooch Nannies are always on hand for special-needs animals, such as seniors and those who are post-surgery. Elise Vincentini was inspired to open this posh pet salon in 2002 after her own dog fell ill. She has since created a micro-community designed to promote canine happiness. Ensure that your favorite furry companions are receiving the care they deserve when you can't be there by taking them to the Downtown Dog Lounge.

1405 Elliot Avenue W, Seattle WA
(206) 282-3647
305 Bell Street, Seattle WA
(206) 441-6160
420 E Denny Way, Seattle WA
www.downtowndoglounge.com

Theresa's No Place Like Home Pet Care LLC

Theresa's No Place Like Home Pet Care LLC is a lot like other day care services; it offers great indoor and outdoor play areas, comfortable furniture, lots of toys and loving care from a professional staff. The big difference is that this particular center is designed for our four-footed charges rather than the two-footed kind. Theresa's No Place Like Home is owned and operated by founder Theresa Kotas who left her nursing career in 1977 to take care of her ailing and beloved dog Pepper. After Pepper's death Theresa decided to devote her time to other animals in need and, along with her newest family member Raisa, a German shepherd puppy, began canvassing her neighborhood offering pet care and services to her neighbors and friends. Her business has since outgrown its original location, and services have grown to include such things as massage, pet boarding, grooming, positive reinforcement obedience training and agility training. Pets also enjoy private cottages, a secure cat apartment and other amenities. Theresa's No Place Like Home specializes in geriatric and special needs animal care, and professional staff members are always on hand to properly distribute medications. Theresa and her caring crew treat each and every pet like family and ensure that every dog and cat receives the individualized attention they need to feel safe and secure, whether you're away from them for a few hours or a few days. Treat your pet to a day out at Theresa's No Place Like Home Pet Care LLC.

14720 58th Avenue E, Puyallup WA (253) 531-2422 *www.theresaspetcare.com*

Dog Daze Natural Pet Market

For anyone who watched Erin Walker bringing home stray animals as she was growing up, it would have been obvious that the Dog Daze Natural Pet Market was the result of a natural progression. A former obedience trainer and exhibitor, rescue coordinator and 4-H leader, she understands animals' needs and behaviors and feels strongly about treating them with the same care we would ourselves. At Dog Daze Natural Pet Market, you'll find natural foods, treats and supplements to keep animals healthy, alert and physically beautiful. The selection is impressive for a non-corporate shop, including frozen raw foods for cats and dogs. You'll also find high-quality collars, beds and gifts and toys for pets and owners. Erin makes a point of supporting the small manufacturer, so you will find many specialty items at the market. There is even a backpack specially designed to carry your pet. Erin and her husband own several dogs, most of whom she rescued and fostered. She continues to work closely with Compassioned Animal Rescue and Education (CARE), offering a foster home for abandoned animals until they can be placed in permanent homes. She has over 15 years in the natural pet products industry and personally guarantees everything in the store. Treat your pet with gifts and groceries from Dog Daze Natural Pet Market.

116 S Meridian Street, Suite A, Puyallup WA (253) 445-3647
www.dogdazenaturalpet.com

Great Egret

WESTERN WASHINGTON

Attractions
& Recreation

Camano Sail

Experience Camano Island from the sea's perspective with a chartered cruise or sailing lesson provided by Captain Lawrence Baum, owner of Camano Sail. Captain Baum puts his love of the sea and his geological interest in the land together to bring clients an unusual set of insights into the sea-exposed cliffs of Camano and Whidbey Islands. He holds a hefty set of credentials in sailing and is a semi-retired geologist, capable of conducting an onboard geology class as well as sailing instruction, and day or overnight cruises aboard his Hobie 33 or J24 sailboats. Captain Baum introduced sailing to Camano Island 15 years ago and has also worked as the head sailing instructor for Seattle Parks and Recreation ever since. He is a nationally certified instructor through the U.S. Sailing Association and holds a Captain's license with sailing endorsement from the U.S. Coast Guard. Fifty years as a sailing enthusiast has sharpened his perspective, ensuring that your time with Captain Baum will be memorable. Learn to catch the wind, try a boat-based geology class, or sit back and feel the sea spray. Captain Baum's skippered charters allow you to enjoy the solitude and adventure that first captured Captain Baum's attention so many years ago. For insights on the land and exploration of the sea, set sail with Camano Sail.

51 S East Camano Drive, Camano Island WA (425) 314-9824
www.camanosail.com

Lee's Martial Arts—Puyallup

In Downtown Puyallup, you will find the fastest growing Tae Kwon Do school in the Puget Sound area. Chief Instructor, Matthew Ray, has been involved in all facets and levels of Tae Kwon Do for 26 years, and had always dreamed of having his own school. In 2004, he started Lee's Martial Arts – Puyallup, when he was finally able to devote himself full-time to his passion. This has resulted in one of the most comprehensive and elite Martial Arts schools in the state of Washington; including a premier, nationally-ranked, Olympic-style competition team. Matthew and his wife Lynell are dedicated to assisting in the development of responsible, independent, confident, self-sufficient and productive individuals through quality Tae Kwon Do instruction. They believe that the values which are taught through Tae Kwon Do can benefit all kinds of people, all ages and from all walks of life. LMAP offers high quality instruction in a professional and encouraging environment, in the largest facility, and with the most flexible class schedule that you'll find anywhere. In addition to being a Martial Arts school, LMAP regularly hosts fundraisers, philanthropic events and many extracurricular activities each year which are strictly meant to entertain. They hold several large parties for kids each year, summer barbecues, holiday events and parties, and they participate in social gatherings together such as golf, theater, potlucks, and concerts. Feel free to visit LMAP, where they value equally the Spirit, the Sport, the Discipline and the Tradition of Tae Kwon Do.

115 W. Meeker, Puyallup WA (253)770-1101
www.onetkd.net www.onetkd.org

Jae Hun Kim Tae Kwon Do Institute

The instructors at the Jae Hun Kim Tae Kwon Do Institute are busy, teaching more than 40 classes weekly at all levels. Interest in the martial art is high, and this facility meets the demand with a schedule of morning, afternoon, evening and weekend classes that can accommodate anyone. Top reasons for learning Tae Kwon Do include self-defense, physical fitness and the development of self-confidence. At the Jae Hun Kim Tae Kwon Do Institute, there is the added attraction of training with someone who learned from the recognized master who lends his name to the facility. General Choi, often called the Father of Tae Kwon Do, personally taught only a handful of instructors, and Jae Hun Kim was one of them. Grandmaster Kim opened his own school in Boston in 1974. That school now serves as the headquarters for a worldwide network of training facilities. The Seattle branch was established in 2005, and is headed by Ms. Gailyn Perrin, who was personally trained by Grandmaster Kim. She operates a premier martial arts facility, fully equipped with punching bags, weight machines and training equipment. Enroll at the Jae Hun Kim Tae Kwon Do Institute and become part of a proud martial arts tradition.

1900 N 45th Street, Seattle WA (206) 632-2535
www.tkd-seattle.com

Anytime Fitness

The owners of Anytime Fitness in Seattle envisioned a fitness club where people feel comfortable, cared for and inspired. They have succeeded with the Seattle Anytime Fitness club. Exercise has always been a part of the owners lives and they wanted to share the life-enhancing benefits of working out on a regular basis with others, yet realizing many people have problems with their schedules. The goal of Anytime Fitness is to provide top-notch service and equipment 24 hours a day, 365 days a year. From the moment you walk into the lobby, you can sense that you are joining a friendly and supportive group. Everyone is welcome regardless of their fitness level or ability; there is nothing intimidating about this gym. All of the staff members are certified, highly experienced, effective and encouraging. Anytime Fitness has state-of-the-art equipment that it maintains to the highest standards. You are sure to get the results you want in the safest, most beneficial way. Tanning is also available. Members can work out and feel secure even when staff members are not there with the 24-hour Lockmatic system. The system is interfaced with check-in software and the security system to assure safety. Staffed service hours are clearly posted, and you can rely on those postings to access service professionals. Come into Anytime Fitness in Seattle and enjoy the great neighborhood location, supportive family feel, wonderful staff and the best in equipment.

3601 Fremont Avenue N, Seattle WA (206) 545-4FIT (4348)
www.anytimefitness.com/clubs/seattlewa

WESTERN WASHINGTON

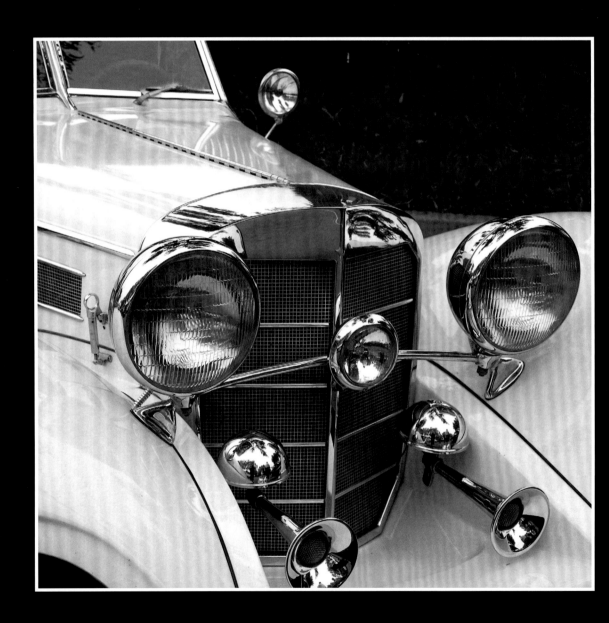

Automotive

Bowen Scarff Ford

It's one thing for a car dealership to say that its business is built on honesty and integrity. It's another thing for it to back up its claim with proof. In the case of Bowen Scarff Ford, the 12 Ford President's Awards it has won speak volumes in assuring potential car buyers of the impeccable reputation that this business enjoys. Because the President's Award is based on customer voting, it reflects the truth about how the community views a business. Only two percent of all dealers nationally have been recognized that many times. The Scarff name has been associated with Ford since the days of the Model T. Way Scarff began selling Fords in 1922 along with iron-wheel tractors. Bowen Scarff carried on the family tradition, opening his own Ford dealership in Kent in 1958. By 1964, the dealership had outgrown its corner lot and moved to its present location. Recognition as *Time* magazine's Dealer of the Year followed in 1975. Its 40th anniversary in 1998 coincided with its being named the Ford Distinguished Dealer for the 25th year in a row. You should be getting the idea by now that this is no fly-by-night enterprise, but a business that has been treating people with respect, customers and employees alike, for three generations. Mark Scarff runs the dealership these days. He and his staff invite you to come by and experience the trustworthy Bowen Scarff Ford way of servicing your automotive needs.

1157 Central Avenue N, Kent WA (253) 852-1480 *www.bowenscarff.com*

Sunset Chevrolet

A love of money might be what motivates the owners of some car dealerships, but for Jerry Yoder of Sunset Chevrolet in downtown Sumner, it's always been about his love of cars and people. He cleaned windshields at a local Texaco station when he was 12 just so he could be around those beautiful Bel Airs and Impalas that rolled up to the pumps. In 1959, he signed on with Sunset Chevrolet as a lot boy. He would have done the job just to gaze at the cars on the lot, so getting paid 75 cents an hour was icing on the cake. Jerry's partner Ray Sparling came on board in 1980, two years after the dealership completed a new building. The two began the process of buying the dealership in 1983, and finally took ownership in 1996. Today, Sunset Chev is one of the top Chevrolet dealerships in the Pacific Northwest. The secret behind its success is that staff members treat customers just as nicely after the sale as before it. Sunset Chev invites its new car owners to attend Right from the Start clinics where, in just 30 minutes, technicians teach most everything you need to know to keep your car running smoothly. At the end of the session, which typically attracts a crowd of 250, all owners in the room receive a card good for a lifetime of oil, lube and filter changes. Sunset Chev gives back to the community in part by supporting the local high school, which has named its stadium after the dealership. Who wants to be hustled when buying a car? Get spoiled instead at Sunset Chevrolet.

910 Traffic Avenue, Sumner WA (800) 201-4444
www.sunsetchev.com

Scarff Motors

At popular car dealership Scarff Motors, President Way Scarff will tell you that his business is to serve people first and to be a dealership second. Scarff Motors believes building positive relationships with customers and employees is the secret behind its 84 years of success. Way is the third generation Scarff to run the family business. In 1922, his grandfather, Wayland, founded the dealership, and Way's father, Bob, continues to serve as a consultant and chairman of the board. Way, like his father and grandfather, is active in several community organizations, including Rotary, YMCA and local museums. He takes pride in helping to improve Auburn and the lives of its residents. The old-fashioned values of the company are evident in the honesty and integrity each customer receives from the moment they walk through the door. Pre-owned vehicles here go through a certification process that assures a nearly new condition, and a complete vehicle history is available. Scarff Motors believes that happy employees who are treated well will, in turn, create happy customers. Some employees have been with the company for more than 35 years. Scarff makes it easy to find the car or truck that suits your needs with a huge selection of new Fords and Isuzus and superior pre-owned vehicles. The service department keeps your car in top condition and stays open late to accommodate busy work schedules. Come to Scarff Motors for the treatment you deserve and the vehicle of your dreams

501 Auburn Way N, Auburn WA (253) 833-1500 *www.scarff-ford.com*

Sharp & Sons USA of Yesterday

Own a piece of American automotive history or simply stroll down memory lane at Sharp & Sons USA of Yesterday, where owner and founder Walter Sharp lovingly shares his passion for collectible cars. This memorabilia-packed tribute to our wheeled heritage is housed in what used to be the largest car dealership in the nation. Built in 1948, the lot was originally home to the Mueller-Hawkins Motor Company, which was considered to be an elite place to work at the time and boasted the highest paid mechanics in the Tacoma area. Since then the facility has undergone extensive renovation and now visually recreates the automotive era that spanned the 1930s through the late 1960s. This architectural showplace comes complete with circular glass showrooms, turntables for the cars and a nostalgic essence that takes you back to the time of tail fins and bebop. In addition to a fine selection of classic cars, USA of Yesterday features an indoor re-creation of a quaint 1950s town, complete with a diner, soda fountain and drive-in movie screen. USA of Yesterday specializes in selling antique, classic and collector cars to the public. It can arrange financing, insurance and on-site appraisals. The facility is also available for private events and offers both private and public tours. Grab your best gal, set your radio to the classic station and cruise on down to Sharp & Sons USA of Yesterday.

455 St. Helens Avenue, Tacoma WA (253) 627-1052
www.collectorcar.com

Private marina on Puget Sound with Tacoma's waterfront in the distance.

WESTERN WASHINGTON

Bakeries, Markets,
Coffee & Tea

L-R: Kathleen Young, Production Manager; Pam Montgomery, Founder; JT Montgomery, CFO

Chukar Cherries

Pam and JT Montgomery, Kathleen Young and the Chukar Team are pleased to introduce to you what they feel captures the best of the Pacific Northwest in naturally dried and chocolate-covered cherry, berry and nut treats. Most days they're busy in the Chukar kitchen creating a sleighful of luscious new sweets such as Pinot Noir Chocolate Cherries and Dark Chocolate Cocoa Pecans. They create high-protein snacks like Triple Cherry Nut Mix, flavorful savories such as Peach Cherry Salsa and a wide variety of beautifully packaged, delicious gifts. All are 100 percent natural, of course. As always, their approach is pretty simple. Use only the finest ingredients. Combine them in delicious and creative ways. Listen to their customers and employees. And have fun. It's a recipe they have strictly followed, from the first dried cherries developed on the family farm to the sumptuous array of pure fruit preserves and fillings, sauces and confections, fruits and nuts. They invite you to visit Chukar Cherries throughout the year for your personal and business gifts, and promise outstanding quality, flavor and value for every season, reason and occasion. One taste and you'll know that Chukar is synonymous with the Best of Nature and Best of Chocolate. Visit the website or stop by a Chukar Retail Outlet and taste for yourself. Cherry Cheers!

320 Wine Country Road, Prosser WA
(509) 786-2055 or (800) 624-9544
www.chukar.com

All Photos © 2006 Chukar Cherry Company Inc.

Bella home and garden

Bella means beautiful, and Bella home and garden is beautiful indeed. The flagship store, featured in the *Seattle Times*, is located in historic downtown Kent, with a second location recently opened in Kent Station. This European garden market features upscale design, French-style fresh flowers and imported foods. You'll see packaged pastas, olive oils and other specialty items from Italy and France, plus local favorites. Since opening in 2003, Bella has become an integral part of the neighborhood and is a favorite among local shoppers. Owner Marci Wainhouse brings a sense of style and love of color and texture to every corner of her stores. From the earliest age, she can remember wanting to be a florist. Today, you still see that passion in every design. She often uses fresh mint, garden roses or lavender to bring a delightful fragrance to her stores. If you're looking for a perfect thank-you gift, you might choose the organic honey from Tuscany or a lavish bouquet. At Bella, Marci celebrates the idea of living a simple and beautiful life. Bella home and garden brings a distinctive style to Kent. The spirit is energetic, the inventory constantly changes and the service is wonderful. Stop by and see what's new at Bella home and garden.

212 1ˢᵗ Avenue S, Kent WA (253) 852-9945

Cupcake Royale & Vérité Coffee

When you step inside Cupcake Royale and see the light of the pastry case shining like a beacon of sweetness, beckoning your inner cupcake to come and partake of the goodness, you will feel like you're five years old again in your grandma's kitchen. Anna Beard, head baker at Cupcake Royale, attributes this virtual transportation to three things: bake 'em fresh from scratch daily, hand-frost each and every one, and do it with love. The café fills with people from all over Washington who've made the trek to treat themselves the Royale way. Cupcake fans love the homemade goodness and the welcoming atmosphere created by people who enjoy their jobs. Owner Jody Hall values quality over quantity, making sure that only the finest, all-natural ingredients make it into these tasty treats. Located inside each Cupcake Royale bakery is Vérité Coffee, specializing in hot cups of coffee crafted by baristas who care. Meaning *truth* in French, Vérité embodies the original ideals of coffeehouse culture by supporting the community and the arts, and by providing a welcoming spot for conversation and contemplation. To satisfy your sweet tooth or to sip a hot latte and discuss the latest news, art and literature, come to Cupcake Royale & Vérité Coffee.

2052 NW Market Street, Seattle WA (206) 782-9557
www.cupcakeroyale.com
www.veritecoffee.com

Espresso Vivace Roasteria

Espresso Vivace Roasteria's motto is *una bella tazza di caffe* (a beautiful cup of coffee) and that's just what you will find here. Owners Geneva Sullivan and David Schomer even found a way to show their love for coffee in the name of their company—*espresso vivace* translates loosely as great enthusiasm for coffee. One drink of this specially roasted coffee and you'll share that enthusiasm. The roasting process at Espresso Vivace is the result of 15 years worth of research on preparing espresso. That expertise has led to a book, *Espresso Coffee: Professional Techniques,* and two instructional videos that are delivered worldwide. That worldwide acclaim is reflected in a review in the *London Independent* that refers to the coffee at Espresso Vivace as "the best in the country." You'll delight in the sights, sounds and smells of the company's coffee bars, which have gorgeous inlaid art. Bring home that experience with a bag of one of Espresso Vivace's specialty blends, which can also be ordered in bulk for businesses. A beautiful cup of coffee awaits you at Espresso Vivace Roasteria.

901 E Denny Way, Seattle WA (206) 860-5869
227 Yale Avenue N, Seattle WA (206) 388-5164
www.espressovivace.com

Dilettante Mocha Café

Delectable chocolate is the family business at Dilettante Mocha Café. Owner Dana Taylor Davenport comes from a long line of confectioners—one of whom created chocolate fit for an emperor. Julius Franzen, the family's first chocolatier, served in the court of Franz Josef I of Austria in the late 1800s, before settling on the West Coast. Some of Dana's favorite memories are of learning the chocolatier's trade from his father and grandfather, along with his brother Brian, who has helped run the company since it was founded in 1977. The family tradition of excellent chocolate has carried on—as have those early recipes, kept in their original notebooks. The chocolate of royalty includes the Ephmere Truffle, with its rich bittersweet flavor, created by Dana's grandfather. The signature pastry is a *Rigó Jansci* dessert of chocolate Genoise, mousse and glaze. *Newsweek* has proclaimed that Dilettante offers the best chocolate in the world. Dilettante also offers fine coffee. The atmosphere here is as sweet and rich as the chocolate, with romance in the air. Come enjoy imperial chocolate at Dilettante Mocha Café.

416 Broadway E, Seattle WA (206) 329-6463
1603 1ST Avenue, Seattle WA (206) 728-9144
17801 Pacific Highway S, Seattle WA (206) 433-7476
411 108th Avenue NE, Bellevue WA (425) 451-8518
2300 E Cherry Street, Seattle, WA (206) 328-1955
514 Ramsay Way, Kent WA (253) 852-3555
1300 5th Avenue, Seattle WA (206) 223-1644
400 Pine Street, Seattle WA (206) 903-8595
www.dilettante.com

Chocolati Café

Seattle is getting a lot sweeter as Christian Wong continues to add new Chocolati Café locations. So far, Chocolati is at Greenwood, Greenlake and Wallingford, plus the Seattle Public Library and some bank branches. At any shop, you can take a break in the relaxing atmosphere while sipping on a gourmet chocolate-infused espresso beverage. You don't have to order coffee, though—Chocolati offers seven straight chocolate drinks, such as the Chocolate Europa, reminiscent of the dense, velvety hot chocolate served in Italy. In warm weather, consider the Chocolati Chill. Of course, you can also purchase handmade truffles and other chocolate creations. Chocolati has its own small chocolate plant and outlet store on Aurora Avenue, where it hand-makes its chocolates with the utmost attention to detail. The result is a taste like no other. Owner Christian Wong has had the entrepreneurial fire within him at least since high school. In 2000, he purchased the long-established Sutliff Candy and CBM Chocolate companies, and Chocolati was on its way. Check Chocolati's website for locations and then take a break from your busy day at a Chocolati Café.

Original location: 7810 E Greenlake Drive N, Seattle WA
(206) 527-5467
www.chocolati.com

Tacoma Union Station
Photo by Jan Tik

Brindles Marketplace

Brindles Marketplace puts the necessities and pleasures of life under one roof for Camano Island residents. Arrayed before the shopper, are quality products and a commons area for music, art fairs and other special events that draw a community together. Bonnie and Don Brindle of Brindles Market are at the heart of this enterprise. The market specializes in the best premium meat and wild-caught seafood. Family-owned ranches and farms provide much of the natural and organic meat, turkey and chicken, and meats are cut-to-order. Don's seafood expertise assures selections from Canadian rivers and pristine Alaskan waters. The Brindles also provide recipes to assure your triumphs. A visit to Great Blue Heron Wine Cellars promises that your meal will have the very best accompaniments with wine tastings every Friday, Saturday and Sunday. The market's bistro creates specialties such as fish 'n chips from halibut or cod and salmon seafood chowder with catering specialties. The attractions continue with Bonnie Z's Place for island living and special occasion women's clothing. Also included is the Gallery in the Loft for artwork by Camano Island artists which represent the finest. The Snow Goose Bookstore carries a selection of books to suite every reader; Island Custard & Gelato will keep you refreshed with frozen desserts; and Camano Island Coffee Roasters will treat you to the best shade-grown, organic coffee in the world. Karen's Kitchen will also supply all of your gift needs in and out of the kitchen. To complete the marketplace atmosphere, music by local musicians provides entertainment on Friday and Saturday nights. Next time you need it all, visit Brindles Marketplace at Camano Commons, the gateway to Camano Island.

848 N Sunrise Boulevard, Camano Island WA
(360) 722-7480 or Fax (360) 722-7481
www.brindlesmarket.com

Firehouse Coffee

Ed Robinson and his son Brian have turned Firehouse Coffee into a community sensation since they first opened the doors in 2002. Firehouse Coffee offers a select menu of oh-so-tasty pastries, muffins, soups and salads. A terrific array of specialty coffee drinks will turn your daily caffeine buzz into a sensuous reward to the taste buds. This father-and-son team has deep roots in the Ballard area. Brian, who holds a degree in international business, put himself through college by working in the coffee house industry. Upon graduation, the idea of a coffee shop, where friends and neighbors could come to charge up or unwind, seemed perfect. Cozy, family-oriented Firehouse Coffee features a separate space for moms and kids, along with a selection of kid-friendly edibles. There's also a quiet seating area that is perfect for reading a book or browsing the newspaper. Take a muffin and mocha break and connect with fellow coffee enthusiasts or sit back and lose yourself in a latte at family-friendly and always welcoming Firehouse Coffee.

2622 NW Market Street, Seattle WA (206) 784-6004

Gosanko Chocolate Art

Ronnie Roberts started Gosanko Chocolate Art because he got tired of hollow chocolate bunnies. Instead, he wanted solid gourmet chocolate that makes your mouth water. At Gosanko Chocolate Art the chocolate is really, really good and the company artistically molds this irresistible chocolate into thousands of delightful shapes. The shop is well known for its chocolate fish, but you will also find sculpted animals, flowers, delicious handcrafted truffles, confections and much, much more. Gosanko Chocolate Art uses more than 10,000 different molds and creates more everyday. The company exclusively uses the award-winning chocolate of the Guittard Chocolate Company, a firm that makes dark, milk or white chocolate using European methods and a special blend of rich handpicked cocoa beans. When you drop by the store you will find more than just wonderful chocolate, you can also enjoy ice cream served in a chocolate bowl, an espresso or pick up a gift or card. In addition to the store, Gosanko Chocolate Art runs a nationwide wholesale business. One division can create custom chocolates for companies, organizations and special occasions. This wholesale division has reproduced the logo of dozens of major corporations in chocolate. Ronnie and his wife Susan have assembled a team of employees who are huge contributors to the success and friendly atmosphere of the enterprise. Stop by Gosanko Chocolate Art's retail store when you are in Auburn and pick up a gift for someone important, perhaps for yourself.

116 A Street SE, Auburn WA (253) 333-7567 or (800) 584-7790
www.gosankochocolate.com

Island Freeze Smoothie & Nutrition Center

You may feel like you are on vacation when you walk into Island Freeze Smoothie & Nutrition Center. The décor is decidedly tropical. Palm trees and bamboo surround you as you are greeted with friendly smiles. The atmosphere is warm and relaxing, so take your time deciding on one of the more than 25 different smoothies offered. Randall Pruitt is the brainchild behind Island Freeze. He and his wife, Shannon, have been in business since 2003. Randall had almost 20 years of experience as an executive chef, and it disturbed him that he couldn't find a really great smoothie with fresh ingredients instead of artificial flavoring and syrups. He set out to create a bold-tasting smoothie that didn't just taste wonderful, but was nutritional, too. Island Freeze Smoothie uses the finest and freshest fruits and real fruit juices. You won't hear a can opener opening a single can or find a drop of syrup in the place. There's an entire menu of nutritional supplements to add to your smoothie as well, for that extra healthful punch to your wildly-good-for-you drink. Another fun thing about Island Freeze is that the staff is crazy about their customers. They're happy to make you happy, and if you don't see the smoothie you want on the menu, think up your own and they'll be glad to make it for you. Come in and fuel up in a healthful way that'll keep you going all day.

13210 Meridian Avenue E, Suite 104, Puyallup WA (253) 841-7304

WESTERN WASHINGTON

Fashion
& Accessories

LeRoy Jewelers and the Art Stop

Steph Farber tells his customers at LeRoy Jewelers and the Art Stop that jewelry is not just something to wear, but something that holds memories and meaning. Since Steph's parents, Irving and Hazel Farber, opened the family business in 1941, the shop has created many priceless memories. In 2003, Steph and his wife, Phyllis, took ownership of the family business and added the Art Stop, a contemporary gallery with a focus on ceramics. Together, they give the store a colorful mix of traditional jewelry and eclectic art. Steph's custom jewelry pieces are gorgeous. He offers customers more than 35 years of experience as a jeweler. Steph can skillfully repair precious family heirlooms, or create new ones by working closely with a customer to create an original design. Phyllis, who runs the Art Stop, values the importance of connecting the right piece to the right person, whether it is jewelry or art, and enjoys working with artists and customers. Her friendly, hands-on gallery features hand-made crafts in glass, wood, fiber and metal as well as ceramics. Phyllis and Steph are very involved in the community and are proud to be founding members of the Tacoma Downtown Merchants Group. Visit LeRoy Jewelers and the Art Stop for special pieces of jewelry and art that is full of meaning.

940 Broadway, Tacoma WA (253) 272-3377

Annette B.

When Doreen Jensen was pregnant, she refused to be seen in mundane or matronly maternity clothes. Her quest for stylish, sexy tops and tunics led nowhere, so she decided to open her own shop. The result is Annette B., a boutique in downtown Tacoma. Named after Doreen's daughter, Annette B. offers upbeat, fashionable maternity clothes and accessories for ladies in waiting. Doreen has an eye for color and comfort and wants to make sure you find the right look to show off your shape. Choose a jaunty stretch denim skirt, a cute striped knit shirt, or select a shirred knit top or beautiful tunic. The latest fashions from Olian maternity wear adorn the shop, accompanied by hip items from Maternal America, Momzee and Ripe Maternity. Added to the wardrobe choices are nursing accessories and skin care solutions for mother and child. Select from an array of luxurious Tummy Honey skin care products, including creams that address the moisture and toning needs of stretched skin. All natural Erbaviva products let you pamper yourself and your baby with lotions that employ essential oils and extracts. The perfect designer diaper bag can set off your chic look. Satisfy your craving for style and visit Annette B. to find a fashion statement that fits your form.

2712 N 21ˢᵗ Street, Suite B, Tacoma WA (253) 761-0984
www.annetteb.com

Bliss

If you're a 25 to 35-year-old trendsetter with an eye for fashion, Bliss is your place to shop in Seattle. Bliss has been the subject of editorial pieces featured in *In Style* and *Lucky* magazine. The shop carries men's and women's designer collections ranging from obscure to highly sought after labels: T bags, Nu Collective, Zooey and fcuk (French Connection). The shop emphasizes casual, fun and sexy. From the launch of Rock & Republic and True Religion to Fidelity Denim, Sling & Stones and Aristocrat, designer jeans continue to be their specialty. *Nylon* magazine declared Bliss to be one of the 100 best places in the world to purchase jeans. Expect to find more than clothes here; there is also a large collection of Voluspa candles, C-IN2 underwear for men, Tano handbags, and jewelry designed exclusively for Bliss by Gorjana. You will be greeted by professional service and a fun atmosphere when you visit. The staff is trained to fit you in the perfect pair of jeans, and the store is always changing and reinventing itself, moving forward at the speed of fashion. Let Bliss help you set the pace.

3501 Fremont Avenue N, Seattle WA (206) 632-6695
www.blissfremont.blogspot.com

Bonaventure

Owner Jeanne Carras is fulfilling her dreams with an upscale boutique catering to women. Located in the New Caldonia building, her shop is called Bonaventure. Jeanne and her staff are dedicated to helping people buy shoes, as well as handbags and hosiery. They focus on educating customers in buying the correct shoes for their feet, personal style and needs. They serve customers by measuring and fitting them in the old-fashioned shoe store style. Jeanne's commitment to quality came from her parents, but her daughter was the inspiration behind opening the store. Jeanne initially considered opening a clothing shop. She quickly realized the one thing downtown Olympia lacked was a shoe store and Bonaventure was born. The name of her boutique is very important to her, as it came from her old family Bible. Bonaventure was a saint whose name means good fortune, and he was known to spread peace in the community. Jeanne is also a peace spreader; she believes in giving back and appreciates all of those who have helped her succeed. She has strong convictions about contributing to the community and is involved in the Olympia Downtown Association, Thurston County Chamber and the Olympia Symphony Orchestra. Jeanne believes that shoes aren't just an accessory, but the most important part of a woman's wardrobe. Visit her at Bonaventure on your next trip to Olympia.

116 5th Avenue SE, Olympia WA
(360) 943-4899
www.bonaventureshoes.com

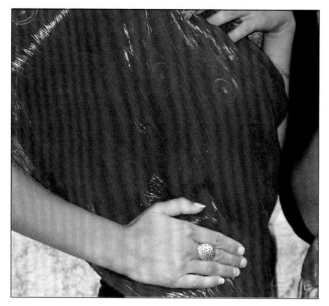

Endless Knot

Make a true fashion statement without sacrificing comfort or breaking the bank at Endless Knot, a charming shop that's packed with personality. Owner Anne Gavzer, who opened Endless Knot in 1997, is as vibrant and exciting as the clothing she sells, much of it funky fashions from Asia that run the gamut from ethnic to anime. The store is all color—scarves, hats, dresses, nightgowns, tops and more. You name it, they have it in multi-color. In addition to owning the store, Anne is also the designer for the shop's exclusive clothing line. With a focus on natural fibers, comfort and color, Endless Knot has something for women of all shapes, sizes and ages. It's best known for soft, comfortable designs that are equally suited for day or night. Endless Knot carries a wide selection of accessories that are well suited to the eclectic styles that line the stores racks. Anne displays necklaces, rings and other accoutrements that will add class, style and pizzazz to any ensemble. The shop even has rugs designed by Anne and made in Nepal. Discover your new favorite boutique for everyday living with a trip to Endless Knot.

2300 1ˢᵗ Avenue, Seattle WA (206) 448-0355

Precious Metalsmith

The true art of custom jewelry design is alive at Precious Metalsmith, located in the New Caldonia Building in the heart of Olympia's historic district. Precious Metalsmith is a full-service jewelry store with a knowledgeable and talented staff who combine Old World quality with modern craftsmanship. From the initial idea to the production, manufacturing and sale of their items, Christopher and Joanna Thornton pride themselves on creating distinctive pieces. They specialize in uniquely crafted wedding rings and appreciate being part of the special moments in the lives of their customers. They use an ancient Japanese technique called Mokume-gane that forges different contrasting metals into one—a fitting metaphor for marriage—to achieve a wood-like pattern. Many cultures are represented here, including Celtic-inspired pieces that reflect Chris and Joanna's shared Scottish ancestry. Precious Metalsmith is well-known for taking on challenging repair work. Joanna began her design career by making souvenir jewelry for tourists in her Michigan hometown. Chris uses his background in computers to design jewelry with the aid of high-tech equipment. You are invited to stop in or visit their website and see the wonderful artistry on display at Precious Metalsmith.

116 5ᵗʰ Avenue SE, Olympia WA (360) 870-4391
www.preciousmetalsmith.com

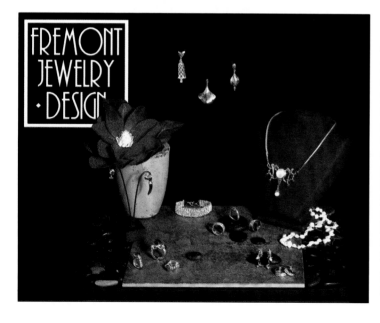

Fremont Jewelry Design

There is true passion when it comes to designing jewelry at Fremont Jewelry Design. It flows from owner Lisa Magetteri's desire to make her customers' dreams come true. She has 10 years of experience behind each custom-designed piece in her distinct selection. Design elements are drawn from customer's ideas as well as her own sense of style. Her husband, James, does all of the casting for her beautiful designs, which further adds to the personal attention to detail. Lisa loves helping the young man pick or design a beautiful and unique wedding ring for his love. The heart of the business is in understanding you and creating the perfect piece. The store also features other local artists' work, which is of the same high quality as Lisa's creations. Other services offered are jewelry and watch repairs, engraving and pearl re-stringing. Visit Fremont Jewelry Design, where happy occasions are what it's all about.

3510 Fremont Place N, Seattle WA (206) 547-5551
www.fremontjewelrydesign.com

Doria's

In the heart of downtown Olympia is Doria's, a women's boutique designed to meet all aspects of a lady's fashion needs from prom to mom. Tami Perman created her shop in 2000, naming it after her late grandmother who was a tremendous inspiration and a contributor to her flair for fashion. Like its namesake, Doria's is very involved in the community, and the staff of this fine enterprise believes it is the giving back that measures success. The staff of Doria's is well versed and experienced in assisting with a wide variety of fashion needs. While perhaps best known for their formals, this shop has everything else a woman might need, from cute tops to shoes and accessories. The energy present during the busy times of the year, such as a prom or holidays/special events, is only part of what makes this place special. It is the old-fashioned service and care that the staff shows to each and every customer that really stands out, and it is said that you won't leave Doria's without making a friend. For a chance to experience why people come all the way from Seattle, start a new friendship at this special place next time you're in Olympia.

418½ Washington Street SE, Olympia WA (360) 753-1088

Me 'n Moms

With expanded space and a hip new look, Me 'n Moms is Seattle's consignment destination for kids and moms. The walls of the airy loft space are green, orange and purple. Kids enjoy a train track play table, not to mention Tonka trucks. The aisles offer ample room for baby carriages. Consignment is a great system for mothers-to-be, who must often set aside their maternity wear while it is still in perfect condition. Brands include A Pea in the Pod, Motherhood Maternity, Japanese Weekend, In Due Time and Liz Lange. Me 'n Moms also has racks of name-brand kid's wear in all sizes, plus diaper covers, socks, cute locally made hats and underwear. The large selection of footwear includes RobEez leather shoes. Me 'n Moms is roomy enough to stock large items such as car seats, hand-painted furniture and tricycles. Cribs and high chairs are also on display. One of Puget Sound's most trusted children's stores since 1980, Me 'n Moms offers a fun, easy way to recycle and save money. The shop offers some new items as well. In addition to the original Ballard outlet on Market Street, Me 'n Moms has expanded to Issaquah and Lynnwood locations. Come to Me 'n Moms, and you too can enjoy well-dressed kids.

2821-B NW Market Street, Seattle WA (206) 781-9449
1480 NW Gilman Boulevard, Issaquah WA (425) 427-5430
19800 44th Avenue NW, Lynnwood WA (425) 778-6200

Photos by Angelic Digital Photography, 2007

Red Line

Residents of the Pacific Northwest are a whole lot closer to Southern California fashion thanks to Red Line, a shop that delivers tomorrow's fashions today, straight from Los Angeles to Tacoma. Owner Ranee Hickam started the business in 2000 as a personal shopper and eventually opened her boutique in an effort to bring sexy, casual fashion to the area. At Red Line you will find designer selections that appeal to young, hip shoppers. Dressing rooms are large and a kid friendly area offers movies and games that keep little ones occupied while Mom and Dad try on the most fashionable denim, tops and jackets around. If you're too busy to come in, Ranee offers personal shopping services that involve getting to know you, your needs and your personal tastes. She frequently shops for individual clients while in Los Angeles, selecting brands like BCBG, Stitches, True Religion, Twisted Heart, 2 B Free, 575 and Morphine Generation. When she returns to her store with treasures in hand, she will even set up a dressing room for you before you arrive, taking into account that your time is precious. Whether you're looking for clothing, bags, accessories, gifts or just the right funky shoes to go with that perfect little black dress, Ranee invites you to shop for it at Red Line.

2503 6ᵗʰ Avenue, Tacoma WA
(253) 627-9910
www.redlinestyle.com

Horseshoe

You'll find finery for fillies at Horseshoe, a quaint boutique which brings a Western chic to Seattle that's cute, not kitschy. Jill Andersen's shop has plenty of denim and T-shirts, and loads of designer wear as well. The clothing assortment is Jill's take on practical contemporary fashion. You'll find collections from unique designers such as Prairie Underground, Porridge and Kara-line. Jill sources each season to find fresh product lines, especially in the world of denim. Look forward to consistently finding stylish designer jeans that will make your derriere swing. You'll also find the best Tees by Ogle, Aude, Grassroots, C&C California and more. Seattle women will find expressions of themselves at Horseshoe—with classic vintage cowboy boots and stylish belts, country is sexy at this shop. Timeless fashions are displayed hanging on worn pitchforks and among Jill's personal collection of quirky horseshoes. The spacious fitting rooms are made from salvaged doors in their naturally distressed state. Coming from five generations of Nebraskans and Coloradoans, Jill reflects on her heritage for the design of her store and her lifelong interest in fashion to select high-quality garments and accessories. She also designs her own line of jewelry made from precious metals. You will find Jill Renae simplistic and bold necklaces, earrings, bracelets and rings suspended from old shoemaker's lasts. Visit Horseshoe; it's a little bit country and a little bit rock 'n' roll.

720 N 35th Street, Seattle WA
(206) 547-9639
www.horseshoeseattle.blogspot.com

Photo by Jennifer Gifford

Zebraclub

When you combine up-to-the-minute fashions with fresh music, you have Zebraclub, where it's as fun to work as it is to shop. Brothers Raj, Amit and Akhil Shah opened this trendsetting clothier in 1984 and continue to make shopping the ultimate recreational sport. Zebraclub is a lifestyle store that specializes in fun and fabulous fashions, footwear and accessories for men and women alike. The shop stocks the trendiest labels—Diesel jeans, Asics and Nike shoes, garments from Luxurie, Obey and Stussy, and many others. Guest DJs spin records, definitely adding to the shop's invigorating ambience. The upbeat staff of fashion professionals is always happy to help you find just the right outfit for every occasion. Zebraclub has expanded to three Puget Sound locations and one in British Columbia, a gratifying success for three brothers whose parents came to the United States from Africa. The *Seattle Times* and many trade publications have featured Zebraclub. The business is also known within the community for philanthropy, including donations and participation in charity benefits. Turn your next shopping excursion into a fashion party extraordinaire with a visit to Zebraclub.

1901 1ˢᵗ Avenue, Seattle WA (206) 448-7452
421 E Pine Street, Seattle WA (206) 325-2452
249 Bellevue Square, Bellevue WA (425) 450-5542
www.zebraclub.com

DREAM

Dream is a boutique that caters to the women who love fashion, yet want it to be timeless and elegant. Just as the seasons are sure to change, expect Dream to bring you fresh, up and coming designers and labels. Shopping at Dream is a luxurious experience, made all the better by the stylish handmade shoes, fine jewelry and potent apothecary. There is nothing here that you don't want to touch, smell and see. From the sumptuous fabrics of Majestic tees to the heady scent of True Grace candles and the handmade gold jewelry of Rebekah Brooks, you'll delight and satisfy all of your senses. Owner Neil Silverman and his partner, John Tseng, believe that every customer should be pampered and receive the utmost attention when they step through the door. Come explore Dream and you'll see how well this boutique is named.

3427 Fremont Place N, Seattle WA (206) 547-1211
www.dreamfremont.blogspot.com

Photo by Christopher Potter

Bonaci Fine Jewelers

Master Jeweler Robert Bonaci believes a good piece of jewelry is timeless and should last forever. At Bonaci Fine Jewelers, customers can find beautiful pieces that meet Robert's exacting standards. They also can have their own designs produced or have a special piece repaired or restored. The jewelry shop, which opened in 1962, offers top quality diamonds and other fine gemstones. Robert travels to Belgium twice each year to personally choose the finest cut diamonds in the world to bring back and offer to his customers. Knowledgeable staff members are happy to educate customers on the cut, color, clarity and carat weight of diamonds and how these features impact your diamond choice. Choose from a variety of precious metal settings to complement the gems. With more than 30 years of experience, Design Artist Jeff Prevette creates stunning custom pieces to the customer's specifications and has received awards for his original designs. Though the store has served customers for nearly 45 years, Bonaci Fine Jewelers continues to stay on the cutting edge of technology. The state-of-the-art design center uses lasers to repair delicate jewelry without damage to surrounding stones. Come to Bonaci Fine Jewelers for a special piece of jewelry you will treasure forever.

302 E Smith Street, Kent WA (253) 852-2222
www.bonaci.com

Dame Lola

Rebecca Dashow may own a boutique in Tacoma, but she has her eye constantly on New York. Located in Tacoma's downtown theater district, her shop is called Dame Lola, and it carries the latest fashions before they hit the rest of the Northwest. Rebecca does all of her buying in New York, where she has access to the best designers and to what's hot at this very moment. Among the many lines that you will find at Dame Lola are Rebecca Taylor, Theory and Hudson Denim. The difference between her boutique and others, says Rebecca, is that, although she has a broad price range, she specializes in dressier, harder to find items. When asked about the focus of her business, Rebecca says without hesitation that customer service is her foremost concern. She offers personalized service, private appointments and style consultations. "There's nothing better than making someone feel great," she says. "I love it when someone leaves pleased with how they look and what they've purchased." An admitted fashion nut, Rebecca loved clothes and began dressing herself at the age of two. She is proud to be carrying fashion forward in Tacoma by offering discounts for students, men and frequent shoppers. To create a little fashion envy, wear the latest from Dame Lola.

711 St. Helens Avenue, Suite 101A, Tacoma WA (253) 272-4140

Earthworks Gem Design Studio

Earthworks Gem Design Studio stands apart from everyday jewelry stores. Featuring the design inspiration of owners Steve and Donna Saint Louis, the studio has quickly established itself with discriminating jewelry lovers, those looking for one-of-a-kind, high-quality jewelry creations. At Earthworks, each showcase is a voyage of discovery, a feast for the eyes. The shop has exclusive rights to designs from more than 20 acclaimed jewelry artists—you'll find their exciting jewelry at only at Earthworks. You'll see eye-catching items that blend styles in attractive ways, such as pieces from the Reflective Images collection that combine Celtic symbols with a Santa Fe style. You'll thrill to Steve's own Etienne Ethos collection, which features ecologically responsible materials and techniques. The Trigem Designs collection by Kathe Mai also consists only of fair-trade gemstones. With 30 years of jewelry design experience, Steve and Donna opened Earthworks in a century-old brick building. They chose the First Avenue South neighborhood because of its inviting boutiques and delightful restaurants. Steve and Donna believe jewelry is a form of personal expression. They can help you bring your own sense of style to pieces you bring in for reconditioning or help you to create an all-new piece of precious art. Earthworks also provides jewelry repair, performs appraisals and buys estate jewelry and watches. If you're looking for artistic jewelry that's all your own, come to Earthworks Gem Design Studio.

235 1ˢᵗ Avenue S, Kent WA
(253) 859-4112
www.earthworksgem.com

Jewell's Premier Consignment

Owner Jewell Guaglianone employs a simple trick to please her customers. She buys only the very best new and gently used apparel for women and teens to stock her downtown Puyallup store, Jewell's Premier Consignment. From a finely-made August Silk top to a beaded evening gown worthy of a starlet, Jewell matches the items to the season with sassy capris and lightweight fabrics in early spring, wool sweaters and back-to-school corduroys in autumn. Her particular buying practices ensure that her inventory is wearable the day it is purchased. Her quaint resale shop is a boutique experience that blends high-end department store quality with affordable pricing. Jewell's is chock-full of name brand labels, ready-for-business slacks and flowing summer dresses. In addition to a wide variety of everyday wear, Jewell's stocks an ample selection of swimwear and skiwear. The store's formal gowns are popular for proms and other special occasions. The wide selection of belts, purses and shoes allows you to accessorize your new look. With prices so affordable, it is easy to experiment with the latest trend. Turn your extra clothing into cash and find quality fashions and accessories for ladies and teens at Jewell's Premier Consignment.

124 S Meridian, Puyallup WA (253) 864-7619 *www.ijayg.com*

The Tux Shop

The bridegrooms of Washington and any other man requiring formal wear can be sure their needs are topmost on the agenda of the Tux Shop. With 19 Washington locations, the Tux Shop offers the largest selection of designer tuxedos and accessories in the Northwest.

With 20,000 tuxedos in its inventory, this formal wear shop can fit you and your party in any size and style of tuxedo you could want. Rent or purchase what you need right down to the cuff links and choose from such prestigious designer labels as Calvin Klein, Joseph Abboud and Ralph Lauren. Look also for Perry Ellis, Liz Claiborne and Oscar de la Renta designs. Owner Ed Honeycutt has been working with high fashion formal wear since the 1970s and brings plenty of savvy to his operation. You can count on a staff of trained specialists to assist you with your purchase. They understand when a cutaway coat is acceptable and when a white dinner jacket is best. They can tell you how to store your tuxedo after the wedding and provide a checklist of the groom's responsibilities on the wedding day. The Tux Shop also carries wedding invitations, gifts for the bridal party and favors for the guests. An informative website helps guys get their look and their etiquette straight. For outstanding fit and choice in formal wear, visit the Tux Shop.

3827 S Meridian, Puyallup WA (253) 770-2761 *www.thetuxshops.com*

Seattle, Washington

DeCaterina's Fine Jewelry

If you haven't been to DeCaterina's, then it's too early to conclude that you just can't afford fine jewelry. Bonnie Boyer and her daughter, Casey McKee, agree with you that most jewelry seems overpriced. That's why they pledged to try a different approach when they took over DeCaterina's Fine Jewelry in 2004. The store has been around since 1949, and the current owners are proud to continue the legacy of its good name, though with their own spin. Specializing in custom designs, designer settings and loose gemstones, Bonnie and Casey provide the community with fine quality pieces of jewelry at affordable prices. Services include appraisals, repairs and pearl restringing. You will never be hassled into buying at DeCaterina's, because the product and prices, say Bonnie and Casey, speak for themselves. They understand that because jewelry makes such a personal statement, folks often need to go home and sleep on it before making a decision. Their no-pressure style is essential to preserving the customer relationships that they inherited in 2004 and the new ones that they have forged since then. For diamonds and precious stones that won't give you sticker shock, try DeCaterina's Fine Jewelry in downtown Sumner.

1202 Main Street, Suite 101, Sumner WA
(253) 826-9211
www.decaterinasfinejewelry.com

WESTERN WASHINGTON

Galleries
& Fine Art

Jelita Arts

Jelita translates as "beautiful" in Indonesian, and that's an apt description of the gorgeous antique pieces you'll find at Jelita Arts. Owner Julia Clauset was born in Indonesia and grew up in Asia. In her childhood, she worked in her grandfather's store and inherited her grandmother's love and appreciation for antiques. She also gained skills as an artist, hand-painting art nouveau-inspired designs on jackets, vests, porcelain, tiles and glass. In 2005, Julia created an origami paper crane sculpture with 1059 cranes, which she donated to the Whatcom County Peace and Justice Center. At her store, Julia's art mixes with a splendid variety of authentic Asian art and antiques. You'll see intricate Chinese reverse paintings, painted in reverse on the back of glass to allow light to shine through. Beautiful jade flowers bloom eternally here. The Chinese are renowned for their beautiful vases, and Jelita Arts features a large selection of the delicate porcelain pieces. You'll also find a variety of Western antiques and vintage items, including fiber and glass art, masks, ceramics, photographs and paintings. Julia's goal is to make customers more aware of the various kinds of art that surround them. If you're in the market for Asian or Western art and antiques, visit Jelita Arts.

1139 11ᵗʰ Street, Bellingham WA
(360) 756-1949
www.jelita-arts.com

Designs by Bonnie
—Bonnie Burns Glass Blowing Studio & Gallery

It started with a simple good-luck-token Bonnie made for her son who was going off to war in the Middle East. Now Bonnie Burns is known throughout the armed forces and even in the White House as the Heart Lady. The reason is the glass Hearts of Hope she makes for the troops. Bonnie displays these with her other glass arts works at her studio and gallery, Designs by Bonnie, which is a registered trademark. A Tacoma fixture since 1982, the gallery features such diverse works as custom lighting, jewelry, vases and bowls. Folks drop by to browse the pretty things and to watch Bonnie at work. You can even take a class at Designs by Bonnie to learn the art of glassblowing. Designs by Bonnie is a family-owned and operated business, and Bonnie's three sons, Sean, James and Anthony, are all actively involved. Support an inspired glass artist with a visit to Designs by Bonnie.

1334 S Fawcett Avenue, Tacoma WA
(253) 627-6556
www.bonnieburnsglass.com

Frame Up Studios

Frame Up Studios can do the job. Regardless of the dimensions, shape or depth of the item you want to frame, Frame Up Studios delivers topnotch work and beautiful designs. Owners Gail and Robert Bradley consider framing to be an art, and the creative designs that this studio has delivered over the past 20 years are the proof of this. Frame Up's staff members are specialists who put their knowledge and artistic skills in photography, art history and the fine arts to work for each client. In the shop's comfortable design studio, the staff works with you to learn about your piece and its significance. They'll discuss preservation techniques with you and ask about your home décor to ensure the frame fits in. In addition to framing services, the studio offers a variety of creative gift items and home accents from handmade Peruvian pots and funky brass bookends to fine greeting cards, stationery product and beautiful handmade papers. Gail and Robert actively support local artists and student groups and regularly contribute to the community. On the first Friday evening of each month, the studio participates in Fremont's First Friday Art Walk by hosting an artist reception. Frame Up also carries an ongoing collection of limited-edition prints by regional artists. Come to Frame Up Studios to find creative solutions, from custom framing to gift giving.

3515 Fremont Avenue N, Seattle WA (206) 547-4657
www.frameupstudios.com

Glasshouse Studio

Glasshouse Studio, the oldest glass-making studio and gallery in Seattle, was founded in 1972 at the beginning of what became known as the Northwest Glass Movement. Initially located in the basement of the Grand Central Arcade Building, the studio later moved to its present location on historic Pioneer Square. When the original owner retired in 1998, three of its artists, Chris Sternberg-Powidzki, Don Inthapany and Craig Maxwell, partnered to take on the business. The artists bring a wide variety of backgrounds and philosophies to their work. Their commitment to their craft and each other has created an opportunity to design and produce one-of-a-kind and limited production editions of fine handmade glass. The artwork—chandeliers, lamps, jewelry, vases and many other glass creations—ranges in price from $100 to $1500, and is sold and shipped to galleries nationwide. The Glasshouse Studio is a must-see for tourists. The facility can accommodate groups of up to 40 people, and is a frequent destination for elementary school field trips. When you're in Seattle, come to the Glasshouse Studio and watch the artists at work. Something beautiful might catch your eye that you'll want to buy to remember your visit.

311 Occidental Avenue S, Seattle WA (206) 682-9939
www.glasshouse-studio.com

Edge of Glass Gallery

James Curtis uses the shifting beauty of blown glass to explore the concept of change. He is the artist-in-residence at Edge of Glass Gallery in Fremont, where his work as a glass artist and poet combines to gently challenge others. James began exploring glass as a medium for his artistic voices in 1997. He and his select staff are known for their custom designs and for working closely with clients to discover their personal tastes and color preferences. Their creations include functional lighting and large, glass wall displays made up of dozens of blown-glass platters. Visitors can sometimes see these artists at work in the hotshop. James offers one-on-one instruction to anyone interested in learning and growing. He wants everyone to have access to good art and donates dozens of pieces each year to benefit schools and charities. His work appears in public and private collections in several states and in his Northeast Asia homeland. The gallery displays many types of glass art created by Pacific Northwest glass artists. Shake up your thinking with a visit to Edge of Glass Gallery.

513 N 36th Street, Suite H, Seattle WA (206) 632-7807
www.edgeofglass.com

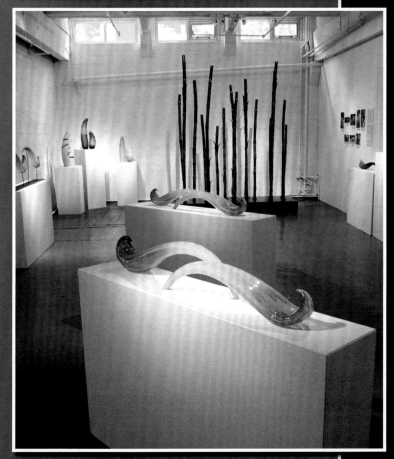

Canlis Glass

Jean-Pierre Canlis pushes the boundaries of glass art by translating forms found in nature into clean-lined glass artwork. J.P.'s wife, Leigh, uses her eye for design and business savvy to bring J.P.'s work to the public's attention. This dynamic pair forms Canlis Glass, a hip Denny Triangle gallery that attracts collectors and art lovers. J.P.'s organic, deceptively simple forms include blown glass pieces and sculpted cold work. He works with residential and commercial clients to create custom three-dimensional installations, such as a 10-foot tall bamboo installation at a Seattle jewelry store. His Ocean series shows an insight into the action of water gained from a childhood spent in Hawaii. In fact, J.P. and Leigh opened Canlis Glass Gallery in 2005 following four years of working in Hawaii. J.P. first met Leigh in 1997 while they were both working at Dale Chihuly's studio in Seattle. Leigh credits Chihuly with inspiring them to sell J.P.'s art from their own studio, a concept that has led to great success and community involvement. The couple passes the concept on to younger artists, teaching them how to run profitable businesses. Canlis Glass has been featured in *USA Today, Seattle Homes and Lifestyles* and on the evening news. The *Puget Sound Business Journal* named Leigh one of the 40 Under 40, and *Seattle Magazine* called the "golden couple" Trendsetters for 2006. Prepare for a visual thrill with a visit to Canlis Glass.

3131 Western Avenue, Suite 329, Seattle WA
(206) 282-4428 *www.canlisglass.com*

Oasis Art Gallery

Do you feel that a home is complete only when it has a few original works of art in it? If so, then you possess what might be called an Italian outlook. Alex and Jeannie Strazzanti, owners of Oasis Art Gallery, possess one, too. They were inspired by their Italian heritage to open their gallery, where you can find everything from tapestries and glass art to watercolors and furniture on display. Alex, a self-

taught photographer with a gift for the art, always keeps a large selection of photography on hand. Oasis Art Gallery represents about 50 artists, some local and some from as far away as Germany, Russia and Nepal. It has the bright, open feel of a tastefully adorned living room, complete with large, cushioned chairs for lounging. Holding free art workshops for the disabled is one way that the owners encourage others to get involved in the arts. They also donate generously to neighborhood auctions and local schools. Alex and Jeannie note that, in Italy, people live with art all around them, therefore they encourage their customers to develop an eye for art and to express their sensibility in their own homes. Find art for everyday life at this beautiful gallery in the Wallingford neighborhood.

3644 Wallingford Avenue N, Seattle WA
(206) 547-5177 or (888) 35-OASIS (356-2747)
www.oasisinseattle.com

Bergen Reflections
Photograph © Laurie O'Donnell

Lucas Art & Frame

Mt. Rainier looms grandly in many of the paintings on display at Lucas Art & Frame. Owner Karen Lucas enjoys a magnificent view of the mountain from her place, which showcases the work of about 30 Northwest artists. The gallery has been around since 1979,

founded by Paul Chalk, a palette knife artist acclaimed for his depictions of Rainier. Karen is known mainly for her marinescapes, which are featured in many galleries, though just how deeply she, too, has fallen under the spell of Rainier can be seen her painting, *Mountain Retreat.* Alongside works of realism, you are likely to find the gentle surrealistic visions of Tim Wistrom. Tim's orcas swim past Seattle's Space Needle; they come up for air in a martini glass and generally show up in the oddest places. Also known as the Gallery on the Hill, Lucas Art & Frame serves as a classroom for art instruction. People come from all over Washington and from as far away as Oregon to sharpen their skills in oils, acrylics and many other mediums. Karen brings in guest instructors from throughout the United States. In her own classes, she guides students through the process of depicting such specific subjects as pansies or a river canyon. View the work of Northwest artists, and enjoy the spectacular view outside, at Lucas Art & Frame.

25201 Meridian Avenue E, Graham WA
(253) 847-0858 *www.lucasart.net*

Mt. Rainier
Photo by Jennifer Gifford

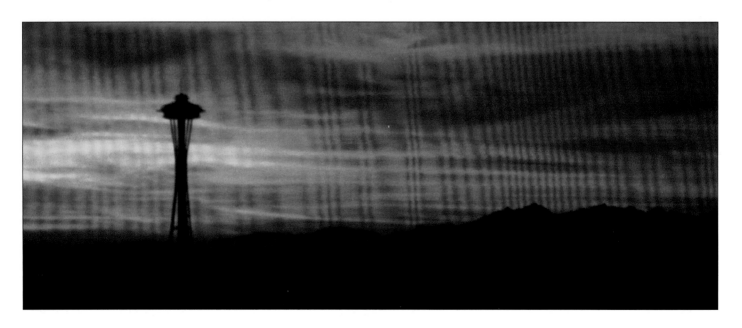

WESTERN WASHINGTON

Health
& Beauty

Revitalize! Health Spa & Organic Store
—Modalities from Around the World

Whether you're looking to balance your mind, body or spirit, Revitalize! Health Spa & Organic Store has what you need. This shop in the recharged historical district of downtown Kennewick is a center for modalities from around the world. Customers enjoy shopping from one of the widest selections of gluten-free and sugar-free products around. To help you with your health concerns, browse through a diverse number of self-help books on topics that range from cooking, diet and wellbeing to taking control of and managing your finances. Owner Erickson is a living testament to the effectiveness of the therapies and techniques offered at her shop. Before opening the spa, Erickson, a 14-year mail carrier, faced debilitating asthma. Her use of healing modalities from across the globe has transformed her life and she now prides herself on helping others to discover the techniques that helped her. People from around the world and professionals from many fields have come to Erickson and her knowledgeable staff for help. Revitalize offers a variety of therapeutic options. While listening to tranquil music in the Infrared Sauna, you can lose weight, burning up to 900 calories in a 30 minute session. Experience a reduction of cellulite, muscle soreness and pain relief. Another favorite is the Australian Energy Spa, a detoxifying foot bath. The Solo System uses far infrared, the healing rays from the sun, for everything from skin conditions and stiff joints to strengthening cardiovascular. Revitalize yourself with a trip to Revitalize! Health Spa & Organic Store.

Photos By Barrett Brown Photograhy

Photos By Barrett Brown Photograhy

Revitalize! Health Spa & Organic Store boasts a number of licensed and certified biofeedback therapists and specialists. Having such, it is well-suited to sell to health professionals, offer therapy and provide training on a number of bioenergetic and biofeedback devices from around the world. Biofeedback refers to techniques in which people receive feedback on the state of their body, allowing them to alter their own bodily state through conscious or unconscious responses. Two biofeedback systems offered are the LIFE system and the EPFX/QXCI/SCIO. These noninvasive devices screen for organ weaknesses and check toxicity, pH balance and hormone imbalances. They are useful in leveling out stress and releasing emotional traumas on a cellular level. Erickson has been awarded exclusivity in sales of the Electro Interstitial Scanner (EIS) in the state of Washington. The EIS is capable of scanning the body for 69 parameters in two minutes, with 87-percent repeatable accuracy. Revitalize's top seller, the SCENAR, a therapeutic device small enough to fit in your pocket, generates electrical signals that feed information back to the brain and body. Therapy with the SCENAR can greatly reduce or even eliminate pain in just minutes. Revitalize! has a hard time keeping this product in stock. If you or someone you know is in need of relief, come in and visit the Little Shop with Big Variety. Revitalize your health and your life by experiencing this unique gem in Washington's treasures.

311 W Kennewick Avenue, Kennewick WA
(509) 586-6574
www.BiofeedbackPlus1.com

Studio 271

Surround yourself with vivacious professional service providers and a tranquil atmosphere at Studio 271 on Camano Island. The salon and spa, bought by Shoaleh Monadjemi in 2004, has been in the business of relaxing and beautifying patrons since 1990. Smooth your skin with microdermabrasion or one of the luxurious facials, such as the one hour and 15 minute Signature Facial, which offers deep cleansing, exfoliation and a treatment mask along with a relaxing massage of the face, neck, shoulders and scalp. A facial just for men is every woman's favorite, because it improves the texture of masculine skin. Alleviate your aches and pains with a massage that combines relaxing Swedish massage techniques with deep tissue work, or feel muscle tension melt away with the application of hot stones as part of the massage therapy. Studio 271 can prepare you for everyday beauty and special occasions with full hair services, manicures and pedicures. For times when only the most special care will suffice, like weddings and proms, Studio 271 offers makeup applications and fancy updos. Take in the calm, ask for the latest trend, and feel ever so much at home with high-end salon and spa services from Studio 271.

1143 E SR 532, Camano Island WA
(360) 629-3555

Photo by Jennifer Gifford

Cristy Carner Salon & Spa

When Cristy Padilla opened Cristy Carner Salon & Spa in 2000, she had already amassed a lifetime of beauty experience. Cristy started styling friends' hair in the third grade—and started charging for it in the seventh. Pampering people has always been a passion for Cristy, and she's surrounded herself with a staff that feels the same way. It's that dedication to the needs of the customer that sets this spa apart, Cristy believes. Your sensory experience begins the minute you enter the spa, slip into a plush white robe and sink into one of the leather chairs in the waiting room. Dim candlelight flickers, soothing music plays and relaxing essential oils waft subtly in the air. Put your body in the hands of a highly trained masseur or polish it with salt and sugar scrubs. The manicure and pedicure rooms are completely private. Facials are available for men and even for your back. Cristy and her salon staff can transform your hair in any way you please, cutting, shaping and styling it to compliment your unique features. You'll also find an array of premium makeup, skin care and hair care products to choose from. Come to Cristy Carner Salon & Spa and let the staff tend to the comfort and beauty of your mind, body and spirit.

100 NW 36th Street, Seattle WA
(206) 548-8224
www.cristycarnersalon.com

Ballard Health Club

Fitness. Health. Exercise. Ballard Health Club makes sure that you enjoy yourself as you pursue these goals. All members receive the personal attention they deserve, whether they're just starting out or making a final push for top-level fitness. When you join, you can meet a personal trainer who designs an individual program suited to your specific needs, and who helps you stay on track. If you're not ready to commit to a full lifestyle change, Ballard offers a complimentary day to check out the club to see if it's for you—the staff is confident you'll find it to your liking. They focus on making each member feel comfortable and important, so whether you're attending a relaxing yoga class, an invigorating step class, working with their full range of cardio and strength equipment or attending any of the 45 available classes, you'll feel right at home. All classes and periodic fitness training are included in the cost of membership. Ballard Health Club means individualized attention, just what you need to get in shape. The club is located in the Ballard Building in the heart of the historic downtown Ballard neighborhood. Pay the friendly staffers a visit and see what makes Ballard Health Club stand out from the crowd.

2208 NW Market Street, Seattle WA
(206) 706-4882 *www.ballardhealthclub.com*

1st Choice Acupuncture and Herbal Medicine

The moment you step into 1st Choice Acupuncture and Herbal Medicine clinic, you understand its name. Someone hands you a steaming cup of herbal tea and as you relax in the waiting room with its elegant décor, the bamboo flooring, greenery and gentle sound of the fountain envelope you in tranquility. At 1st Choice Acupuncture, you are what they care about and Howie Sun, nationally board certified and licensed acupuncturist and Traditional Chinese Medicine (TCM) practitioner, together with his entire staff, is dedicated to helping you achieve and maintain holistic personal wellness at the highest level. TCM is a means of healing that has been in use for

over 5,000 years. At 1st Choice, every treatment plan is tailored specifically for the individual and part of the clinic's unique approach is to provide lifestyle counseling and support for each patient's treatment plan. TCM encompasses systematic medicines and techniques that include acupuncture, oriental massage and herbal medicine. Howie is a part of the third generation of healers in his family and has earned a BS degree in holistic science, a second BS in biochemistry, a third BS in molecular cellular developmental biology and a MS degree in oriental medicine. With this unique background, Howie is able to fuse the best of both Eastern and Western traditions of medicine with his own dedication and passion for healing. Begin your journey to radiant health in the compassionate and caring world of 1st Choice Acupuncture & Herbal Medicine.

13401 Bel-Red Road, Suite A-12, Bellevue WA
(425) 392-8881 *www.1stchoiceacupuncture.com*

Beaux Cheveaux

There's a salon in downtown Puyallup with a snappy French name run by a lady who knows all the latest hair styles, and women aren't lining up to sit in her chair. They can't, because this one is just for guys. Rhonda Kaech-DeLong owns Beaux Cheveaux, which is French for *beautiful hair*. She thinks of herself as being more upscale than your typical barber and says that her place is where men who are tired of the $8 haircut can come for some real style, personal care and great conversation. We might add that, for you girls, it's a great place to send your boyfriend or husband if you're tired of his $8 haircut. Give him a gift certificate and see if he gets the message. Even without your girlfriends' help, you guys could probably come up with a whole list of occasions, such as a job interview or your best friend's wedding, that would require you to look your best. Of course, there's your wedding, too. Maybe you would just like to indulge yourself. Rhonda offers coloring in addition to haircuts and styling. For hair sharp enough for the streets of Paris, go to Beaux Cheveaux.

504 2ⁿᵈ Avenue NW, Puyallup WA
(253) 848-3249

Angela & Co. Salon

Located in Tacoma's renowned 6th Avenue business district, Angela & Company Salon is a full-service facility, where customers can obtain a long list of desired beauty services under one roof. Owner Angela Glagavs jumped at the chance to acquire this property when it became available, because it allowed her and several friends who each operate their own beauty businesses to come together in one location. Angela's salon is a multifaceted upbeat salon with charismatic overtones and a welcoming atmosphere. She specializes in hair extensions and hairstyling. Patricia Huesers is a licensed aesthetician who provides waxing and makeup services. Michelle Stanzel offers airbrush tanning services. Andrea Jager specializes in hair extensions, colors and cuts. Regina Steed applies permanent cosmetics and eyelash extensions. Irish McCutchan, the receptionist, is also a makeup artist who works with mineral makeup applications. The comprehensive range of services is so popular that customers travel from all over the state of Washington to have their beauty needs met here. For a salon that concentrates on beauty services for all of your self indulgences, visit Angela & Company Salon.

3401 6th Avenue, Suite H, Tacoma WA
(253) 756-1952

Mother Nature's Natural Health Store

Mother Nature's Natural Health Store is the place in Seattle for expert nutrition advice, friendly and caring service, top-quality supplements and a fun and welcoming atmosphere. It's been serving Queen Anne, Uptown, Magnolia and Belltown neighborhoods since 1979, and prides itself on its vast knowledge in nutrition and healthy healing. It is here to provide you with the finest quality nutritional supplements, body care products, healthy homemade deli fare and health information in a relaxed, comfortable, clean and open environment. If you prefer to shop locally in a place where the people truly care about your health, then stop in and discover what makes Mother Nature's different.

516 1st Avenue N, Queen Anne, Seattle WA
(206) 284-4422
www.mothernaturesstore.com

Emerald City Smoothie, Capital Hill

Running on empty? Head to Emerald City Smoothie on Capital Hill, where flavor-filled recipes provide meal-in-a-cup goodness that energizes and satisfies. Blended with fresh fruit, pure juice and quality supplements, these high protein drinks fill you up, not out. Lose weight or buff up with a hand-made delight. One sip and you'll taste why smoothies serve as a meal substitute or anytime snack. Naturally high in vitamins and minerals, Emerald City smoothies boost your immune system and escalate your feeling of well-being. You can choose no-fat and low sugar selections. Try a tangy Guava Sunrise, a combo of fresh guava, berries, orange juice and energy mix. The low-calorie Apple Andie is a blend of apples, bananas, nonfat milk and protein supplements. All items can be made dairy-free by substituting soy milk or whey. Since 2002, co-owners Sam Harris and Chris Matty have served as Seattle's ambassadors of good health. Their mission is to provide you with energy boosting drinks to maintain physical strength, stamina and mental sharpness throughout your day. Their staff are trained to help you select a blend that best suits your lifestyle. Stop by Emerald City Smoothie on Capital Hill and see why their delicious concoctions are good to the last drop.

428 Broadway E, Seattle WA (206) 322-1994
www.emeraldcitysmoothie.com

Images Hair Design & Skin Care

Patricia Miller and her daughter, Amber Franklin, offer clinical skincare and hair design at Images Hair Design & Skin Care. "Your skin and hair are the only things you always wear," says Patricia, who has 30 years of experience, holds a CIDESCO certificate and is a licensed instructor. The duo opened Images Hair Design & Skin Care in 2001 and are committed to educating clients. Services include hair styling and dermo-corrective clinical skin treatments, many of which feature G.M. Collin products. Body treatments include Bioterra products, therapeutic massage and education on bio-identical hormone therapies. Professional makeup application services use Colorescience mineral makeup, which is free of perfumes, dyes and synthetic preservatives. Ask about available packages and browse the product selection, which includes Aromababy organic baby solutions, vegan, sulfate-free hair care from PureOlogy and Mead Labs bio-identical hormone replacement products and tests. Ask Patricia about body and skincare classes and continuing education classes. The treatment rooms are luxurious, and the courtyard is relaxing and can be rented for a special event. For attentive service in a serene environment, visit Images Hair Design & Skin Care.

1528 8th Street NE, Auburn WA (253) 939-2517
www.imageshairdesign.com

Red

There are many excellent salons and spas in this world, but you'd be hard-pressed to name a place that offers the spectacular upscale services you'll find at Red. Clients know that this elegant salon, spa and lounge sets trends rather than following them. Red has been featured in more than 20 top fashion magazines, including *In Style* and *Allure*. Stop by for hair styling, coloring and cuts, skin and nail care, as well as waxing, massage and body treatments. Red has been awarded Best Of for its amazing facials and provides incredible make-up services for both weddings and daily wear. Key to the Red experience, however, is its Spotlight service, in which a team of artists gather round to help you make the most of what you've got. Spotlight's specialists can focus on brow design, personal styling, hair color, skin health, make-up, wardrobe and other topics. Red's specialty services include customized wardrobe tutoring, shopping trips and even closet-clean ups. Services are not even limited to clients in metro Seattle. Red is prepared to fly a consultant anywhere in the country to assist you with wardrobe and other services. Red also loves to host spa, wedding and special event parties. Angela Bern Castagnola traveled the world visiting first-class salons and spas before she settled down to create Red. Her vision has come to glorious fruition. Experience the ultimate in pampering and personal care at Red.

1925 3ʳᵈ Avenue, Seattle WA
(206) 256-6214
www.redseattle.net

Salon & Spa Sabre

Sabre Sathern, owner and founder of Salon & Spa Sabre, has been cultivating her love affair with hair and all things concerned with beauty since the ninth grade, when she began cutting her family's hair. She has long since completed her initial education and continues her training annually, along with her employees, in order to stay on top of new trends and techniques. In 2005, after more than 15 years of honing her skills, Sabre opened Salon & Spa Sabre, which offers a complete range of rejuvenating spa treatments along with a full selection of salon services, such as hair cuts, color treatments, hair straightening and perms. In the spa you can enjoy back treatments, facials and body waxing, as well as receive permanent makeup, eyelash extensions, manicures and pedicures. Salon & Spa Sabre offers a complete line of beauty supplies, including the skin and hair care products used in-house. Sabre works closely with her staff and listens to her clients' feedback in an effort to grow and offer the services that are most beneficial for her customers. The facility's intimate atmosphere is conducive to setting a slower pace, relaxing and truly enjoying a pampering session. Take time out for a well-deserved break at Salon & Spa Sabre.

6017 Parker Road E, Sumner WA
(253) 863-6316

Sooji's Day Spa

When you come to Sooji's Day Spa in Tacoma, you will discover a soothing and healing experience for your mind and body. Nurturing, educated staff has one thing on their minds—your total well-being. Owner Sooji Hartzell believes that her staff's commitment to treating body and soul is a vital component to your overall good health and balance. This will give your self-esteem a healthy and positive boost. Sooji, a skin care specialist, along with Shelia N. Gomillion and Adrienne Locke, both licensed massage practitioners, want to heal your body by nurturing it from the inside out, while providing a peaceful environment for you to relax and feel pampered. Men and women take comfort here in luxurious treatments like Reiki energy healing, facials and body wraps. Stress and negativity will melt away as you enjoy Swedish or deep tissue massage or schedule an appointment for their unique sugaring hair removal. Other options include hot stone and Shiatsu massage, peeling treatments and facials. Sooji has created a positive place for practitioners to care for their clients and achieve holistic goals. Treat yourself to an afternoon at Sooji's Day Spa and unearth your spirit again.

3021 6th Avenue, Tacoma WA
(253) 404-0024
www.soojisdayspa.com

Photo by Jennifer Gifford

WESTERN WASHINGTON

Home
& Garden

Chair & Trellis

You can buy a singular gift of lasting value or get help with the design of an entire home at Chair & Trellis. Owners Harvey Rook and Mark Mandelin guarantee that a gift from their store will never be regifted. Underlying their confidence is a collection of finds worth treasuring for a lifetime. The Kent store, opened in 2005, carries its own line of furniture and ironwood art objects, as well as many European furnishings, designer floor coverings, chandeliers and antique replicas. You might find a crystal eperne, a bronze statuette or a life-size marble carving. Dishes by Rosanna bring good cheer to any table. You'll also find the kind of expertise you need to reinvent your home. The store's interior designer staff specializes in all aspects of interior design, and the company can fulfill many an artistic vision with special order and custom fabrications. Upholstered furniture by such companies as Van Gogh can be fitted with custom fabrics. The store also designs and creates hand-hammered iron gates, specialty draperies and mosaic inlays. Harvey and Mark are committed to helping customers create soul-soothing environments. Even the name Chair & Trellis speaks to their focus. The chair represents a place of rest, while the trellis represents the vineyards that define the lifestyle of the region. It is easy to see why these business owners have made so many friends among their customers. They've also embraced the community through charity work. For adornments that change the way you'll feel at home, visit Chair & Trellis.

321 W Smith Street, Kent WA
(253) 852-8520
www.chairandtrellis.com

Continental Furniture

Continental Furniture is a third-generation family business offering quality furniture in contemporary and traditional styles. Owners Al and Sam Moscatel continue the high product standards and devotion to service that have earned Continental Furniture the loyalty of customers since 1946. The brothers have also taken a penetrating look at the business to make the hard calls that separate the survivors from the temporary players in the furniture industry. Today Continental Furniture has expanded to include stores that represent individual product lines as well as a beefed-up furniture rental business. You can still visit the flagship store at 1st Avenue and the nearby Thomasville outlet. At 2200 Western Avenue, the Moscatel family runs a La-Z-Boy store and It's Gotta Go, a center for rentals and consignment furniture. The new focus on used furniture appeals to those seeking to replace the furniture in apartments and condominiums and to real estate companies that need to shed display furniture previously used in model homes. Continental Furniture offers the services of talented designers who can help you with space planning and color selection and recommend window treatments, carpets and bedding for your home in addition to furniture. For furniture know-how that runs in the blood, see Al and Sam at Continental Furniture.

2111 First Avenue, Belltown, Seattle WA
(206) 441-1822
www.continentalfurniture.com

Ballard Home Comforts

Visit Ballard Home Comforts, a long-standing shopping tradition in the heart of historic downtown Ballard. This chic boutique entertains all of your shopping whims. Cheryl O' Conner, the owner, has created a store that is appealing to all age groups. Merchandise varies season to season, but you can always count on Cheryl's trend-forward buying abilities to bring you fabulous accessories, purses and jewelry as well as furniture and home décor—something for everyone. Visit Cheryl and her knowledgeable and energetic staff at Ballard Home Comforts. They promise you a smile, a how-are-you and the satisfaction that your visit is appreciated.

**5334 Ballard Avenue NW, Seattle WA
(206) 781-1040**

Area 51

When a store's staff is as loyal as its customers it is clear that the store is doing something right. At Area 51, co-owners Jason Hallman and Daniel Meltzer have created an atmosphere where staff is like family and the work is meaningful. Offering well-designed quality home furnishings at affordable prices, they are committed to making their showroom an enjoyable place to visit and meeting your home décor needs in a way that will have you coming back for more. Bringing decorating possibilities to life with eye-catching room displays, the showroom is housed in a bright lofty building with oversized windows. The furniture is modern with a retro twist, and most pieces are multifunctional. The store supports local emerging artists as well as sourcing home furnishings from around the world. It also offers customization at an affordable price where most of the upholstered items can be ordered in 90 fabrics and leathers. Area 51 is a full service store, offering design consultations, home delivery and free in-store assembly. The on-site warehouse allows you to take home most items that day. Area 51's designers have a passion for great design, let them help you create a perfect haven in your home.

401 E Pine Street, Seattle WA (206) 568-4782
www.area51seattle.com

Photo by Joe Crawford

Bunksnstuff

When living space gets tight, it's time to free it up with intelligently designed furniture. Bunksnstuff specializes in that traditional space saver, the bunk bed. Its creative solutions extend to kids' rooms, dorm rooms and vacation homes and include innovative loft beds with space underneath for desks and storage. Teens like the sleek metal dressers, nightstands and entertainment centers as well as the poof chairs. The furnishings can be viewed on the e-commerce website or at the storefront in downtown Sumner. Owner Marty Evans appreciates the deep community roots of Store Managers Bobbi Usher and Diane Childers; they know practically everyone and are responsible for much of the store's popularity. Marty previously worked for an industrial business located next door to a manufacturer of children's furniture. Feeling that it would be more fun to sell furniture than steel, he began an on-line enterprise in 1998. His concept was successful, but he missed personal contact with customers and opened his retail outlet in 2003. The stainless steel and wood beds here are stylish space savers. You can put your princess to bed in a pink castle or choose a trundle or platform style for your guest room. What grownup wouldn't smile at the free shipping to all 48 contiguous states? Gain back your floor space with a visit to Bunksnstuff.

926 Main Street, Suite 102, Sumner WA (253) 826-8088
www.bunksnstuff.com

DeLong's Landscaping

The history of art is filled with stories of artists who achieved greatness early in life and then settled into a mellow complacency. After more than 34 years in business, Robert DeLong of DeLong's Landscaping is still waiting to hit that latter stage. His flair for designing beautiful yards for his customers remains as sharp as ever. Robert is an artist, and nature is his medium. Ponds and waterfalls are some of his specialties, as are walls and patios. He could enhance your yard by adding one of these elements to it, or he could create an entire environment from scratch. Either way, his work makes a statement. Customer satisfaction is the make-or-break factor in the landscaping business. You don't survive in it as long as Robert has with anything less than work that exhibits flair, a commitment to perfection and an impeccable reputation for straightforward dealing. With Robert's son, Dustin, on board as vice president and operations manager, this tradition of quality should continue for many years to come. When your yard needs an artist's touch, give the Picasso of Pierce County a call at DeLong's Landscaping.

2729 9ᵗʰ Street, Puyallup WA (253) 848-4709

Masins Furniture

Masins Furniture might have turned into another kind of shop if owner Bob Masins' grandfather Eman hadn't happened upon some bargain furniture in the early days of his dry goods store, which he opened in 1927. Eman's first furniture was factory seconds rejected by the Frederick & Nelson department store, but it wasn't long before Eman was selling new furniture of the highest quality. Today the store with its historic Pioneer Square location carries quality furniture from the most recognized names in the industry. Even though the showroom is large, it can only display a selection of the available possibilities. Most items are custom-ordered in fabrics and finishes suited to a customer's home. The Masins staff includes accredited interior designers who are prepared to help customers with all aspects of their new interior, from floors, paint, color and style choices to furnishings for new and existing rooms. Four generations of family have served at Masins. For Bob's father Ben, now in his 80s, coming down to the store to help out every day just seems like the logical thing to do. Bob's son David runs the newly rebuilt store in Bellevue. The Masins are survivors who have faced the destruction by fire of their Bellevue store and an earthquake at their Seattle location. Their commitment to their stores and their community never wavered, even when they had to rebuild completely. When you want help creating beautiful interior environments, Masins Furniture is the place to come.

220 2nd Avenue S, Pioneer Square, Seattle WA
(206) 622-5606
www.masins.com

Pugerudes

Since 1957, Pugerudes has been providing the best in custom window treatments and the finest in home furnishings. What started out as a widow and her eldest son trying to make ends meet by providing friends with draperies, has evolved into South King County's premier custom home furnishing business. Still family owned and operated, Pugerudes' workroom turns out beautiful window treatments, custom bedding and custom upholstered furniture. They also provide a wide range of blinds, shades, shutters and sunscreen shades. Pugerudes' expertise and commitment to quality décor for the home has given them an unsurpassed reputation. Attention to detail is not just a phrase; it's a daily commitment. From color and texture selection, to fabrication, to measuring and installing, Pugerudes leaves no detail overlooked. So whether it's simply new blinds, or a room makeover, by allowing Pugerudes to assist in your project, you will be pleased with your new look.

118 Railroad Avenue S, Kent WA
(253) 852-2517
www.pugerudes.com

Floor Coverings International

During his more than 20 years in the flooring business, David Jones, owner of Floor Coverings International, has installed miles of tiles and enough carpeting and wood to cover many acres. That's the experience that you want when you're considering a dramatic new look for any room in your home. Floor Coverings International offers more than 3,000 flooring options from the top brands in the industry, all at competitive prices. What's more, David's staff makes house calls. With Floor Coverings International's mobile shop-at-home service, you can view samples under actual lighting conditions together with your wall colors, furniture and accessories. David understands that flooring is the real foundation for the rest of the décor in the home. He encourages customers to set a budget so that he can work with them to provide the flooring that best reflects their style, taste and definition of comfort. His reward comes when folks take their first steps across their new floor and he sees the smile on their faces. He knows that if you are happy with the look of the living room, then you will trust Floor Coverings International when it's time to take on the kitchen, bedroom or bathroom. Put your flooring needs into the experienced hands of David and his crew at Floor Coverings International.

902 Kincaid Avenue, Sumner WA
(253) 891-8573 or (800) DIAL-FCI (342-5324)
www.floorcoveringsintl.com

Relatively Rustic

Joanne Cormier and her daughters, Heather Rowan and Robin Rohr, are the driving forces behind the highly popular and aptly named home decorating store, Relatively Rustic. This inviting store specializes in country home décor, primitives and folk art and has quickly become a favorite stop for locals and tourists alike. The family, all Puyallup natives, takes special pleasure in country-style home

décor. Robin had long dreamt of opening the kind of creative establishment that would allow her to work closely with customers as they decorated their homes. With help from her sister Heather, who handles the business aspects, and her mom Joanne, Robin was able to realize her dream in 2005. Relatively Rustic is a browser's haven, filled with one attention-getting delight after another, including handcrafted country furniture, striking clocks and a full selection of linens, lamps and mirrors. The shop additionally offers whimsical home décor items that make wonderful gifts, along with an array of rustic pictures and country landscapes. Relatively Rustic is also the ideal place to find potpourri and gourmet goodies, as well as a broad range of specialty candles and candle accessories. Spend an afternoon with three charming ladies while finding the folk art, primitives and country décor you love at Relatively Rustic.

107 W Steward, Suite A, Puyallup WA
(253) 445-4784

WESTERN WASHINGTON

Lifestyle
Destinations

Thielsen Architects, Inc.

Despite computer-aided design (CAD), Dave Thielsen still begins project discussions with a graphite and pencil sketch on vellum. Owner of Thielsen Architects, Inc., he wants to make it easy for new home builders to participate in the preliminary discussions about design concepts and functionality. Helping clients realize the vision of their new custom home is Dave's way of assisting himself and his team to expand as architects. They specialize in designing lakefront, oceanfront and other view properties. They'll even take you to see homes designed and built by other customers. Clients of Thielsen Architects are actively involved in every step of the home building process. Dave says, "We try to get clients engaged in the free flow of ideas and information through a series of meetings to find out what's important to them and let them know what's important to us as a design firm." He says this is especially important if you want a house that will grow and adapt with your family. CAD is a program they use to help you visualize your home from a variety of angles. Dave specializes in detailing elements that ensure continuity between the interior and exterior. Thielsen Architects design personalized homes that have broad appeal. Designing both traditional and modern homes, Dave and his design team will work with you to create your dream home. If you want a home that looks like fine art, is functional, energetic and comfortable, Thielsen Architects, Inc. can do it.

720 Market Street, Suite C, Kirkland WA (425) 828-9376 *www.thielsen.com*

WESTERN WASHINGTON

Restaurants
& Cafés

Julia's Restaurant

The smell of fresh baked goods greets customers at the original Wallingford location of Julia's Restaurant. The bakery that creates the enticing aroma is responsible for the breads, cookies and beloved carrot cake that customers have been enjoying since 1978. In 1993, Karsten Betd and Eladio Preciado purchased the café, where Karsten had risen from bus boy to manager after moving to the United States. Today, Julia's has four locations. All rely on the bakery, and all create breakfast, lunch and dinner fare using house-made sauces and local ingredients. Internet access lets you work while enjoying a latte and such treats as granola, pancakes or cookies. No matter where you are in the Seattle area, you'll find a Julia's with its own style. Julia's in Queen Anne gets its character from a Victorian cottage, while Julia's on Broadway uses its stage for Saturday night performances. Julia's of Issaquah takes its ambience from gazebos, gardens and artwork. Julia's has won awards for its community involvement and dedication to the environment. It's often cited for Best Breakfast by Seattle Magazine and other publications. Get comfortable at a Julia's near you.

1825 Queen Anne Avenue N, Seattle WA (206) 282-0680
375 NW Gilman Boulevard, Issaquah WA (425) 557-1919
4401 Wallingford Avenue N, Seattle WA (206) 633-1175
300 Broadway E, Seattle WA (206) 860-1818
www.eatatjulias.com

Photo by Brookelynn Photography

611 Supreme Restaurant & Lounge

Crêpes made with buckwheat, just like they make them in Brittany, have gone a long way in establishing 611 Supreme Restaurant & Lounge as a favorite place for casual French cuisine in all of Seattle, particularly around Capital Hill. Very popular with the after-work crowd, the restaurant features 11 different kinds of crêpes, ranging from the simple Le Fromage, with a choice of Gruyère, Brie, Cambazola or Chèvre, to crêpes more complex in their tastes, such as the Les Crevettes, which features sautéed shrimp with tomato coulis, garnished with white wine cream sauce. Brined pork rack, roasted half-chicken and hanger steak are favorites on the dinner menu. Guests can either dine in the lounge or the restaurant. The lounge offers some of the finest bartenders the city has to offer, making specialty cocktails with an extensive liquor selection to complement the wine. The lounge is open late every evening and is filled with neighborhood regulars. 611 Supreme serves dinner every evening and a busy brunch Saturday and Sunday mornings. All the menu items, from the onion soup to paté, are house made. Owner Margaret Edwins serves only French wines, making it even easier to pretend that you are spending an afternoon or evening on the Breton coast.

611 E Pine Street, Seattle WA (206) 328-0292

Archa Thai Bistro

Archa Thai Bistro offers diners an elegant setting to enjoy artfully prepared authentic Thai food. Owner Tanya Wongvanich, who was art commissioner of Kent, grew up in the high society of Thailand and came to the United States to further her schooling. Tanya holds undergraduate degrees in biology and visual art, and a postgraduate degree in communication, and she puts them all to use in her quaint Thai bistro. The fine décor, quiet ambience and piano bar offer a romantic evening out, all reasons that readers of the *King Country Journal*, *Business Exam* and *Meridian High School Journal* voted Archa Thai the Best Place for a Date. Tanya grows many of the herbs served at the bistro and places an emphasis on healthy, anti-aging organic foods. Fresh summer rolls, coconut prawns, crab delight and spinach-wrapped savory nibbles are flavors to die for. Entrée options include Flaming Duck Curry, Classical Pad Thai, Zingiber Ginger Lover, Thai Basil and Cashew Chicken. The restaurant never uses MSG (monosodium glutamate) in its dishes. While the atmosphere and food reflect the high quality of a fine dining establishment, prices at Archa Thai are very reasonable. Visit Archa Thai Bistro for healthful Thai food in a sophisticated atmosphere.

214 E Meeker Street, Kent WA (253) 373-1868
www.archathai.com

Bittersweet

Bittersweet is an icon in downtown Kent. Voted Restaurant of the Year in 2006, Bittersweet offers the best lunches in town. Owner Jim Krier opened Bittersweet in 2002. The restaurant is a charming, down home, country café where works by local artists grace the brick walls. The aromas coming from the kitchen are incredible. Enjoy the delectable flavors of such homemade soups as clam chowder, lentil sausage, and true mushroom. The Chicken Enchilada Casserole, Chicken Artichoke Bake, and Broccoli Pie are sure to warm your soul. At Bittersweet, they even bake their own bread. Jim and his staff carry their made-from-scratch philosophy right on down to a famous house salad with homemade dressing. For dessert, the Chocolate French Silk Pie is a dream come true, though the signature dessert is a fresh apple crisp topped with fresh whipped cream. On Fridays, you can celebrate the beginning of the weekend with dinner and live music. It is the only night that dinner is available. Visit Bittersweet the next time you're in Kent. Their homemade goodness and warm inviting atmosphere will make them a favorite.

211 1st Avenue S, Kent WA (253) 854-0707

Cutter's Bayhouse

A visit to any seaside city is not complete until you've savored the seafood. You can relish all of your favorite Pacific Northwest flavors at Cutter's Bayhouse, situated just north of Pike Place Market. This outstanding restaurant features attentive service, stunning panoramic views of Puget Sound, Elliot Bay and the Seattle skyline and cuisine that is both exquisitely fresh and expertly prepared. Popular favorites include seared fillets of salmon in a spicy crust, succulent steaks and almond crusted sea scallops. Once you've had such specialties as the cedar-plank roasted king crab legs or the maple chicken salad, you'll want to order them again. They make fabulous compliments to the house salmon chowder and the explosively delicious chocolate volcano cake, to which the *Seattle Weekly* awarded the title Best Chocolate Dessert. You can enjoy intimate private dining in the Bayroom, an ideal spot for business gatherings, receptions and special events of all kinds. The establishment features a warm and welcoming ambience that's perfect for a casual lunch, cocktails with colleagues, a leisurely dinner with friends and family or a relaxed happy hour. Enjoy the quintessential Northwest dining experience at Cutter's Bayhouse.

2001 Western Avenue, Seattle WA (206) 448-4884
www.cuttersbayhouse.com

Chutneys Bistro

Anyone who frequents Chutneys Bistro has met its congenial owner Harish Khurana. Harish is responsible for the Northern Indian recipes that attract patrons to his restaurant. He also manages the floor and takes a personal interest in customers. "Good food is a combination of good spices," says Harish, who has been applying both science and art to his spice combinations since first opening Chutneys in 1999. Chutneys is now in the southwest corner of Wallingford Center, where diners enjoy a patio and an Indian-style interior. You can choose a tandoori dish cooked in a traditional clay oven or an enchanting curry. Diners rave about the mulligatawny soup and the butter-cream sauce that flavors the chicken tikka masala. A spicy masala sauce is the key to the succulent meat in lamb rogan josh. In mango chicken, boneless chicken breast gets tangy treatment from a mango curry sauce. Harish is deeply involved in community festivals and school fundraisers. He's a strong believer in giving back to the people who have made him successful. He's been featured in the *Seattle Times,* and his customers take the time to pass on their delight in Citysearch reviews. For memorable flavor combinations, visit Chutneys Bistro.

1815 N 45ᵗʰ Street, Seattle WA (206) 634-1000
www.chutneysbistro.com

Gateway to India

The family of restaurant owner Surinder Singh wants you to feel like you have had dinner in an Indian home when you visit Gateway to India. The Tacoma restaurant brings the authentic flavors of Indian cuisine to the 6ᵗʰ Avenue business district. Surinder works closely with his brother, CJ, who is general manager, and his sister, Kaljinder, who is also a manager. It was a visit from their mother, however, that provided inspiration for the restaurant. After the two brothers came to America to attend college, they constantly called their mother in India for cooking advice. She decided to come over to teach them to cook, and the siblings agreed to translate what they learned into a restaurant. Food here is authentic Indian fare, not some Americanized version. Each day offers dinner, a lunch buffet and opportunities for take-out. Yes, you can learn a lot about the flavors of Indian meals here and expect to make many visits before exhausting the restaurant's extensive menu. Among the most popular appetizers are the *Samosas*, vegetables dipped in chickpea batter and deep fried. Main dishes can be vegetarian or feature seafood, chicken, lamb or rice. You'll find a selection of Tandoori entrées, made in a clay oven pot known as a *tandoor*. The restaurant's décor is distinctly Indian, accented by soft lighting. Come home to the cuisine of northern India at Gateway to India.

2603 6ᵗʰ Avenue, Tacoma WA (253) 552-5022
www.gatewaytoindia.4t.com

Costas Opa Greek Restaurant

In the heart of Seattle's Bohemian Fremont neighborhood, Costas Opa Greek Restaurant has been cooking up great dishes from the homeland since 1982. With exuberant Grecian décor, Costas Opa is a true trip to the Mediterranean. You can sit on the mezzanine as you enjoy your dinner of gyros, which is ground lamb and beef on pita bread with cool and garlicky *tzatziki* sauce, potatoes and vegetables. Other dinner favorites include *souvlaki*, bite-sized bits of tenderloin beef, chicken or lamb seasoned with pepper, oregano and garlic served on skewers with rice and vegetables. Try the mousaka, baked layers of eggplant and meat sauce topped with creamy Béchamel sauce and cheese. Full bar service is available. Costas Opa is also open for breakfast and lunch. Enjoy a simple workday lunch of lentil soup and a chicken breast sandwich, or a lazy Sunday breakfast of gyros and feta omelettes at 3 pm. Visit the restaurant's website to stay tuned to announcements of belly dance performances, live music and Greek dancing specials. City Search endorsed Costas Opa for Best Mediterranean Food in 2005. Owner Costas Antonopoulos dreamed of coming to America from the time he was a small boy. He arrived in the late 1960s and soon after opened his first restaurant. Visit Costas Opa Greek Restaurant, one man's American dream come true.

3400 N Fremont Avenue, Seattle WA (206) 633-4141
www.costasopa.com

Contour

It's not every day that you find a nightclub with a clientele that includes suit-clad businessmen, punk rockers, and everything in between. A hot spot in downtown Seattle, Contour has a European ambience and offers Mediterranean-inspired cuisine. It draws its guests in early with happy hour drink and appetizer specials. To keep them going 'til the sun comes up, Contour hosts the best in entertainment seven days a week. Fire performers, comedians, DJs, and live bands are sure to get your blood circulating. Once you've hit your dance limit for the night, recharge with traditional Turkish and Greek appetizers. Spanakopita, the classic Greek specialty, and dill-battered button mushrooms are among the mouth-watering offerings. The restaurant serves three meals a day and opens up to the patio and sidewalk in the summertime. Its outdoor dining setup makes it a premier destination when the sun is shining. Contour's passion for the local art scene enhances the club's atmosphere. As a member of Seattle's monthly Gallery Artwalk, this swanky downtown nightclub supports and represents the local art community by adorning its walls with all media of artistic expression. With entertainment every night and its dynamic combination of art and European ambience, Contour is where to go to dance the night away.

807 1st Ave, Seattle WA (206) 447-7704
www.clubcontour.com

Il Fiasco

Il Fiasco owner Mark Gaimster told *Northwest Jazz Profile* magazine that he got into the restaurant business "because it allows me to throw a party for people every night of the week." That explains the festive atmosphere at this Italian Restaurant and wine bar, located in Tacoma. Mark knows the secret of a great party is friendly people and great food and drink, and you'll definitely find all of the above here. Il Fiasco's menu includes everything from the familiar pizzas and spaghetti and meatballs to more exotic dishes, such as the popular wild boar. As the seasons change, so does the menu here, allowing for the finest in fresh vegetables. Make sure to save room for Il Fiasco's delicious desserts, which include tiramisu and Chocolate Heaven, a triple chocolate cake served with mocha sauce and Madagascar vanilla ice cream. Wine lovers will delight in the variety of vintages from Italy, California and the Pacific Northwest. The restaurant offers two private banquet rooms, wine dinners and catering services. Il Fiasco is named for the straw basket around a Chianti bottle, and you can be sure no other kind of fiasco will happen here. For an Italian feast from folks who understand how to throw a party, come to Il Fiasco.

2717 6th Avenue, Tacoma WA (253) 272-6688
www.ilfiasco.com

Hattie's Hat Restaurant

Stiff drinks and good, old-fashioned American cuisine with a classy touch have been traditions at Hattie's Hat Restaurant since the 1940s. *USA Today* has named Hattie's one of the best places to have Easter brunch, and with a menu that includes everything from corned beef hash to crêpes served with Swedish lingonberries, it's easy to see why. Lunch options include soups, salads and scrumptious sandwiches. The dinner menu includes dishes such as the Guinness meat loaf, soaked in Guinness gravy, and country fried chicken, along with hamburgers and vegetarian dishes. The weekend brunch has quite a following, and several reviewers have called it one of the best breakfasts in town. Owners Kyla Fairchild, Ron Wilkowski and Dan Cowan have kept Hattie's looking much the same as it has been throughout its history. The original wood bar, hand-carved in France and installed in 1904, is still here. So is the mural by well-known artist Fred Oldfield, painted in the 1950s. The restaurant is a laid-back, down home place for families and friends to enjoy a meal and socialize. At night, it's a hip bar. Hattie's Hat has an extensive wine list, along with a selection of spirits from around the world. The bar is proud of its first-class Bloody Mary. Poke your head into Hattie's Hat for old-fashioned fun, food and drink.

5231 Ballard Avenue NW, Seattle WA (206) 789-5807
www.hattieshat.com

Kaosamai Thai Restaurant & Caterers

The husband and wife team of Doug and Sumalee Somerville have become an important part of Fremont's dining scene since they opened Kaosamai Thai Restaurant & Caterers in 2001. Doug is a trained engineer and former Alaskan crab fisherman who stays in touch with his old fishing pals to keep Kaosamai supplied with fresh seafood. Sumalee is the chef and knows just how to take advantage of this bounty. Her menu is bursting with seafood combinations, not to mention rice, curry and noodle dishes. Kaosamai's catering assures that delicacies are always hot and fresh. Instead of bringing prepared food across town, the Somervilles bring their cook truck across town to your event and use their specially equipped mobile kitchen for on-site preparation. This service turns weddings, corporate functions and such events as the Bite of Seattle into opportunities to sample a buffet of authentic Thai dishes. You will find plentiful parking at Kaosamai and a giant sun deck for enjoying the outdoors when weather permits. The staff always greets you with big smiles. Rediscover Thai food at the inventive Kaosamai Thai Restaurant, nominated as one of Seattle's 10 best Thai restaurants for 2006 by AOL Cityguide.

404 N 36th Street, Seattle WA (206) 925-9979
www.kaosamai.com

El Gaucho—Seattle

For food preparation laced with Argentinean drama and romance, Seattle turns to the award winning El Gaucho, a restaurant that has been astonishing customers with its food, wine and ambience since it first opened in 1953. Owner Paul Mackay and General Manager Cooper Mills oversee operations here, while Chef John Broulette directs activities in the exhibition kitchen. You can watch your steaks, pork, poultry and seafood being prepared over an open bed of glowing coals, while your filet mignon comes to you on a flaming sword. Staff members excel at tableside preparation of such signature dishes as Caesar salad and Chateaubriand, as well as Bananas Foster and Cherries Jubilee. The staff can make informed wine recommendations, or you can select your own favorites from a first-class wine list that has earned an Award of Excellence from *Wine Spectator* magazine. El Gaucho's lounge features cocktails and nightly piano music. Its private dining rooms offer choice options for special events. Cigar aficionados will appreciate indulging in a fine cigar in the intimate cigar lounge, where you can purchase your own cigar box. On Fridays and Saturdays the Pampas Room features supper club entertainment with music and dancing. For some, dining at El Gaucho has become a family tradition. The staff knows guests who have been coming here since childhood by name. For gracious hospitality, retro-swank atmosphere and meals known for their quality and panache, make a reservation and a memory at El Gaucho.

2505 1ˢᵗ Avenue, Seattle WA (206) 728-1337
www.elgaucho.com

Kickstand Café

Savor artistic expression at the Kickstand Café in downtown Tacoma. Karin and Jeff Green enthusiastically support creativity, whether it's through a perfect cappuccino, a mouthwatering sandwich, a subtle jazz riff or a superb still life. In the morning, invoke your liquid muse with a caramel macchiato accompanied by a tempting breakfast bagel. For lunch, enjoy a turkey and havarti cheese sandwich that the Earl of Sandwich himself would be proud to claim as a descendant. Fun at the Kickstand includes mellow tunes from local musicians, too, since the café is a mecca for music makers. Try out your newest chords at open mic nights or sit back, quaff a Guinness and enjoy the beat. If your creative canvas runs to art, Karin and Jeff want to make sure you have a place to display your work and feature a variety of artistic styles each month in the gallery. The Greens can help you schedule a party or meeting in the colorful Cavalletto Room or offer you a cozy spot to play chess. For high-octane espresso, a delectable lunch, live music and a visual showcase, visit the Kickstand Café.

604 S Fawcett Avenue, Tacoma WA (253) 779-KICK (5425)
www.kickstandtacoma.com

Kitchen 2 Kitchen

Healthy eating is often one of the first casualties in today's fast paced, fast food society. Kitchen 2 Kitchen's mission is to help families keep healthy, home cooked meals in their lives. Here's how the program works. Customers review a monthly menu, choose entrées, choose a date and time, then work with Kitchen 2 Kitchen's staff to create six to 12 entrées that are ready for freezing and reheating as necessary. Kitchen 2 Kitchen provides the recipe planning, prep work and clean up along with 15 menu selections and all necessary ingredients to make the dishes. You'll need a one to two-hour reservation, depending on the number of dishes you plan to create. The staff is on hand to guide even the most inexperienced cook through the process and promises you'll master the procedures in about three minutes. Customers can customize entrées to fit individual or family preferences and choose from an array of side dishes. The only equipment you need to provide is a large laundry basket or ice chest to transport the fresh meals home. Meals cost approximately $2.50 per serving with additional meal bargains for parties of six or more. You'll know the calorie, carb and fat count of each meal. For customers who can't find the time to prepare the meals, Kitchen 2 Kitchen offers a personal chef service to prepare your entrées for you. Save yourself meal preparation time without scrimping on quality with a reservation to cook at either of two convenient Kitchen 2 Kitchen locations.

4312 6th Avenue, Tacoma WA (253) 761-5100
3046 Pacific Highway S, Federal Way WA (253) 946-6870
www.kitchen2kitchen.us

La Isla

At La Isla Restaurant, Alfonso and Marion Gonzalez and their partner Jason Mikos bring the sights and flavors of San Juan, Puerto Rico to Seattle. A tropical drink made from one of several rum varieties will get you in the mood for a meal with all the charms of the Gonzalez family's Caribbean homeland, along with some local twists on traditional Puerto Rican classics. To get a feeling for Puerto Rican delicacies, dive into the appetizers, which include *empanadas* (flakey dough turnovers filled with various ingredients) and *bacalaito* (fried codfish). Anyone who has been to Puerto Rico has sampled plantains, a cousin of the banana. If the specialty is new to you, be sure to try the *Medley de Plantanos* for starters. The dish offers *tostones* (smashed green plantains), *maduros* (thinly sliced, ripened plantains) and *arañitas* (shredded plantain patties). Entrées impart Puerto Rican flavor to fish, chicken, pork, beef and vegetable dishes. Blackened wild salmon gets a tropical twist from mango and pineapple salsa. Plantains and tofu fill Puerto Rican-style vegetable lasagna. Many of the staff members are Puerto Rican, and all are devoted to producing meals that are as delicious as they are authentic. Sit back and take a tropical break in a Puerto Rican paradise at La Isla.

2320 NW Market Street, Seattle WA (206) 789-0516
www.laislaseattle.com

The Pike Brewing Co.

The Pike Brewing Co. deserves to be either your first or your final stop in Seattle. The locale is ideal, near the waterfront and not too far from the famous Pike Place Farmer's Market. The solid lineup of brews makes a visit worthwhile even for Sea-town locals. On your first visit, you'll notice that you're not only walking into a pub, but you've also entered a museum, a brewery and a restaurant. In the old-time tradition, Pike Brewing Co. merges their brewery with their pub, providing a welcoming space for its customers. The pub prides itself on serving dishes that are complimentary to its flavorful beers brewed on-site. The family-owned brew house hopes to get people excited about the history and pleasure of beer by adorning the walls with historical beer displays—plus information on prehistoric beers, extending up to 9,000 years into the past. Acclaimed beers such as Pike Pale Ale, Kiltlifter and Pike XXXXX Stout earn the Pike Brewing Co. its own place in beer history. They have been voted Best Brewpub and Bar by *Where* magazine in 2006, Best Rebirth in Best Restaurants, *Seattle* magazine, 2007 and won a gold medal for Old Bawdy Barley Wine from the North American Beer Awards in 2007. Head to the Pike Place Market for a pint or two—the Pike Brewing Co. is not a destination to miss.

1415 1st Avenue, Seattle WA
(206) 622-6044
www.pikebrewing.com

McCabe's American Music Café

McCabe's American Music Café is a good old-fashioned kind of place, where people from all walks of life gather to eat, drink, dance and just have a fun time. Charles and Jenny Pak own and operate this lively Tacoma restaurant and bar that has welcomed patrons for more than 25 years. The restaurant serves up hearty meals of steak, chicken and burgers. Customers rave about the loaded nachos, quesadillas and Ranch Hand fries. After your meal, get out on the dance floor in the center of the room, where you can swing and line dance into the night. On Sundays, Tex McClish offers swing dance lessons. In fact, dance lessons take place six days a week, so learning to salsa or do a Chicago-style line dance is as easy as planning a visit to McCabe's. After your time on the dance floor, catch your breath and relax by the large fireplace or shoot a game of pool or darts with friends. You'll find two bars to serve you and a nightly drink special. For an all-American good time, visit McCabe's American Music Café.

2611 Pacific Avenue, Tacoma WA
(253) 272-5403

Old Milwaukee Café and Dessert Company

At the Old Milwaukee Café and Dessert Company, Chad and Patricia Kerth will feed you like family sitting down for a meal in their dining room. The pair have worked together since 1992, and moved the business to this location in 1997. They enjoy visiting with their customers and getting to know them on a first name basis. They explain that their goal is to feed you food they would prepare for themselves, with fresh, wholesome ingredients and recipes made from scratch. Start your day off right with a hearty breakfast, such as a skillet full of food you will find in a House Scramble, featuring four eggs, potatoes, and loads of other goodies. Regular customers vouch for the pancakes. The batter is made fresh each morning. Lunch favorites include the homemade soup and deluxe cheeseburger. The Super Clubhouse sandwich piles ham, turkey and bacon on top of your choice of bread and then finishes it with swiss and cheddar cheese and all the trimmings. The culinary delights are just beginning, because Pat is also known for her made-to-order desserts. If you call the café ahead of time, a heavenly Turtle Pecan cheesecake, orange cream cake, or tray of raspberry pecan bars will be waiting for you to take home. Come to the Old Milwaukee Café and Dessert Company, where the Kerths will serve you up delicious food and make you feel right at home.

3102 6ᵗʰ Avenue, Tacoma WA
(253) 761-2602

Photo by Stu Spivack

New Orleans Creole Restaurant

The scent and flavors of old-fashioned gumbo and jambalaya mix with the sweet sounds of Dixieland jazz and the blues to make New Orleans Creole Restaurant a southern-fried treat for all the senses. The restaurant, which opened in 1985, brings authentic Cajun flavors and sounds to historic Pioneer Square in Seattle. Lovers of Louisiana's spiciest cuisine will thrill to the menu, which includes some of the Bayou's best flavors. From the familiar fried catfish with hush puppies, to more exotic dishes such as chicken Rochambeau with poulette sauce, you'll find plenty to tempt your taste buds. You'll also find some of the finest gumbo and jambalaya outside New Orleans. Head to the lounge for some of the South's most distinctive drinks, including hurricanes with rum and fruit and a Cajun martini with double vodka or gin and jalapeno. Live jazz music plays Monday through Thursday. On the weekends, the tempo picks up a bit, with live blues bands. The atmosphere is friendly, with helpful staff and plenty of talkative regulars. Come on in to New Orleans Creole Restaurant and listen to America's music as you enjoy your Cajun cuisine.

114 First Avenue S, Seattle WA
(206) 622-2563
www.neworleanscreolerestaurant.com

Ray's Boathouse, Café & Catering

Ray's Boathouse, Café & Catering on Shilshole Bay is a Seattle landmark that's famous for its preparation and presentation of Northwest cuisine. Guests gaze out at Puget Sound and the Olympic Mountains. Ray's gained popularity as a dockside café with home-cooked meals. It became part of a food revolution in the Pacific Northwest, helping to introduce a fashionable and distinctive regional cuisine built around Northwest products, microbrews and wines. Today's restaurant has been called one of the 10 best seafood restaurants in the country. It draws rave reviews from major food magazines and websites, including *Gourmet Magazine, Wine Spectator* and AOL Cityguide. If you like seafood and prime cuts of meat, you'll love Chef Peter Birk's healthful and tasteful creations, which feature the clean taste of fresh produce and dairy products. Local fishermen deliver seafood from their boats to Ray's, which fits right in with Chef Birk's sustainable approach to food. Two elegant dining areas have seating for 300, and the upstairs café deck seats 75 when the weather allows. The Ray's name came from its original owner, who in 1939 opened a boat rental and bait house. Four partners now own the restaurant. Look for the 50-foot, red flashing neon sign that points you to Ray's Boathouse, Café & Catering. Bon appétit.

6049 Seaview Avenue NW, Seattle WA
(206) 789-3770
www.rays.com

Pacific Grill

Food & Wine Magazine has named Chef Gordon Naccarato of Tacoma's Pacific Grill one of the 10 best chefs in America. That immediately says a lot. Gordon co-owns this popular eatery with his brother Steve Naccarato and Joe Hardwrick. The trio opened the restaurant in 2005, and it has quickly gained rave reviews for its exceptional staff, elegant atmosphere and intensely pleasurable dining. The Pacific Grill is on the magnificently restored ground floor of the historic Waddell building. You dine under a 17-foot ceiling with exposed beams, graced by intimate lighting and original artwork that is skillfully displayed against exposed brick walls. Patrons can find a seat at the bar or in the elegant dining room and relax over their favorite libation. Then comes a tranquil meal of divine cuisine accompanied by gracious service. The Pacific Grill's menu features traditional American cuisine brilliantly prepared with fresh, high-quality ingredients. Highly favored appetizers include crisp Kumamotos, fresh from local waters, and the Pacific Grill's shellfish starter, an array of delicious shellfish and assorted sauces. Chef Gordon offers a selection of salads, such as the Pacific Grill Caesar, as well as savory fish, chicken and beef dishes. Enjoy a classic steak or a perfect chop. You owe it to yourself to dine at the Pacific Grill.

1502 Pacific Avenue, Tacoma WA (253) 627-3535
www.pacificgrilltacoma.com

Porter's Place Southern Cuisine & BBQ

At Porter's Place, Alton and Patrice Porter bring a bit of down-home Southern hospitality and comfort food to Tacoma. Alton and Patrice have fond memories of Southern cooking interwoven with family gatherings as they were growing up. After Hurricane Betsy, the couple relocated to Tacoma and opened the restaurant, where they serve barbecue and entrées inspired by the flavors of Louisiana and Mississippi. One of their specialties is The Man, a smooth and tasty hot sauce with just the right amount of heat. Staff members, who with their friendly demeanor might remind you of long lost friends, serve meals packed full of flavor. Starters include the Kickin' Chicken Wings and Big Daddy Gumbo, a stew full of seafood, sausage and chicken simmered with Creole seasonings and served over rice. Entrées include the barbecue Sandwich, fried catfish and beef or pork ribs. The flavors of the South continue in side dish choices, such as fried okra, hush puppies, and red beans and rice. Be sure to leave room for Porter's famous lemon cake for dessert. You can also find Porter's Place food at many major sporting venues around the area, where the same delicious flavors come to you concession style. Bring the barbecue to your house with Porter's generous buffets and catering services, and everyone will get their fill. Come to Porter's Place, and you too can say that you have met The Man.

2615 E N Street, Tacoma WA (253) 383-7603 or (253) 472-5277 (catering)
www.porters-place.com

Pastrami's New York Eatery and Espresso

Sometimes only a real New York deli-style sandwich will satisfy your hunger. When that craving hits, head to Pastrami's New York Eatery and Espresso in Tacoma. Husband and wife Mike Rovech and Debbi Skraba opened Pastrami's in 2001 and run it with help from their daughter, Rachel, and her boyfriend, Brandon Johnson. Mike describes the restaurant as a real New York deli without the attitude. It has plenty of personality, though, with a warm atmosphere that keeps regulars coming back for the food and the company. The Reuben sandwich, loaded with lean corned beef, fresh sauerkraut and Swiss cheese, is something of a legend in these parts, and folks have been known to travel for 100 miles or more just for a bite of it. The restaurant also offers many other delicious sandwiches, including hot pastrami, turkey hero and prime rib dip specialties, as well as savory soups and custom-baked breads. The exclusive Pastrami's coffee blend is rich, smooth and full of flavor, because, as Mike says, "coffee shouldn't have to hurt to be good." For big East Coast flavors, save the airfare and come to Pastrami's New York Eatery and Espresso in the Rhodes building, on Broadway at 11th Street in downtown Tacoma.

950 Broadway, Suite 100, Tacoma WA (253) 779-0645
www.pastramis.com

El Gaucho—Tacoma

Washington CEO magazine calls El Gaucho the nation's best steakhouse. *Playboy* puts it in America's top 12. These are only a few of the many publications that rave about El Gaucho's exquisite food and grand service. Stop by and enjoy the retro, yet swank atmosphere. Head Chef Tristan Holst has prepared a mouth-watering menu filled with dishes fit for a king. If you haven't tasted El Gaucho's famous Chateaubriand, a 24-ounce tenderloin prepared for two and carved table side, you haven't lived. All beef is 28-day dry-aged Certified Angus Beef Prime. Meats are prepared to perfection over an open bed of glowing coals. Tenderloin, lamb shish kabob and Cornish game hen come on flaming swords. The fresh fish changes nightly, and you can order hard-to-find treats such as venison or ostrich. Spectacular sides and starters include lobster mashed potatoes and the seafood tower. Save room for something fancy or traditional from the dessert menu. The Piano Bar features the cool sounds of top performers every day of the week. Martini Heaven is a collection of fantastic martinis prepared by Tacoma's most skilled mixologists. Try the Menage a Trois, the Bling-Bling, the Ultimate Sidecar or any of two dozen others. For those who partake, El Gaucho even offers a menu of superior cigars in a special lounge. Four rooms are available for private dining. The heart of the El Gaucho experience is the legendary hospitality of Seattle-area restaurateur Paul Mackay. For an evening you'll remember forever, come to El Gaucho in Tacoma.

2119 Pacific Avenue, Tacoma WA (253) 272-1510
www.elgaucho.com/elgaucho/_tacoma

Rockin' Burrito

Rockin' Burrito is open for breakfast, lunch and dinner, serving Belltown's best burritos and wraps with a rock 'n' roll flair. The friendly and patient folks who work here are serious about their burritos, and they can accommodate almost any alteration you want. The burritos are huge, the food is fresh and it's as healthy as you like—vegetarian options abound. Beans can be substituted for meat in many items, and the restaurant has brown rice and low-carb tortillas. Consider a burrito with scrambled eggs, cheese, spinach, sautéed onions, and whatever else you ask for. This is basically a breakfast burrito that you can eat any time of day, a real treat. Try the Abba. Upon first inspection, it's simply a big burrito, but once you bite in, there is nothing else like it. It's got rice, fresh spinach, chicken, cilantro, green onions, Thai peanut sauce and crushed, roasted peanuts. The Johnny Rzeznik includes spicy wing sauce, chicken, rice, shredded cabbage, celery and blue cheese crumbles. The Louis Armstrong gives you andouille sausage, red beans, caramelized onions and zesty rice. You'll love the red wall with all the rock posters. Head over to Rockin' Burrito, the fast, fun way to dine in Belltown.

2501 4ᵗʰ Avenue, Seattle WA (206) 728-5910

The Rock Wood Fired Pizza & Spirits

Don Bellis and Jay Gigandet joined forces in 1996 to create a pizza company. They added classic rock, a generous dollop of great cuisine and plenty of atmosphere. The result is the Rock Wood Fired Pizza & Spirits, a backstage pass to pizza bliss. Don, who originally hails from the East Coast, came to the Northwest with the mission of introducing the craving for wood-fired pizza into the region. He and Jay have always used themselves as models for the business. They aim to create a place where they, self-described average guys, would want to hang out. The Rock Wood Fired Pizza & Spirits prepares all of its dishes from scratch. This includes delicious pasta entrées, such as the Elvis Sighting, colorful ricotta and mascarpone ravioli served in a rich pesto cream sauce. The menu features a full range of appetizers,

salads and soups. Pizza choices include the Classic Rock, Sweet Emotions or the Bohemian Rhapsody, which is made with chicken, roasted peppers, cream sauce and spicy Cajun seasonings. The Rock stocks a full range of your favorite beers and spirits, and the background pulses to the beat of your favorite classic rock. The Rock Wood Fired Pizza & Spirits is so popular that Don and Jay have opened many new outlets.

1920 Jefferson Avenue, Tacoma WA (253) 272-1221
4010 196ᵗʰ Avenue SW, Lynnwood WA (425) 697-6007
1408 Lake Tapps Parkway E, Auburn WA (253) 833-7887
5400 Martin Way E, Lacey WA (360) 412-0300
17809 SE 270ᵗʰ Place, Covington WA (253) 630-7404
34817 Enchanted Parkway S, Federal Way WA (253) 835-ROCK (7625)
www.therockwfp.com

Red Door

Like any true Northwestern bar and restaurant, Red Door serves a diverse crowd. You'll find workers, artists, techies, families, students and hipsters all enjoying this establishment. Red Door fills at lunch with professionals working downtown. As a neighborhood hub, Red Door entertains Fremont folks who play cribbage and snack on appetizers weeknight evenings. WiFi is available throughout. On Friday and Saturday nights, Red Door shakes it up with lively, young professionals. It's a Fremont neighborhood institution that defies classification. Hungry patrons come for the American pub food that incorporates a healthy dose of salads, local meats and seafood. The fruits of the Northwest are used liberally throughout the menu. Consider the Dungeness crab, artichoke dip and the Fremont salad, mixed greens tossed with Granny Smith apples, seasoned walnuts and bleu cheese in a sherry vinaigrette. A cold sandwich at lunch is a treat—try Red Door's curried chicken salad sandwich. The Red Door chicken club stacks grilled chicken, provolone cheese, avocado, bacon and crispy onions on a kaiser bun. The large beer and spirit selection makes it easy to pass an hour or two on the outdoor patio. Be an honorary local and join the happy mix at Red Door in Fremont.

3401 N Evanston Avenue, Seattle WA (206) 547-2022
www.reddoorseattle.com

Sea Grill

Elegantly appointed, Paul Mackay's Sea Grill adds top seafood dining to downtown Tacoma's cultural renaissance. General Manager Mike Neumann plans and orchestrates a symphony of hospitality, and his warm and friendly staff is ready to serve your every need. Chef Travis Nash's menu stars seafood with a hint of nostalgia. Travis brings in fresh lobster, king crab and oysters from around the world. He prepares daily changing selections of fish on an open-pit charcoal grill in the exhibition kitchen. The menu extends beyond seafood. If beef is your preference, Sea Grill serves 28-day dry-aged certified Angus prime steaks. The rack of lamb is epic. Among the sharable sides are creamy polenta and the addictive lobster mashed potatoes. For dessert, try the Mount Rainier Volcano, a baked Alaska that provides a fiery climax to an evening of culinary delight. After a play or show, stop by and enjoy a signature Mai Tai or a Zentini in the remarkable circular bar with shades of glowing marine blue. Bar snacks include sea delicacies such as Wicked Shrimp, Dungeness crab cake and the bar prawn cocktail. Weather permitting, enjoy your drink on the outside deck. Sea Grill is also open for lunch. Come by mid-day and try the warm seafood Caesar, the Oregonzola burger or the Maine lobster linguini. Visit Sea Grill soon and savor the experience.

1498 Pacific Avenue, Suite 300, Tacoma WA
(253) 272-5656
www.the-seagrill.com

Tango Restaurant & Lounge

The food at Tango Restaurant & Lounge is inspired by the lands where the tango is popular, namely Spain, Cuba and South America. As scintillating as the dance, the restaurant has earned rave reviews since opening in 2000 for both its cuisine and ambience. "This sophisticated tapas bar supplies sexy snacks for an even sexier crowd," notes Citysearch. Sip a mojito from the bar as you check out the scene and wait for your food to arrive. Ceviche and an assortment of hot and cold tapas are the main attractions, though this is a place for much more than just appetizers. Executive Chef Michael Bruno's paella is exquisite, and his grilled lamb with a fruity crust is a marvel. Pastry Chef Anna McKinley deserves the credit for the chocolate Diablo cake, which Citysearch named one of the best desserts in 2004 and 2006. *Seattle Metropolitan* magazine agrees that this cube of chocolate creaminess surrounded by a cayenne-infused meringue is "the single best dessert in this city." Housed inside a 1908 brick building on the cusp of Capitol Hill, Tango Restaurant & Lounge is located just a short walk from the convention center, Paramount Theater and ACT Theater. Make it your choice for a meal that will arouse your passions.

1100 Pike Street, Seattle WA (206) 583-0382
www.tangorestaurant.com

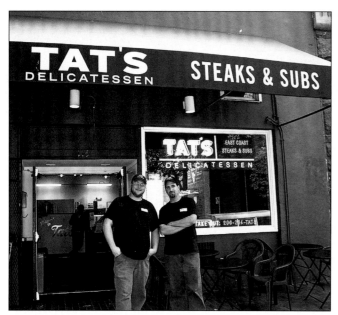

Tat's Delicatessen

Where do you go when you're craving an authentic cheesesteak sandwich but are 3,000 miles from Philly? Seattle's Tat's Delicatessen in historic Pioneer Square, that's where. Luckily, folks from the Emerald City no longer have to hop a flight back East to enjoy such regional classics. Tat's specializes in authentic East Coast cheesesteaks and subs, including hot pastrami, grinders, Italian, chicken cheesesteaks and many more. Interested in lighter fare? Tat's also offers a variety of delicious fresh salads and homemade soups and stews. In the morning, you can choose from a selection of breakfast egg sandwiches. Hosting a meeting or party in Seattle? Tat's is a must for all of your catering needs with a tempting array of sub trays and platters. Brian "Tat" Tatman and Jason Simodejka established the deli in 2004 to bring a taste of their hometowns to their newly adopted city. Tat and Jason grew up in Philadelphia and New Jersey respectively. Tat's Delicatessen is the place if you're looking for some authentic East Coast grub served in a friendly and efficient manner.

115 Occidental Avenue S, Seattle WA (206) 264-TATS (8287)
www.tatsdeli.com

Wild Orchid

Lim Po, owner of Wild Orchid, delivers authentic Thai and Oriental food in Tacoma's 6th Avenue business district. Mr. Po assures authenticity by hiring employees of Thai and Oriental descent who have a deep understanding of proper ingredients and food preparation secrets. Dishes here feature fresh ingredients, and menu selection is extensive with appetizers, soups and salads for every taste. Sautéed dishes, offerings from the grill and noodle delicacies abound. Curry dishes, rice entrées and many seafood selections assure you'll find your favorite Asian foods here. Mr. Po was born in Cambodia, lived in Bangkok, and moved with his family to Europe. He fell in love with America after vacationing here and dreamed of opening his own restaurant. The dream sprang as much from his love of people as from his love of food. He is renowned for his ever-present smile and loves the notion of helping to make positive changes in what he considers a small community. For delicious Thai and Oriental cuisine in a welcoming place that makes you feel you have been transported miles away from the everyday cares of life, visit Wild Orchid.

3023 6th Avenue, Tacoma WA (253) 627-5889

Three Chicks Catering

From boxed lunch to black tie, Three Chicks Catering promises to, Make Fun of Your Parties. That's the playful attitude of Owner Nems Scarim. Nems, along with Vice President Chick Becky Jorgensen, Executive Chef Jackie Westergaard and Sous Chef Michael DiMiceli, create delicious and creative food displays for all sorts of events. Voted Best Caterer in South King County and Northeast Tacoma by the *Federal Way Mirror,* Three Chicks delights guests with fun food preparations, which include antipasto trays with dipping sauces served in bell peppers, twisted breadsticks and garlic chicken satays displayed in artistic, vertical arrangements. A veggie tray isn't a tray at all at Three Chicks. Served in clear glass vases and displayed like a floral bouquet, these *veggie vases* are edible art. The Candied Walnut Spinach salad comes topped with juicy diced apples, bleu cheese crumbles, sweet and spicy candied walnuts and the most delicious cranberry vinaigrette you've ever tasted. Chilled salmon comes adorned with flowers cut from sweet peppers and the International Cheese Tray is an amazing presentation of hand selected hard and soft cheese of the world. For a sweet ending, savor a fresh baked chocolate chunk cookie or a fudge truffle with port wine pipette. The fun food from Three Chicks Catering features popular homemade dressings, marinades and herb rubs. Nems loves a party and works to make your event a smash with your guests, whether your occasion is casual, corporate or classy. Three Chicks offers drop-off or full-service off-site catering in your home, office or other venue. For a good time, call Three Chicks Catering and feel like a guest at your own party.

3822 S Union Avenue, Tacoma WA
(253) 475-8333
www.threechickscatering.com

Harmon Brewery & Restaurant

One of the pioneers of Tacoma's urban renaissance, Patrick Nagle, is a local Tacoma product, and so is his beer. After graduating from Washington State University, Patrick opened the Harmon Brewery & Restaurant in 1996 to bring Tacomans a product that they could celebrate as their own. His pride in the Northwest is declared in the names of his award winning microbrews, from the golden Pinnacle Peak Pale Ale to the hoppy Brown's Point ESB and the dark and rich Puget Sound Porter. Mike Davis is the brewmaster who presides over the 15-barrel system. With a casual atmosphere suitable for the whole family, the restaurant is the home of $3 steaks on Mondays. Many folks consider the big burgers and calamari the best in town. The Harmon made local history when it became Tacoma's very first microbrewery. Its location in the heart of downtown Tacoma is just a block away from the city's historic Brewery District, once the home of such breweries as the Heidelberg and the Columbia. While Patrick is very proud of Tacoma and aware of his place in its history, his favorite quote comes not from a local statesman but from one of the country's Founding Fathers. Ben Franklin said, "Beer is proof that God loves us and wants us to be happy." Raise a pint to Ben and to Tacoma at the Harmon Brewery & Restaurant.

1938 Pacific Avenue, Tacoma WA
(253) 383-BREW (2739)
www.harmonbrewing.com

Tacoma Dome at Sunset
Photo by J. Poth

Troiani Ristorante Italiano

Spaghetti and meatballs may hit the spot for everyday Italian comfort food, but when a special occasion arises, you can count on Paul Mackay's Troiani Ristorante Italiano to provide the atmosphere and Italian cuisine that make the evening magical. The restaurant reviewer for the *Seattle Times* was certainly enchanted. "One valet took my car while the other escorted me to the door," she wrote. "Within minutes, I had a well-mixed cocktail in hand, bread at my elbow and an opportunity to view Troiani at its bustling best." After this very promising start, diners view a menu that presents so very many appealing options for a traditional full-course Italian feast. A dream meal might consist of the *pancetta*-wrapped prawns from the antipasti selections, followed by the house salad of Bibb lettuce, hazelnuts, goat cheese and golden beets. For the pasta course, the lobster ravioli would be hard to pass up, though you could not go wrong with any of the choices. The second main course could be anything from *branzino*, that is, shaved fennel and orange salad, to lamb rack chops or *osso buco*. A vegetable side dish, such as the baked squash with brown sugar, *parmigiano reggiano* and sage, completes the meal. Consider also the a wine list that can, without exaggeration, be called massive, and you'll see that Troiani Ristorante Italiano aims not just to satisfy an appetite but to provide a dining experience that you will remember for years. Reserve your table now.

1001 3rd Avenue, Seattle WA (206) 624-4060
www.troianiseattle.com

CRAVE

Located in Seattle's chic Capitol Hill Arts Center, Crave serves contemporary comfort foods that reflect the vivacious, renaissance spirit of founder and Executive Chef Robin Leventhal, who believes food should be beautiful but unpretentious. Crave was featured on the February 2007 cover of *Seattle Metropolitan Comfort Food Magazine* and was voted Best Breakfast in 2004 and Best Restaurant in 2006 by *Seattle Weekly*. With its hand-crafted tables and booths, candle-lit corners and large picture windows, this is a delightful place to dine. Crave is open for breakfast, brunch, lunch and hearty dinners. Almost everything is made in-house from scratch with the best-quality ingredients. Only free-range, grass-fed organic meats are used here, along with artisan breads and locally-grown produce, as available. Signature dishes include the locally-famous Shiitake Mac & Cheese, goat cheese gnocchi, duck *confit* and apple Dutch babies, a thick apple crepe. Early risers enjoy the espresso bar, which features Caffé Umbria coffee and fresh pastries as well as free wireless Internet access. Chef Robin offers off-site catering, working with you to create the right menu for the season and occasion. For a dining adventure with international flavor, visit Crave.

1621 12ᵗʰ Avenue, Seattle WA
(206) 388-0526
www.cravefood.com

Farrelli's Wood Fire Pizza

Farrelli's Wood Fire Pizza is more than just a great family restaurant with excellent pizza at affordable prices. It's also a genuine family to its workers, many of whom have grown up here. When the Farrell family opened this restaurant, they made the commitment to treat their workers like valued members of the family, offering full benefits to all employees. Take, for example, Tacoma General Manager Mike Rutledge, who started working here at age 15 as a dishwasher and has moved up through the ranks to run his own store. As well as they treat their workers, it's the customers at Farrelli's who are in for a real treat. Delicious wood-fired pizzas top the menu, with a full range of toppings. The restaurant uses only the freshest ingredients and the finest applewood to seal in the best flavors. You'll also find a full array of appetizers and sandwiches for lunch and dinner. You'll delight in watching as your food is prepared in the open kitchen. The atmosphere is friendly and inviting. Kids will enjoy balloons and handling uncooked pizza dough. For adults, there's a happy hour in the evening where you can taste the Farrelli's Five, a mixture of five different fruit cocktails. Farrelli's is dedicated to the community as well, sponsoring athletic teams and arts events. Come and be treated like part of the family at Farrelli's Wood Fire Pizza.

Tacoma WA (253) 759-1999
Sumner WA (253) 447-2227
Parkland WA (253) 538-0202
DuPont WA (253) 912-5200
Lacey WA (360) 493-2090
www.farrellispizza.com

Volterra

Don Curtiss and Michelle Quisenberry named their Seattle restaurant after the Italian town of Volterra where they were married. The couple's love for food and for Tuscany has become an avenue to pleasure for their customers, accomplished through Don's masterful and artistic preparations. Volterra opened in 2005 in Ballard, one of Seattle's hottest neighborhoods. Don's 20-year culinary career has been inspiring to-date with praise from culinary experts throughout the country. Michelle is an international accounting consultant and ably handles the business end of Volterra. The majority of the foods served here are organic, and the menu changes seasonally. A favorite appetizer is the Bruschetta Volterrana, an intriguing mix of mushroom and truffle puree and minced artichokes served on Tuscan bread. For a main course, consider such popular choices as lamb ragu served with house-made noodles, wild boar tenderloin or a polenta custard with a mushroom ragu. The choice of Italian wines here has earned Volterra a *Wine Spectator* Award of Excellence, and Volterra's signature cocktail list stands apart with such selections as Volterra Sky, which features blue Curacao and vodka combined with sage, orange flower water and lemon. Artistry and authenticity, right down to the coffee served with French sugar and special cookies, come at a neighborhood price at this eatery, which produces wine and several foods under its own label, including a fennel seasoning salt. For meals inspired by Tuscany, visit Volterra.

5411 Ballard Avenue NW, Seattle WA
(206) 789-5100
www.volterrarestaurant.com

Asado

The exotic flavors and smells of fine Argentinean cuisine await diners at Asado. The Tacoma restaurant features all natural Black Angus beef grilled on an open mesquite fire and served with *chimichurri* and *salsa criolla*. You'll also find traditional seafood, pork, lamb and chicken dishes here. A choice of side dishes featuring seasonal vegetables promise a rotating mix of fresh flavors throughout the year. The restaurant's name, *Asado*, means *grilled meat* and rightly describes the high protein meals characteristic of Argentina. At Asado, you'll find a uniquely Argentinean mix of European and South American flavors, with Executive Chef Sean Quinn demonstrating a Spanish-Italian influence. The Peruvian purple mashed potatoes are always popular, while lamb shank and vegetarian tamales provide tastes particular to this fascinating culinary tradition. If you're looking for something a little less formal, try dishes from the restaurant's bar menu, which includes such enticements as lamb and beef empanadas or the Asado burger, a ground sirloin burger served with fried provolone, ham and yucca fries. You'll find a comfortable, friendly environment here that's both dressy and casual along with an energetic and helpful staff. Experience the special favors of Argentina from the vantage point of the Pacific Northwest at Asado.

2810 6th Avenue, Tacoma WA
(253) 272-7770
www.asadotacoma.com

Canlis Restaurant

Awards line the stairwell up to the private dining areas at Canlis Restaurant. It's one of the most celebrated restaurants in the nation, and it's all in a day's work to win such honors as the 2007 James Beard Foundation Outstanding Service award and placement in *Gourmet Magazine*'s 2006 list of America's Top 50 Restaurants. Founder Peter Canlis set out to create an ideal fine dining experience in Seattle's Queen Anne district in 1950. The stone building is an architectural wonder, with wide views of Lake Union, the city lights and the

Photo Copyright Brian Canlis Photography, 2006

Cascades. Your servers operate as a team, sharing tips and profits in a style Peter believes best serves his guests. Canlis defines contemporary Northwest cuisine with seasonal selections, seafood delicacies and Wagyu steaks, a Kobe-style beef that comes from American-raised Japanese cattle. The house salad is a masterpiece of meticulously crisped romaine leaves and fresh herbs. Presidents and movie stars dine at Canlis. Plan to don your best evening wear and make a weekend reservations well in advance. Today, Peter's son Chris and his wife, Alice, run the restaurant with their sons. "Like us, Canlis is steady, trustworthy, and honest. Yet like us, it carries a sense of adventure, romance, and fun," says Alice. Mark is manager; Brian is head of the new Department of Adventure; and Matt is the chaplain and whiskey consultant. They invite you to be their honored guests at Canlis.

2576 Aurora Avenue N, Seattle WA
(206) 283-3313
www.canlis.com

Waterfront Seafood Grill

Fresh seafood, aged steaks and panoramic views are just some of the qualities that set Waterfront Seafood Grill apart. You are sure to notice the attentive service and beautifully appointed surroundings from your seat at the end of Seattle's Pier 70. The restaurant, part of the MacKay Restaurant Group, features the creativity of Executive Chef Steve Cain, backed by General Manager Chris Sparkman's 22 years of experience. Sip your cocktail from a deck that cantilevers out over the bay or watch the colors change at the illuminated wave bar, the longest bar in Seattle. Floor to ceiling windows offer diners sweeping views of Elliott Bay, the Olympic Mountains and the Space Needle. Start your meal with such seafood appetizers as fresh West Coast oysters or spicy crab bisque. The menu abounds with seafood choices that are grilled simply and served with various sauces. Try the king crab legs from the Barents Sea or the Alaskan weathervane scallops, flanked with the trademark lobster mashed potatoes. Meat lovers appreciate the 28-Day Dry-Aged Certified Angus Beef prime steaks or the savory rack of lamb. Many of the dishes are prepared on an open-pit charcoal grill in the exhibition kitchen. Desserts are equally spectacular and include such temptations as Bailey's chocolate bread pudding or the flaming Emerald City Volcano, the restaurant's signature version of Baked Alaska. For dining that's as exciting as it is delicious, come experience Waterfront Seafood Grill.

2801 Alaskan Way, Seattle WA
(206) 956-9171
www.waterfrontpier70.com

Wild Wheat Bakery Café & Restaurant

Wild Wheat Bakery is a bakery, café and restaurant all rolled into one. Owner Mark Handman has been a baker since the age of 18. His folks had a bakery, and he has owned the Greenwood Bakery and the Ballard Baking Company. After he married Marja, a Dutch woman, they baked in Holland for years. When they moved to Kent, Mark and Marja never wondered what they would do. The only question was where. First Avenue South in downtown Kent has become a bit of a restaurant row, and anchoring that row is Wild Wheat Bakery. The baked goods here are some of the finest in the Northwest, including sweet braids of challah, rye, ciabatta and sourdough. They offer organic breads encrusted with olives, herbs, fruits and nuts. The pastry case features flaky puff pastries, fresh fruit pies, croissants, bagels, cream-filled cakes and giant cookies. Wild Wheat Bakery embraces Old World tradition with a commitment to quality that's second to none. Mark and Marja serve breakfast, lunch and dinner, with a diverse menu that includes their own cold-smoked lox, pastrami they cure themselves, grilled salmon tostadas, and lamb or beef burgers built on homemade rolls. If you like blintzes, try Russian Grandma Minnie's blintzes. They are the best. The next time you're in Kent, head down restaurant row to Wild Wheat Bakery. This is one place you won't want to miss.

202 1ˢᵗ Avenue S, Kent WA (253) 856-8919

Photo by Jennifer Gifford

WESTERN WASHINGTON

Shopping
& Gifts

Revitalize! Health Spa & Organic Store

Shopping for someone with diabetes, high blood pressure, gluten or lactose sensitivities? Feel it's a monumental undertaking to find great taste and still make that lifestyle change? Revitalize! Health Spa & Organic Store offers a wider variety for people with special dietary needs than any other store in the entire Columbia Basin. Revitalize stocks the most popular, and tasty, gluten-free baking mixes and pastas by brands such as Bob's Red Mill, Gluten Free Pantry, Pamela's, Arrowhead Mills, Gifts of Nature, Tinkyada and Namaste. To start the morning out right, try gluten-free cereals from Erewhon, Enjoy Life and Glutino. For those who enjoy hot dog and hamburger buns, toast or sandwiches, there is an entire line of Ener-G baked goods that are wheat, dairy and gluten free. Indulge yourself with a bowl of the highly sought after certified Gluten-Free Oats. For those who are watching their glycemic index and for no diabetic spiking, Revitalize carries Xylitol, which is highly recommended by dentists, plus fructose, agave nectar and kurlu for baking. Sugar-free cereals, snacks and chocolate bars are also on-hand. Just in, try adding flavored Stevia to your favorite beverage, or make your own soda from seltzer water. Eco Friendly and Mrs. Meyers, which are environmentally friendly, toxin-free household cleaning and pet care products, line the shelves. To help you with your health concerns, browse through a diverse number of self-help books on topics that range from cooking, diet and wellbeing to taking control of and managing your finances. The Little Shop with Big Variety is ready to serve you.

Photos By Barrett Brown Photograhy

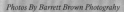
Photos By Barrett Brown Photograhy

If your partner's snoring raises the roof and keeps you awake, then step into Revitalize! Health Spa and Organic Store, the little shop in friendly downtown Kennewick where you can purchase Himalayan Crystal Salt Lamps. Not only are these lamps beautiful, but the negative ions they emit kill bacteria, purify the air, increase well being and soothe the mind, body and soul. Negative ions are abundant where nature is unspoiled, such as waterfalls, caves, mountains and the air following a thunderstorm. Customers swear by the salt crystals' therapeutic abilities, and they love the good night sleep they get when the effects of the crystals' negative ions quiet or even eliminate their partner's snoring. Some clients have reported that even their dogs have stopped snoring. However, snoring reduction isn't the only benefit people realize from the lamps: allergies, the common cold, sinus conditions, anxiety, fatigue, insomnia, migraines, depression, headaches and more have been relieved. The lamps can also protect you from harmful electrical magnetic frequencies, such as are emitted from computers, televisions and other electrical devices. Himalayan Crystal Salt Lamps are one of the shop's most popular items and Revitalize is noted for having the largest selection of these lamps for miles around, priding themselves on having the shapes and sizes to fit every décor and budget. Let the helpful staff assist in selecting a lamp that is right for you.

311 W Kennewick Avenue, Kennewick WA
(509) 586-6574
www.BiofeedbackPlus1.com

Mud in Your Eye Pottery

The sounds of 30 table fountains and assorted wind chimes let you know you have found Mud in Your Eye Pottery, located in one of Fairhaven's turn-of-the-century buildings. Further investigation reveals dozens of functional pieces, including oil lamps, birdbaths and cookware. Frank and Cate Howell owned a store by the same name in Los Gatos, California, which opened in 1971 and sold the work of 100 artists at three locations before closing in 1989. In 1996, the Howells moved their operation to a historic district on Bellingham's south side, known for galleries, crafts stores and restaurants. Cate handles management and Frank has returned to throwing pots, with several house potters working under his direction. He also uses his contacts to bring in the work of about 70 production potters, making the shop the largest retailer of U.S. made pottery on the West Coast. Mud in Your Eye concentrates on useful vessels made of watertight stoneware and porcelain, including kitchen bowls, tableware and bathroom accessories. The dense stoneware is watertight and transmits heat evenly. Foods won't stick to the glazed surfaces. You will find porcelain vases and carved dinnerware by Bill Campbell, known for his distinctive blue-lavender glaze, and place settings by Sunset Canyon Pottery. Put art to work in your life with a visit to Mud in your Eye Pottery.

911 Harris Avenue, Bellingham WA
(360) 650-9007
www.mudinyoureyepottery.com

Photo by Jennifer Gifford

Grassi's

Grassi's is Tacoma's landmark floral and gift shop, now in two locations. People from throughout the Northwest marvel at the dazzling flower artistry in the windows at Grassi's Center Street site. The shop also features a European-style cut flower market, delicious, locally made chocolates and hundreds of expressive cards. You'll find one-of-a-kind silk and dried flower arrangements, distinctive lamps, wall art and gardening gifts. Downtown, the Pacific Avenue site is housed in the charming old triangular Mack building, which provides a stunning backdrop for the enchanting women's boutique. Grassi's attracts savvy customers from around the South Sound in search of stunning fashion, not found in the mall. Look for colorful, fun purses and beautiful jewelry, scarves and shoes, plus clever gifts that make this a not-to-miss shopping experience. Upstairs is the Garden Café, which overlooks Union Station across the street. The Garden Café seems to float above the flowers and gifts downstairs. You can start the day with a Grassi's breakfast and try Grassi's Seasonal Sensation lunch entrees. Remember to save room for one of their fabulous desserts. The café provides a catering service and prepares tasty box lunches for patrons who are short on time. "We are family owned and operated," explain owners Ken and Kim Grassi. "We are dedicated to making your experience a pleasant one. That is why we always go the extra mile." Both locations offer gift baskets and delivery. Stop by Grassi's, have a bite to eat and see the gorgeous gift and flower combinations for yourself.

1702 Pacific Avenue, Tacoma WA
3602 Center Street, Tacoma WA
(253) 627-7196 or (800) 758-2764
www.grassisflorist.com

Bead Factory

Whether you are just beginning to make bead jewelry or are an expert, you'll find the stones and beads you need at the Bead Factory in Tacoma. Most people find beading and jewelry making to be very relaxing, and you'll experience this for yourself when you participate in any of more than 50 classes offered here each month. You can also walk right in and ask the friendly staff for help any time you need it. Owners Mark and Viki Lareau, who also sponsor the annual Puget Sound Bead Festival, believe service sets their store apart. One look at the selection, and you will think you're in the supermarket of beading. Mark and Viki import beads from all over the world, including Swarovski crystals, cultured pearls, Venetian blown glass and vintage glass, as well as semi-precious and precious stones. Prices

range from three cents to $200 a bead. The store even carries its own WireMaster brand. Regular customers get the royal treatment with such offerings as the Bead Club customer loyalty program, customized bead parties for any age and skill level, and the always-free Sunday morning Bead & Breakfast program, which features tips and tricks alongside coffee and pastries. You can also take advantage of the kid's playroom to drop off the little ones while you bead or shop. Discover the pleasures of beading with a visit to the Bead Factory.

3019 6th Avenue, Tacoma WA
(253) 572-5529 or (888) 500-BEAD (2323)
www.thebeadfactory.com

Renaissance Yarns

Revel in the rhythmic clicking of knitting needles while searching for new patterns, finishing up a project or learning to knit at Renaissance Yarns in Kent. Owners RoxieAnn Harvey and Nancy Skorupa first met on the bleachers while attending their sons' baseball games. Such common interests as crafting and gardening drew them together, and they soon became friends and then business partners. The duo is dedicated to keeping the art of knitting alive and chose the title Renaissance, which refers to the revival of art and learning, to express that dedication. Renaissance Yarns offers a diverse selection of quality yarns and needlework accessories, as well as an array of fine patterns and books. Colleague Liz Arcamo, who has over 30 years of knitting experience, has been schooled in the art of design and acts as one of the shop's instructors, along with Nancy and RoxieAnn. They teach knitting and crochet to people of all skill levels as well as specialized classes that focus on technique, sock making, sweaters and gifts. The shop is highly active in the community, works with local scout troops and offers prescheduled stitching circles, where you can receive help with your project and visit with other knitters. The shop is open late on Friday evenings where you will find knitters gathered to socialize, encourage and support each other as they create beautiful works of art. A visit to Renaissance Yarns will inspire you to express your artistic side.

207 E Meeker Street, Kent WA (253) 852-YARN (9276)
www.renaissanceyarns.com

Guitar Emporium

If the next great blues guitarist comes out of Seattle, you might see that guitarist playing an instrument from Guitar Emporium. Owner Robb Eagle has assembled what he believes to be the Northwest's finest selection of handmade acoustic instruments. He works directly with several top guitar makers in the Pacific Northwest, including Larrivée and Webber, to bring you instruments that are a delight to behold as well as to play. When you drop by, ask him to explain why he considers Webber to be the best value available in the acoustic guitar market today. While you're there, you might even spot that long-sought-after guitar of your dreams among the Guitar Emporium's vintage and used instruments. The day we came by, the 1940 Martin 000-28 made us wish we had won the lottery so that we could afford to take this masterpiece home with us. Robb provides a relaxed environment where customers can sit down and get comfortable with an instrument without feeling pressured to buy. In addition to guitars, he carries mandolins and banjos along with a full line of accessories. Lessons and repairs are also available. Robb enjoys being part of the Ballard District of Seattle, which, he says, retains its older character while appealing to newer, trendier tastes. Sounds just like some of the guitars in his shop. Play a few licks at Guitar Emporium today.

5349 Ballard Avenue NW, Seattle WA (206) 783-7607
www.guitaremporium.com

Sweets, Treats & Designs

Whether you are looking for a gift, specialty chocolates, apparel or home décor, Sweets, Treats & Designs has it all. Located in North Tacoma, the store specializes in its own signature chocolates and cookies, created by Owners Mike and Jerri Turner. Knowing that their wide range of clients have different tastes and needs has inspired such innovative confections as hand-dipped chocolate licorice, fresh lemon zest bark, espresso bark and customized chocolate dipped fortune cookies. If you are looking for something special and unique to serve at your next event, Sweets, Treats & Designs can work with you to customize favors and desserts for your function. Not all treats here are edible. Jerri and Mike are known for traveling the States to find fun and fabulous merchandise that you will not find in your typical boutique. Whether your taste is shabby chic, girlie girl or simple elegance, Sweets, Treats & Designs will have you coming back again and again. With merchandise from such designers as Chandra Michaels of Sugarluxe, Jaqua, Illume and Empress Art, Mike and Jerri know that they have something for everyone. They invite you to visit their website or stop by their boutique to enter the extraordinary world of Sweets, Treats & Designs.

2209 N Pearl Street, Suite 103, Tacoma WA
(253) 752-7343
http://sweetstreats.com

Sip & Ship

In days of old, the local post office was more than just a place to collect the mail. It was a place to meet with neighbors and trade gossip and goods. It is this sense of community and camaraderie that Diana and Stephen Naramore have created at Sip & Ship, their unique contribution to the art of letter writing. Sip & Ship offers you a distinctive venue in which to deliver or collect your mail, enjoy fragrant fair trade coffee or find supplies for your stationary box. At the shipping bar you can order your favorite coffee drink, drop off a few packages and pick up your own mail from a private mail box. You can also grab a treat from the assortment of freshly baked goods, prepared and delivered daily by local bakeries. Once your missives are stamped and you've enjoyed a snack, you can browse the gift area and choose from an array of writing papers, pens and desk accessories, as well as photo frames, stylish clothing, jewelry and bath items. The shop also features an old cobble loft with cozy chairs where parents and kids alike can relax and write letters or fill out their cards, notes and invitations. Come to Sip & Ship, where you can step away from the computer, enjoy a cup of coffee, put pen to paper and practice your calligraphy.

1752 NW Market Street, Seattle WA (206) 789-4488
www.sipandship.com

Second Hand Pianos

Second Hand Pianos is an exceptional piano shop where store owner Marci Bagley is firmly committed to the quality and reliability of the instruments she sells. Beautiful vintage pianos, selected for their structural stability, are restored on-site. Customers can watch as the instruments are brought back to their former glory and today's industry standards. Marci utilizes the skills of a Master Technician, assuring that all work is done by someone with over 25 years of experience. One member of the team is a cabinet finisher who has one of the highest reputations in the Pacific Northwest's piano industry. This shop also sells instruments that have been restored by piano technicians throughout the region. You will find newer used pianos that are in very good condition when they arrive at the shop as well. All of the instruments originate from the U.S. or Europe. Due to Marci's careful research, it's not unusual for her to show you a piano's representation in a 100-year-old catalog, or a picture of the man who designed it. Shopping at Second Hand Pianos is a relaxing experience, where browsing is encouraged. With no salespeople, you will feel at home in the cozy, zero pressure environment, and can even play the pianos if you want. Marci is happy to provide visitors with as much information as they request. She says, "I don't sell pianos. I let people buy them."

414 W Meeker Street, Kent WA (253) 850-0649
www.secondhandpianos.net

BKB & Company

Among the art you will find at BKB & Company are scarves to help keep yourself warm and rugs to make your home feel warm and inviting. You will discover handcrafted tools for the garden and lovely vases in which to display the flowers that you grow there. Wearable and decorative art is the dual focus at BKB, located in the Museum District of downtown Tacoma on the campus of the University of Washington in Tacoma. Displaying the work of 30 jewelry artists alone, the gallery is remarkable for its selection as well as for its variety of functional art. Made from such material as glass, clay and fiber, the pieces are as much products of the heart as they are of the hands. "We cannot stress enough how special are the things that people make with their hands," say Corky and Victoria Brown, the mother and daughter artists who own BKB. "They come from the heart, and there is so much spirit that goes into every piece." If you are an artist who shares the BKB vision, you should speak to the owners about showing your work at the gallery. You may also be interested in participating in the Featured Artist Program during Tacoma's 3rd Thursday ArtWalk. For art that that you can wear and use, check out what's on display at BKB & Company.

1734 Pacific Avenue, Tacoma WA (253) 272-6884
www.bkbcompany.com

Alan Gorsuch behind one of the three Alaska Yukon Pacific Exposition windows.
Largest beveled windows in the world

Buzzard's CDs & Stadium Video

Thousands of tantalizing titles await customers who love music, videos and games at two Tacoma shops, Buzzard's CDs & Stadium Video. In 1992, Marriott employees Marty Campbell and Mark Botts started the CD company as a hobby. Two years later, they used funds from CD sales to purchase Stadium Video. One year later, growth caused the company to relocate to larger quarters and a year after that, in 1996, Buzzard's CDs opened in its current location. Mark moved on to other ventures in 1999, and Marty continues to operate Stadium Video on North Tacoma Avenue and the jumping Buzzard's CDs on Jefferson Avenue, which offers new and used videos as well as CDs and DVDs for an inventory of some 30,000 titles. You'll find boxed sets and laser discs here too. Video games are also well represented along with a vintage collection of cassette tapes and LPs. The friendly staff at these related stores can help you locate hard to find and out of print materials and guarantees your purchase against defects. Both Buzzard's CDs and Stadium Video have been repeatedly voted Best in Tacoma by various publications, and Marty now serves as president of the Downtown Association and is well known in the community for his humor, generosity and kindness. Find your favorite things and a whole lot more at Buzzard's CDs & Stadium Video.

1916 Jefferson Avenue, Tacoma WA (Buzzard CDs) (253) 591-0183
29 Tacoma Avenue, Tacoma WA (Stadium Video) (253) 572-1190
www.buzzardsdiscs.com

Jerry's Rock & Gem

Are you a rock hound? Do you love to spend a weekend searching for the earth's treasures? If so, then Jerry's Rock & Gem is for you. Do you merely love fine jewelry? Jerry's has something for you as well. Jerry Appleton, a serious rock hound, opened this geologists' dream shop in 1954 as Jerry's Agate Shop. By 1982 it was time to retire. He passed the reigns to a jeweler and rock hound named Tom who grew the business to include jewelry design, manufacturing and repair. Tom then sold the shop to Glen Saurdiff, who holds degrees in jewelry design and geology and who added gems to the shop's already impressive inventory. At this point Jerry's was a rock, lapidary, jewelry and gem store and the only thing missing, geologically speaking, was fossils. This is where co-owner Joan Simpson, who holds a Ph.D. in Paleontology, came in. At this point it occurred to the owners that the name Jerry's Agate Shop was a trifle restrictive, and so they adopted the name they bear today. Jerry's Rock and Gem now offers a truly amazing collection of rocks, minerals, gems and crystals. It also has a vast inventory of equipment and supplies for locating and working on gems and minerals. Whether you seek gems to add to your collection, need a repair for an existing treasure or need equipment to mount your own geological expedition, you're sure to find it at Jerry's Rock & Gem.

804 West Valley Highway, Kent WA (253) 852-0539
www.jerrysrockandgem.com

Learning Sprout

Put the fun back into learning with a trip to Learning Sprout, a one-stop shop filled with toys, games and learning aids for children of all ages. Founder Rose Calvin, who owns the shop along with her husband, Dan, opened this specialty store in 1996, after several years spent in the childcare business. As an owner of childcare centers, Rose knows how important good quality learning tools, such as games, toys and puzzles, are to cognitive development, especially in younger children. The business resides in a charming building from the early 1900s. Both children and adults appreciate the shopping experience here, because mom and dad can shop while children try out the toys. The first Saturday of each month is a dedicated play day. Clifford the Big Red Dog shows up periodically to visit with his friends at the Learning Sprout. The shop's friendly, dedicated staff is delighted to help you find the perfect gift or toy and provide complimentary gift wrapping and good advice. Let your child's imagination soar at Learning Sprout.

809 Pacific Avenue, Tacoma WA (253) 274-0136
www.learningsprout.com

Cake Apparel & Home

Stop telling your kids that you used to look great in jeans. You can look sensational today in a pair from Cake Apparel & Home. Mary Johnson, Brianna Evans and their staff are fashion experts who pride themselves on being able to fit a flattering pair of jeans on anyone who walks through the door, regardless of their shape, size, age or gender. In fact, you'll find a variety of men's and women's clothing here, from denim to dressy. Cake is also the place to turn for gifts and everything you need for a fashionable home and a fashionable you. You'll find glassware and candles, jewelry and purses, bath and body products as well as couches and even some antique furnishings. Mary and Brianna, who both have design backgrounds, promise that they will never let you walk out of the store with something that isn't right for you. Their friendship was solidified during many shopping trips together, when they would talk about bringing a high quality, affordable boutique to the Tacoma area. They have assembled a highly personable staff at Cake Apparel & Home who are ready to assist you with a full array of boutique services, including tailoring and honest opinions. The shop is easy to find in the Green Firs Shopping Center. Whether you need a coffee table or a pair of shoes, when you want items that fit you and your lifestyle, come to Cake Apparel & Home.

3838 Bridgeport Way W, University Place WA
(253) 564-2253
www.cakeapparelandhome.com

Pioneer Square Antique Mall

With 65 quality dealers displaying their wares in the 6,000-square-foot basement of the 1889 Pioneer building, Pioneer Square Antique Mall is a treasure hunter's paradise. Owned by Dr. Richard and Dorothy Sikora, the mall has been attracting visitors and residents to the historic heart of Seattle since 1985. It's known for costume and estate jewelry, vintage sterling silver and Bakelite jewelry kitchenware. You'll also find relics from the Seattle World's Fair, porcelain, toys and clothes. The mall offers objects in many styles, including Art Deco, Art Nouveau, Arts & Crafts, Mid-Century Modern, Native American and Southwest. Marion Anderson is the knowledgeable general manager, known nationally for her Raggedy Ann collection. A visit to the mall fits well into a tour of the entire Pioneer Square, where Seattle originated in the mid 19th century. Henry Yesler, who owned a steam-powered sawmill in the vicinity, lived on this corner. Whether you seek something particular or just enjoy browsing through historical items, plan to visit Pioneer Square Antique Mall, the oldest antique mall in Seattle.

602 1st Avenue, Pioneer Square, Seattle WA (206) 624-1164
www.pioneer-building.com

Venue

Located in the heart of historical Ballard, Venue incorporates work studios for artists with a retail boutique. Although owner Diane Macrae was already selling her custom handbags at fairs and festivals, she wanted a local venue for designing, crafting and selling her products. Realizing that most artists have similar needs, she opened Venue in 2005. The building is new construction, built to replace the old Sunset Motel that burned down in 2000. It provides eight studios and gives over 30 Seattle artists and designers high-profile space for showcasing their best work. Because the artists work here, customers can sometimes meet the artists and commission custom work. The ever-changing collection at Venue features everything from artisan chocolates, jewelry and pottery to photography and home accessories. The variety makes Venue an ideal place for gift shopping. The building's minimalist interior and fresh, trendy colors set it apart from its historic surroundings and make it fun to shop for everything from fine art to personal embellishments. You can also tap into your creative side when Venue offers special programs. Past classes involved learning to make chocolate truffles and Polaroid image and emulsion transfer classes. Visit Venue, where the proximity of working artists seems to charge the air.

5408 22nd Avenue NW, Ballard WA (206) 789-3335
www.venueballard.com

Urban Gourmet

If there's a gadget to simplify a certain kitchen task, you will probably find it at Urban Gourmet. Gadget Land is one of the popular departments in a shop that is as eclectic as the diverse 6th Avenue neighborhood it serves. Owners Robin Jensen and Cathie Attebery live in the neighborhood and take an active interest in its welfare with donations to local causes. They carry kitchenware and gourmet foods. Customers prize the selection of gifts, bulk teas and spices at the shop. You will also find desirable cookware lines, such as Le Creuset and All-Clad, along with natural cleaning supplies and just the right accessories for a home bar. Gift giving is easier when you start your search at Urban Gourmet, where you can purchase gourmet foods, gift baskets, candles, artwork and iron garden accessories. Robin and Cathie run the shop along with Robin's sister Terry Wong, who works as buyer and manager. The threesome shares their love of cooking through their product line and at classes taught by some of Tacoma's best chefs. Recharge your cooking interest with a visit to Urban Gourmet.

2602 6th Avenue, Suite B, Tacoma WA (253) 272-3111

Romanza Gifts (Ballard)

John Sterlin and Vince Harris, the owners of Romanza Gifts, often find nose prints on the windows of their Ballard store, because they fill those windows with eye-catching seasonal displays. Romanza's gift items fulfill longings you didn't even know you had. John credits his mother, who opened a shop in Walla Walla over a decade ago, with the inspiration for his Seattle-area and Walla Walla stores and thriving e-commerce business. The shops bring together remarkable fragrances, accent pieces, wine and chocolate. You'll find candles that ignite the imagination. The bath and body products invite you to bring spa luxury into the lives of you and your loved ones. Clocks by Timeworks turn a wall into a statement. Many of the shop's colors and products evoke Tuscany, but you'll find influences from France and England, too. Currently, Romanza prepares the gifts for every celebrity guest on the *Ellen Degeneres Show*. John and Vince opened the store in 1999 and used their natural sense of style to guide their initial efforts. "Vince and I love boutiques," says John, "and this gave us the chance to bring all the things that we love together in one place." Romanza is Italian for romance, and visitors experience that giddy otherworldly feeling that accompanies amour. A combination of intriguing offerings, a peaceful interior and a friendly staff account for the store's loyal following. Next time you need a gift or just inspiring surroundings, visit Romanza Gifts.

2206 NW Market Street, Ballard WA
(206) 706-1764 or (888) 519-3475 (online store)
www.romanzagifts.com

Votiv

Sometimes having too much of a good thing is a good problem to have. When Meredith Ida and renowned glass artist Ian Lewis got together, they discovered they had far too much fine glass art to fit in their home. This problem prompted Meredith to open Votiv, a quaint little art shop located right in the middle of the Wallingford neighborhood in Seattle. Votiv features a variety of glass art from Seattle artists. The primary artisan is Ian, who has shown his work in galleries worldwide, from Boston to Tokyo. Ian has been making glass art for more than two decades, in forms ranging from ornate glasses to colorful lighting fixtures and beautiful hanging sculptures. You'll also find the delicate glass candle containers from which the store takes its name, in addition to bowls, vases and garden accents. Meredith's emphasis on the artist means patrons can actually meet the person that created the work in the store. Votiv also deals in custom pieces, which can be made to order. Meredith delights in turning ideas into reality. The selection here is constantly changing, with a variety of new pieces available. For beautiful and useful glass pieces for any home or location, come to Votiv.

3516 Carr Place N, Seattle WA (360) 224-8534
www.votivglass.com

West Coast Awards & Athletics

Since 1976, West Coast Awards & Athletics has been Kent's number one resource for trophies, awards and promotional gear of all kinds. Founder, co-owner and area native Liner Flaten has always loved athletics. He is joined in the business by his wife Chris, sister Stafne Birditt, mother Nancy Flaten, and a staff of positive, caring and committed people, all of whom share his passion for outstanding customer service and community involvement. The business began when Liner collaborated with a co-student while attending Highline Community College to form a small trophy company named Trophies Unlimited. The business was moved to its current location on Smith Street around 1980 and bloomed into a retail store for trophies, awards, athletic equipment and shoes, uniforms and apparel. The owners also changed and West Coast Awards & Athletics was re-born with total family ownership. Today, West Coast Awards & Athletics offers its customers anything from a full line of corporate or athletic garments for screen printing and embroidery, to laser engraving or sand-blasting for the most elegant corporate award. All work is done in-house. West Coast Awards & Athletics features a wide variety of products from firms such as Hanes, Nike, Champion and Richardson Caps. They also supply Letter Jackets for the local schools as well as having a full line of promotional products. West Coast Awards & Athletics backs any product or service they sell100%, and pride themselves in their customer satisfaction.

515 E Smith Street, Kent WA (253) 854-4973
www.westcoastawards.com

Mt. Rainier
Photo by Jennifer Gifford

WESTERN WASHINGTON

Weddings
& Events

Blitz and Co. Florist

Flowers from Blitz and Co. Florist have been pleasing the eye and touching the heart for more than 20 years. There is hardly a segment of the Tacoma community that Blitz has not served in this time. Besides adding beauty to weddings and other private events, Blitz has provided flowers for the universities and museums as well as for corporations and hospitals. Owner Steve Barbazette's inspiring

story began when he was a teenager. He took a job driving a flower truck and thereby developed a fascination with the business that has now lasted 30 years. From this modest beginning, Steve is now in charge of a company that ships worldwide and has earned a stellar reputation throughout the city. Blitz is well known for its theme flowers, and much of the credit for these goes to Carrie Carlson Keller, the head designer for many years. The core members of the Blitz staff, all of them educated in colors and designs, have been with the company for 10 years. Blitz is not just a florist but a gift and home décor store, too, where customers enjoy shopping for a variety of high-end but affordable items. Blitz also offers custom home decorating, a service much in demand during the holidays. For the sake of beauty, consider Blitz and Co. Florist for your floral needs.

909 Pacific Avenue, Tacoma WA
(253) 572-2327
www.blitzflowers.com

Bayview Limousine Service

Bayview Limousine Service started in 1990 as a single car operation from a one-bedroom apartment. Owner Rob Hansen had been racing motocross bikes at a professional level when a crash broke his neck and left him a quadriplegic. He was only 19. After nine months in the hospital he moved in with a friend who was a chauffer. Rob, now paralyzed from the neck down with no college education, got an idea. He borrowed $5,000 from a family member, bought his first limo, and launched Bayview Limousine Service. Rob now has 84 employees and a fleet of 48 limos, the largest and most diverse fleet in all of Washington. In 1999 Bayview was voted The Best

Limousine Service in America by *Limousine & Chauffeured Transportation Magazine.* South King County Commerce rewarded Rob with the business excellence award. The Association of Washington Business awarded Bayview with the workplace and training advancement award and the *Seattle Metropolitan* listed Bayview as one of the Top 25 Best Places to Work. Bayview's chauffeurs are the best-trained and most experienced professionals in the industry. The Bayview fleet is fully equipped with GPS in all vehicles, 24-hour live dispatch, a full time auto-detail and mechanic staff. They offer six, eight, and 10- passenger limos, SUVs, 15-passenger vans, and a wheelchair accessible van. The next time you need a limo, call Bayview Limousine Service. You will be in an exceptional vehicle driven by the most capable hands.

Serving Tacoma, Seattle and the Eastside Area WA
(206) 223-6200 *www.bayviewlimo.com*

Ballard Blossom

High-quality fresh flowers at affordable prices have been the family business at Ballard Blossom since 1927. David Martin, who has owned this full-service Seattle florist since 2002, maintains the traditions of value and friendly service established by his grandfather, who founded the store 80 years ago. Since the business took root in the 1920s, it has grown to one of the largest florists on the West Coast, and been recognized as a Top 50 member of FTD. Ballard Blossom has flowers for every occasion, ranging from carnation bouquets for St. Patrick's Day to red rose arrangements for anniversaries. You'll also find a large variety of decorative houseplants. The shop's expert designers can create an arrangement to meet any need. Ballard Blossom has a large selection of gift items, including gourmet food and delectable candies, bath products and home décor items. The store also offers a variety of baskets appropriate for use as corporate gifts. It can deliver anywhere in the world, with same-day delivery offered in the local area. Come to Ballard Blossom and take advantage of the family tradition of fresh flowers and excellent service.

1766 NW Market Street, Ballard, Seattle WA
(206) 782-4213 *www.ballardblossom.com*

Floral Masters

Flowers are an ideal way to say a myriad of things, from thank you to job well done. You can say these things even better with blooming designs from Floral Masters. Owners Roya and Bijan Khorrami, who purchased the company in 2000, are proud of their astonishing floral designers. The staff members collectively have more than 25 years of experience. All of them bring something different to the design table. Floral Masters is a full-service florist that can assist you with all your floral needs, including wedding arrangements, special event designs and simple, yet elegant displays for everyday happenings, such as birthdays, anniversaries and holiday celebrations. Floral Masters will also take the time to decorate your home or office for the holidays. In addition to spectacular flowers for every occasion, Floral Master's also stocks an assemblage of home décor and art pieces and offers specialized consultations for interior design. Roya has more than 20 years of interior design experience and has beautifully incorporated the two fields of design and floral arrangements into one stunning shop. She can help you design any room or office. Roya's successes include designs for Seattle's Street of Dreams and the Seattle Symphony. Send an elegant gift, pick up some fragrant blooms or redesign your entire home with a little help from the experts at Floral Masters.

2303 1ˢᵗ Avenue, Seattle WA (206) 441-1122
Two Union Square Lobby, 601 Union Street, Seattle WA (206) 838-7290
www.floralmasters.net

A Rhapsody in Bloom

From flowers to coffee, A Rhapsody in Bloom hits all the right notes. The Tacoma florist's owner, Denise Smith, believes in providing great service to the community in every way possible. She says her favorite aspect of her job is creating floral arrangements for special events, such as weddings, because it allows her to satisfy an individual need. Denise can also meet your need for a great cup of espresso. Add a sandwich, salad or dessert, then savor the flavors in the courtyard, where you're likely to hear some live music at least twice a week. Denise created the funky, quaint environment to foster a sense of community. It's that desire for community that has compelled Denise to become involved in many community organizations as well. This oasis of calm along busy 6th Avenue delights and surprises those who discover it. Come on in to A Rhapsody in Bloom for flowers, food and a joyous environment that will put you in harmony with your world.

3709 6th Avenue, Tacoma WA
(253) 761-ROSE (7673) or (800) 579-0557

Capitol Hill Flowers & Garden

Sok Lee's wife is an inspiration to him in more ways than one. Sok had always been fond of beautiful flowers, but it was observing Mimi's creativity in flower design that prompted him to open Capitol Hill Flowers & Garden. Mimi is now the head designer at Capitol Hill, which is renowned for its huge selection of fresh-cut unusual and exotic flowers. You'll find more than 75 different varieties, including tropical flowers from Hawaii and South America. It also has more than 70 vases to pick from and a large selection

of gifts, including assorted plush animals and balloons for all occasions. Mimi and the staff at Capitol Hill excel in creating custom arrangements for any need or occasion, from weddings to corporate events. You'll also find plenty of gourmet fruit baskets and plants. This fully equipped FTD florist can wire flowers anywhere in the U.S. and worldwide. Capitol Hill is located in the center of Seattle's Hospital District and is very close to most funeral homes and downtown. It delivers daily to the Puget Sound area and serves all Seattle zip codes. Looking for a quick bunch of flowers? Check out Sok's street market, Blooms on Broadway, in the Broadway Market, which caters to walk-in traffic. Beauty, fun and convenience are in bloom at Capitol Hill Flowers & Garden and Blooms on Broadway.

300 15th Avenue, Seattle WA
(206) 325-5068 or (800) 888-5068
www.flower4gift.com

Hansen's Florist

When one family owns a florist shop for three generations, you can be sure of two things: they sell excellent flowers and they love what they do. Hansen's Florist, with locations in Georgetown and Fremont, can make those claims. It's been in business since 1945 with a standout reputation throughout Seattle. Hansen's flowers are fresh and long lasting; its arrangements offer an ever-fresh approach to floral artistry while rendering congratulations, sympathy, best wishes, love and romance. Seattle's brides cherish their Hansen's bouquets long after the blooms fade. Hansen's expertise also encompasses live plants and European dish gardens. Greeting cards of floral photography compliment your gift of flowers. The store also sells balloons and gift baskets loaded with fruit or gourmet goodies. Let Hansen's Florist help you honor every occasion with flowers.

1201 S Bailey Street, Seattle WA (Georgetown)
(206) 767-3280 or (800) 432-7092
3415 A Fremont Avenue N, Seattle WA (Fremont)
(206) 632-9330
www.hansensflorist.com

Patriot Limousine Service Inc.

The next time your special occasion calls for luxurious transportation, contact Patriot Limousine Service. Patriot Limousine is available any time of the day or night with reliable and safe professional service for weddings, proms, funerals and corporate accounts. Perhaps you need to get to the airport or want to miss the parking dilemma at a sports game. Whatever your needs, Patriot Limousine is ready to put its resources to work for you. Patriot is a member of the National Limousine Association, and all limousines at Patriot are fully insured, licensed and inspected by the Washington State Patrol. The inside of a super stretch Lincoln limousine is a world apart, with soft leather seats, the fixings for your favorite drink and an opportunity to listen to tunes on the stereo or watch a movie on the flat screen television. You'll have access to a cell phone and can speak directly to your chauffeur through the intercom system. Sit back and rest assured that you will arrive at your destination in comfort and style. Owners Robert and Cathy Powers, along with their professional and courteous team of drivers, pride themselves on providing superb service. Robert and Cathy follow a family tradition and represent the second generation of the Powers family to run Patriot, a business that got started in 1956. Come to Patriot Limousine, where the Powers promise Your Occasion Is Our Occasion.

3823 S Meridian, Puyallup WA
(253) 848-7378 or (877) 848-7377
www.patriotlimo.net

Olympia Harbor

WESTERN WASHINGTON

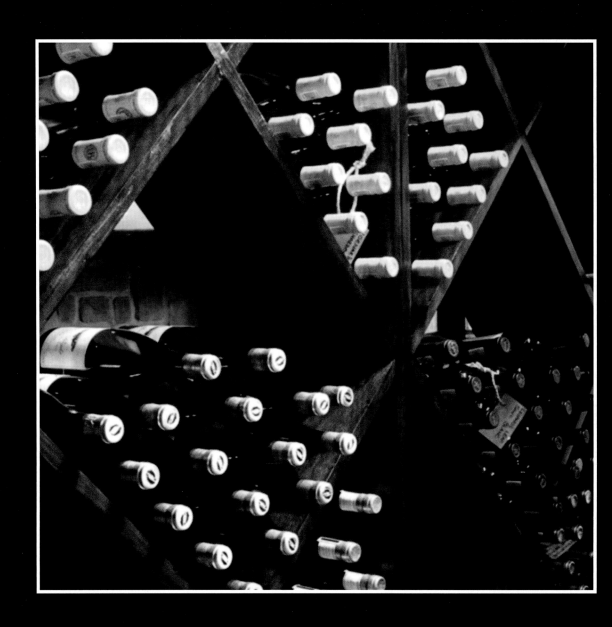

Wineries

Wicked Cellars

If you think fine wine is only for the wealthy or that you have to spend a decade learning the nuances of nose and bouquet to fully appreciate the ancient beverage, think again and head to Wicked Cellars for a memorable lesson you will thoroughly enjoy. Wine aficionado Kevin Nasr and his wife Bonnie purchased the existing wine shop in October 2004 and have since brought it to new heights in popularity by offering a whimsical atmosphere that's free of pretension. Wicked Cellars features a terrific array of wine from all over the world, including numerous vintages from the boutique wineries of Washington. Kevin and Bonnie choose the 2,000 labels they house from more than 60,000 varied selections. They also offer an assortment of specialty beers and ales. Kevin and Bonnie host four wine tasting events weekly, on Tuesday, Wednesday, Friday and Saturday. The tastings are ideal occasions for discovering your own preferences and the world of wine in general. The shop offers a members wine club and a delightful array of wine-related gifts and accessories, such as furniture, artwork and accessories. Discover for yourself why wine should breathe and the importance of decanting, while you search for new favorites with a visit to Wicked Cellars.

2616 Colby Avenue, Everett WA (425) 258-3117
www.wickedcellars.com

EASTERN WASHINGTON

EASTERN WASHINGTON

Accommodations
& Resorts

Cabin Suites Bed & Breakfast

Flexibility is a specialty at Cabin Suites Bed & Breakfast, a luxurious home with three guest suites. With the innkeepers living next door, guests have the privacy and comfort of staying in their own home away from home. Innkeepers Dave and Cherie Rockstrom go out of their way to cater to your needs. You can partake in the full morning meal where the signature dish is French toast. If this doesn't suit your schedule, you can choose a continental breakfast or even walk to a nearby café, show a card from Cabin Suites and eat for free. The flexibility is great, because with so much to do in and around Kennewick, your time is valuable. Foremost on the list of things to do is touring the booming wine country. Your hosts at Cabin Suites can arrange a memorable tour package for you, including transportation and a picnic lunch, or you can set off on your own to visit the scores of local wineries. If you would like a cozy dinner at the inn after a day of wine touring, your hosts can arrange that as well. Cabin Suites is an ideal choice for groups celebrating any kind of family get-together because, once again, flexible sleeping arrangements provide many options. A pop-up trundle bed can be added in any of the three suites, and full-sized futons are available in both living rooms. "We have had up to 16 stay overnight," say the innkeepers, "and even more for breakfast." Explore your possibilities at Cabin Suites Bed & Breakfast.

115 N Yelm Street, Kennewick WA (509) 374-3966 *www.cabinsuites.com*

Cozy Rose Inn Bed and Breakfast

Mark and Jennie Jackson go the extra mile to ensure that you will truly experience the luxury and privacy you are looking for in this beautiful country setting. After all, they are experts when it comes to knowing how travelers like to be treated. They have traveled around the world and have visited more than 400 inns and bed-and-breakfasts. From the moment you enter one of the five suites, you will feel like you have stepped into another country, perhaps France or Italy. The rooms catch the sunlight, while providing views of waterfalls and other lovely vistas. An air of freshness rises from the garden, where the Jacksons grow fruits and herbs for the inn's gourmet, intimate dinners in the beautiful new Tuscan-style dining room. The grounds are dotted with fruit trees and two acres of a lush green oasis of yards, flowers and gazebos. Stroll through the family vineyards and enjoy sweeping views of both grapes and hops. Modern amenities complement the Old World charm. Each room is very large with a private entry, large jetted or two-person soaking tub and shower. All suites host king-size beds, fireplaces, wireless Internet and satellite television. A candlelight breakfast can be delivered to your suite. An 18-hole golf course is located just five minutes away. With 50 wineries and breweries within 30 minutes of your door, the inn is perfectly located for tasting tours. *Bed and Breakfasts in the Northwest & California* awarded the Cozy Rose Inn its highest five-star rating. It is the perfect balance of pampering and privacy. If you are ready to be pampered, let the Jacksons be your hosts. Wine and roses are available upon request.

1220 Forsell Road, Grandview WA
(509) 882-4669 or (800) 575-8381
www.cozyroseinn.com

Sunnyside RV Park

Martin and Peggy Beeler wanted to find a business where they could slow down the pace of their lives and involve the whole family. They found it when they stumbled upon the Sunnyside RV Park, a place that needed the kind of tender loving care they could give. The Beelers, with the help of their daughters, Melissa and Patricia, rolled up their sleeves and worked as a team to re-landscape the grounds and turn Sunnyside into a clean, efficient and comfortable place for families. Sunnyside is pet friendly, offers free wireless Internet, a spotless laundromat and a playground with a playset, basketball, horseshoes, badminton and volleyball. The Beelers offer 35 RV sites with 50-amp service, many pull-thru sites and access for big rigs. Tents and groups are also welcome. They're located close to the Interstate with paved roads all the way to the park. The Beelers are great hosts. They love people, and they live on the grounds, so they are right there to make sure your stay is comfortable. Local attractions include wineries, casinos, shopping and museums, plus golf, auto and hydro racing, river cruises, fishing, hiking and much more. The next time you're in the area and need a place to pull in, call on the Beeler family at Sunnyside RV Park.

609 Scoon Road, Sunnyside WA
(509) 837-8486

Marcus Whitman Hotel & Conference Center

When the Marcus Whitman Hotel was built in the 1920s, it offered visitors luxurious accommodations and fine dining. Years went by and the historic building began to decline, until Kyle Mussman stepped in to restore the landmark. The completely renovated Marcus Whitman Hotel & Conference Center takes its place once again as a leader in world-class dining and accommodations in the Walla Walla Valley. The lobby welcomes you with luxurious décor, dark wood and comfortable oversized chairs. Rooms are equally well appointed with handcrafted Italian furniture in deluxe rooms and luxury suites. A fitness center and a full business center, with free access to computers, printers and a copier, meet the multiple needs of all guests. The conference center can accommodate events of varying sizes with 10,000 square feet of meeting space and a full-service kitchen. Original chandeliers and beautiful wall sconces in the ballrooms create an elegant venue for special occasions. Each morning, the on-site Marc Restaurant serves a complimentary full breakfast with eggs, waffles and fresh fruit. You'll want to return to the Marc to sample Executive Chef Bear Ullman's Pacific Northwest cuisine. The Marc offers an extensive selection of Northwest wine, as well as locally grown organic produce, freshly baked breads and certified Angus beef. The Marcus Whitman places you just steps from downtown shopping and wine tasting. Experience Walla Walla's past and present from the stylish Marcus Whitman Hotel & Conference Center.

6 W Rose Street, Walla Walla WA
(509) 525-2200 or (866) 826-9422
www.marcuswhitmanhotel.com

Walla Walla Inns

The Walla Walla Inns, a small all-suite hostelry, offer two superior places to stay. One is a fabulous vineyard guesthouse overlooking 10 acres of terraced vineyards in a lovely country setting. The other is a group of six downtown suites. All suites and the guesthouse provide a full kitchen including cookware, dishware and utensils. You'll also find a washer, dryer and flat screen television. Other features include feather beds, 500-thread count sheets, luxury towels and robes. Large antique desks and a comfortable chair draped with a cozy throw are standard. Owners Rick and Debbie Johnson are sticklers for the important details and know just what guests require for superior overnight and extended stays. The vineyard guesthouse is large with plenty of windows. The home's many skylights provide an abundance of natural light. Attractive, contemporary artwork is plentiful. The house features a heated pool and a sublime view of the Blue Mountains. The downtown suites are located in a historic district and are designed to offer privacy on a par with your own home. The typical hotel front desk is eliminated. Instead, a keypad system allows you exclusive access to the building and your own apartment. The apartment suites are spacious, with a mix of contemporary and antique furnishings, along with attractive artwork. You'll enjoy convenient access to shopping, dining and local wineries. Both sites allow pets—in fact, they'll supply food dishes and animal beds. For thoughtful and luxurious accommodations, come to the Walla Walla Inns.

123 E Main Street, Suite 155, Walla Walla WA
(509) 301-1181 or (877) 301-1181
www.wallawallainns.com

The Quilted Country Inn and the Sewing Basket

With six bedrooms equipped with hand-made quilts and comfy amenities, a living area easily transformed from cozy living space to quilting central, the Quilted Country Inn is perfect for quilting, sewing and craft enthusiasts. Owners Marilyn and Ben Dalstra host many retreats each year for quilters from all over the country and are happy to provide exactly what each group needs. When the inn isn't full of busy quilters, it functions as a restful bed and breakfast. With gorgeous views from the deck and gazebo at river's edge, the Quilted Country Inn is a perfect getaway spot. Each morning, guests are treated to a continental-style breakfast they can enjoy in the dining room or the family-friendly shared living area. Guests don't have to be expert quilters to appreciate the Sewing Basket, conveniently located right next door. In this quaint shop, you'll find more than 3,000 bolts of top-quality cotton fabric from around the world. The store features every quilting and sewing item you can imagine. For an intimate, relaxing stay in the country or the perfect place for a retreat with your quilting group, call the Quilted Country Inn.

1106 Wine Country Road, Prosser WA
(509) 786-7367
www.prossersewingbasket.com

Sunnyside Inn Bed & Breakfast

Revel in luxurious accommodations while enjoying the cozy privacy of a country inn at Sunnyside Inn Bed & Breakfast, where owners Donavon and Karen Vlieger specialize in offering a personal touch. The Vliegers moved to the area from Southern California, where they owned a small hotel, with a desire to raise their three children in a safer and more peaceful environment. The family opened Sunnyside Inn in 1988, which makes it the oldest bed and breakfast in the Yakima Valley. The structure was originally built in 1919 by Dr. W.E. Fordyce to serve as his family home and office. The inn has since undergone extensive renovations and today features 12 elegantly appointed rooms with private baths, 10 of which come with double Jacuzzi tubs and other amenities designed to make your stay relaxing and memorable. In the morning guests receive a full country breakfast. A variety of complimentary beverages and snacks are available throughout the day. Sunnyside Inn Bed & Breakfast also offers wireless Internet access, cable television and movies and an attractive business rate for corporate travelers. More than 40 wineries are nearby, and guests will certainly enjoy the charms of surrounding orchards, farms and historical sites. Explore the Yakima Valley while enjoying all the comforts of home with a stay at Sunnyside Inn Bed and Breakfast.

804 E Edison Avenue, Sunnyside WA
(509) 839-5557
www.sunnysideinn.com

AmeriStay Inn & Suites

AmeriStay Inn & Suites, a family business, has been home to many a traveler for more than 50 years. The inn's professional, enthusiastic and friendly staff maintain a high standard of excellence in both service and accommodations. Owner and General Manager Troy Duzon invites you to make AmeriStay your hometown hotel in Moses Lake. Rooms are spotlessly clean and quiet. All rooms provide pillow-top mattresses, along with a microwave, refrigerator, iron and ironing board. Fiber-optic high-speed Internet access is standard. The décor is traditional, warm and attractive. Suites with whirlpool baths are available. All guests enjoy a free continental breakfast and use of the exercise room, indoor pool and spa. The AmeriStay's unusually large pool boasts a vaulted wood ceiling and beams. Right next door to the inn you'll find Papa's Casino, with a restaurant and lounge, and Lake Bowl. Additional restaurants and shopping are just a block away. You can swim, play baseball, softball, soccer or golf. The City Aquatic Center is downtown and Moses Lake itself offers 100 miles of lake shore. Catch a concert at the Gorge Amphitheater or make a day trip to the Grand Coulee Dam. For a romantic getaway or a family vacation, come to the AmeriStay Inn and Suites.

1157 N Stratford Road, Moses Lake WA
(509) 764-7500
www.ameristayinn.com

Photo by Jennifer Gifford

Juniper Guest House

What better way to visit Walla Walla than to live in a gracious neighborhood of well-kept turn of the century homes? A family or a few friends will find everything from charming vintage décor to high definition television when they rent the three-bedroom Juniper Guest House. John Sterlin and Vince Harris, the owners of Romanza Gifts, have used their exceptional design skills and some of their shop's finest offerings to embellish this 1909 home. The building is Craftsman in overall design, while the interior décor is the Mission Arts & Crafts style. You will find wood floors and appealing details throughout the home, which features queen size beds and sumptuous bedding, two baths and a dining room with six luxuriously upholstered seats. The parlor contains a game table and a desk, while the living room holds a fireplace and a large plasma television complete with movie channels. You will find DVD and CD players plus Wi-Fi. Four can eat a casual meal at the kitchen's island seating. From the pillows on a window seat to Oriental rugs, cozy seating with leather details and lamps with the characteristic Arts & Crafts wrought iron, Juniper Guest House projects comfort and beauty. You're just blocks away from Whitman College and Pioneer Park and close to art galleries and wineries. Move into Juniper Guest House and experience Walla Walla inside and out.

320 Juniper Street, Walla Walla WA
(206) 650-6077
www.juniperguesthouse.com

Clover Island Inn

Locally owned, the Clover Island Inn is the Tri-Cities only hotel directly on the water with its own boat dock, and it is certainly the only hotel on its own island. It has 150 guest rooms, four of which are upscale suites. Clover Island is a full-service hotel with the famous Crows Nest Bar and Grill. It also features some fun summer concerts. It has bikes and is on the 24-mile Sacagawea bike and walking trail. Guests can ride the inn's bikes for free while staying here. The inn has a relaxed and friendly atmosphere and takes pride in the professional staff. Experience Clover Island Inn and see why the slogan says, It's an island thing.

435 Clover Island Drive, Kennewick WA
(866) 586-0542
www.cloverislandinn.com

Wapato Point Resort

Once the site of the Chief Moses Indian Reservation, Wapato Point Resort is still Native American property. The Wapato family, direct descendants of Chief Peter Wapato, have owned the resort for more than 100 years. Known as a family fun destination, Wapato Point offers something for every kind of visitor. Those seeking tranquility will find the peace that the Natives found along the long stretches of waterfront at Lake Chelan or on the smooth-running paddleboats. Folks with high energy and a daring spirit will enjoy the boat, jet ski and kayak rentals. Wapato Point employs a full-time recreation director to plan ongoing events for all ages, including a three-day Kids Camp to keep the younguns entertained. You'll find seven swimming pools and seven lighted tennis courts on the resort. Off-season visitors enjoy ice skating and the indoor Jacuzzi tub. The resort's luxurious condominiums offer between one and three bedrooms, comfortably accommodating up to 8 people. Each condo includes a fully equipped kitchen and a weekly maid service. With so much to enjoy, make Wapato Point Resort your home base in scenic Manson.

1 Wapato Point Way, Manson WA
(509) 687-9511
www.wapatopoint.com

Photo by Jennifer Gifford

EASTERN WASHINGTON

Attractions
& Recreation

RC's Restaurant, Casino, Sports Bar and Valley Lanes

For a lot of Lower Valley residents, eating out means heading to RC's Restaurant, Casino and Sports Bar for prime rib, lasagna or steak. When the occasion calls for a large celebration, RC's is often the destination of choice once again. The menu leans tantalizingly in an Italian direction, and the banquet facilities can accommodate as many as 200 people. From your seat at the restaurant, you will enjoy a nice view of the neighboring Black Rock Creek Golf Course. RC's is also a premier entertainment destination for the Lower Valley, offering nine gaming tables in the adjoining casino. Guests try their luck at Texas Hold-em, Blackjack and Spanish 21, to name just a few of the featured games. The good times carry into the sports bar, where folks follow the pro and college action on the big screens. If you can carry a tune, the mic is waiting for you on Karaoke Nite at RC's. On other nights, you might find yourself in the middle of a friendly dart tournament. Rob Rice, who owns RC's with his wife, Sue, knows something about competition. A pro bowler at the age of 22, he is the veteran of many tours. Rob and Sue also own Valley Lanes, the Lower Valley's only bowling center. They wouldn't be able to keep RC's and the lanes going without the help of their children, Brandon, Courtney and Trey. For good eating and fun times, try RC's Restaurant, Casino, Sports Bar and Valley Lanes.

31 Ray Road, Sunnyside WA (RC's)
(509) 836-7555
1802 E Edison Avenue, Sunnyside WA (Valley Lanes)
(509) 839-6103

Lake Bowl and Papa's Sports Lounge & Casino

When George and Bernice Russell opened Lake Bowl 50 years ago, they not only provided an entertainment destination for bowlers, they also started a family institution. Although George has passed away, Bernice is still seen regularly at Lake Bowl. Bob Russell, the eldest of their three sons and two daughters, is president of the corporation. The original siblings, their husbands and wives, and even the grandchildren, are involved in the business. Through the years a lot of changes have been made to Lake Bowl. What was once a 16 lane bowling center now contains over 38,000 square feet of entertainment, including a sports bar, casino and a restaurant and lounge. The casino features some of the most popular card games such as Blackjack, Pai Gow poker and Spanish 21. Satellite sports on over 60 televisions make the sports bar a favorite place to catch the game. The full-service restaurant features casual cuisine such as pizza, burgers, sandwiches and salads. In nice weather you can sit on the outdoor patio. When visiting Moses Lake, let the friendly staff introduce you to a world of entertainment at Lake Bowl and Papa's Sports Lounge & Casino.

1165 N Stratford Road, Moses Lake WA (509) 765-1248
www.lakebowl.com

Moses Lake

With an average of 300 days of sunshine a year, Moses Lake is an outdoor recreation paradise. World-class golf is available at several area courses. There is always fishing and boating here on the third largest fresh-water lake in the state. One of the largest ORV parks in the region allows thrilling entertainment. Surf & Slide Water Park, one of the finest water parks in the Northwest, offers 200-foot slides, plus the new Lazy River and FlowRider attractions at an affordable price. There is a free summer concert series and free movies in the grass bowl of the award-winning Centennial Amphitheater. A skateboard park, Farmer's Market and the Moses Lake Museum & Art Center (MAC) will satisfy a variety of ages and interests. MAC hosts Native American exhibits, traveling Smithsonian Institute exhibits and 8 to 10 different art shows a year. The surrounding landscape is a geological marvel created by ancient lava flows and ice age floods. There are many parks and campgrounds and over 1,000 hotel rooms. Over 50 restaurants cater to every taste. Moses Lake is only 30 minutes away from the Gorge at George, a concert venue which hosts such acts as Dave Matthews Band, Willie Nelson and more. Moses Lake is located directly in the path of the Pacific Flyway, the migratory path for countless waterfowl, including the Sandhill Crane. Abundant water and habitat, plus the nearby Columbia National Wildlife Refuge, makes this a birders wonderland. Rugged cliffs, canyons, lakes, marshes and sagebrush grasslands bring a plethora of species to the area. Moses Lake is a hunting and fishing paradise with duck, deer, walleye and steelhead, making it a recreational joy for everyone.

Moses Lake WA (800) 992-6234 *www.moses-lake.com*

Moses Lake Museum & Art Center (MAC)

The MAC provides the Central Washington area with its cultural heart. Located in downtown Moses Lake, the MAC is home to two important permanent exhibits: the Shrub-Steppe and Native Voices. The Shrub-Steppe shows the regions plants and wildlife. Native Voices weaves the relationship of three periods of local Plateau Cultural History to that life and to the land. Artifacts in this impressive display include items from the prestigious Adam East Collection. This museum borrows traveling exhibits from the Smithsonian Institute and the Washington State Historical Society. It also presents a wide variety of speakers from the Inquiring Minds Program offered by Humanities Washington. The art center impressively offers 8 to 10 exhibits every year. These shows may feature local, regional or international artists. The art itself could be anything from Native American arts and crafts or home art, such as quilting, renowned sculpture, paintings, textiles, prints, glass and photography. The first Saturday of every month the MAC presents a family activity, demonstration or special exhibit. This intertwines family entertainment with educational or regional history and events. The MAC also offers regular arts and crafts classes or workshops for both children and adults. A complete schedule of watercolor painting, life drawing, sculpture, basket weaving, papermaking and other art forms are available to learn.

**228 W 3rd Avenue, Moses Lake WA
(509) 766-9395**

Moses Lake Surf & Slide Water Park

The Moses Lake Surf & Slide Water Park, a popular city-owned and reasonably priced water park, recently expanded and now features additional amenities. One is the Lazy River, which provides a pleasant circuit of flowing water for those who enjoy a leisurely tube floating experience. It is a relaxing way to escape the heat. Next, the FlowRider, is both a skill and thrill ride. By shooting thin sheets of water over a fabricated padded waveform, a perfect perpetual wave is created. This allows the riders to simply drop in on their own unbroken surf and ride the wave. Safe and as fun to watch as it is to ride, this new attraction is a thrill for novices and a challenge to all boarders from skate to snow. These new rides will expand a park that already consists of two 200-foot water slides, one and three meter diving boards, a tube slide, Olympic size competitive pool and two volleyball courts. There is lots of play area for the small ones too, including the Treasure Island water structure, the zero depth beach area, Baby Octopus slide, a wet sand play area and a children's playground. This is truly a water park with the whole family in mind. Your family can bring their own picnic and enjoy the shaded picnic shelter area or take advantage of the full-service concession stand. A large deck and patio area and security lockers are also available for your use. Located in lovely McCosh Park, close to the lake, hotels and shopping, the Moses Lake Surf & Slide Water Park is open from Memorial Day weekend through Labor Day weekend.

Dogwood Street & 4th Avenue (McCosh Park), Moses Lake WA (509) 766-9245
www.mlrec.com

Anytime Fitness

An ideal fitness club would be open 24 hours, owned by certified personal trainers, have limited memberships to keep down the crowds and provide easy access for quick workouts. Welcome to Anytime Fitness, a neighborhood gym with all of the above characteristics. Tod Hanberg and Tyler Dart are co-owners at Anytime Fitness in Moses Lake as well as certified Professional Trainers. Anytime Fitness is a nation-wide franchise, but theirs is not a cookie cutter operation. Each club is as individual as its owner. The Moses Lake club offers a friendly, safe environment where the latest equipment occupies a carefully maintained facility. Ryan Winzle does double duty as a full-time trainer and manager. Anthony Hamlett is the professional trainer and mixed martial arts instructor, a world champion of martial arts. He teaches cardio kickboxing and Brazilian Ju-Jitsu free to members and is the owner of the Northwest Elite Martial Arts dojo adjacent to the club. Before and after workouts, Anytime offers related products and a sports bar for members. Both Tod and Tyler are ardent supporters of the community, sponsoring schools, baseball teams and Special Olympics. When you want a personalized fitness experience, go to Anytime Fitness.

619 N Stratford Road, Moses Lake WA (509) 764-0933
www.anytimefitness.com

Benton County Historical Museum

Benton County Historical Museum tells stories from the pioneer past using cutting edge technology to keep those stories fresh and interesting. You can watch a DVD about the town of Prosser on a 42-inch plasma television or learn about the *terroir* that gives Prosser wines their distinctive flavor. In the near future, you'll be able to hear old-timers tell their stories as you view pictures of them on the screen. Cora Nessly Mason conducted these interviews in the late 1970s and early 1980s, and Friends of the Library is transferring them to DVD. The museum, dedicated in 1968, contains five rooms and thousands of photos and artifacts, plus a display of an old store, collections of glass and porcelain and a Victorian parlor with gowns from 1843 to the 1920s, including one worn by Flora Prosser, wife of land agent Colonel William Prosser. You can request permission to play the 1867 Chickering Square piano and view displays on space exploration and a depiction of the 1980 Mount St. Helens eruption. The Farm Room includes an 1886 doctor's buggy and a history of area wineries. Bring Prosser's pioneer past to life with a visit to the Benton County Historical Museum.

1000 Paterson Road, Prosser WA
(509) 786-3842

House of Poverty Museum

How many Depression-era hobos do you know who now, at 80-plus years of age, own and operate their own private museum and a steam railroad? There's just been one—Monte Holm, founder of Moses Lake Iron and Metal and the House of Poverty Museum. The museum represents Monte's private collection of machinery, including gasoline engines, fire engines and other stuff. It's a treasure trove of early power equipment, both stream and internal combustion-based. There are also antique automobiles, including a classic 1917 Mitchell. The museum has one of the most extensive collections of stationary engines you'll see anywhere, all in beautiful condition. A small single-cylinder washing machine is one find. A steam locomotive and presidential rail car run on Monte's own Mon Road Railroad—yes, the man who was once kicked off trains came to own a train of his own. Monte was famous in western Washington even before the publication of his life story, *Once a Hobo . . . The Autobiography of Monte Holm*. His grandkids inspired Monte to start the museum, and grandkids Larry and Steven Rimple run it today. Be sure to stop by the House of Poverty Museum the next time you're in Moses Lake.

1502 W Broadway Avenue, Moses Lake WA
(509) 765-1741

Photo by Jennifer Gifford

Nob Hill Bowl

Avid bowlers have a place to keep their game sharp while visiting Yakima. It's called Nob Hill Bowl. A part of the neighborhood since 1965, the center plays host to leagues throughout the year but always welcomes out-of-towners. Whether your average is 200 and you don't want to get rusty, or you are chaperoning a school group and need a fun activity for the kids, Nob Hill Bowl is your place. The action intensifies on Saturday nights when Money Bowl is the game. Teens especially enjoy bowling to the sound and light show from 11 pm to 1 am on Friday and Saturday nights. The restaurant at Nob Hill serves a full lunch and dinner menu seven days a week and is known for its special on Black Angus prime rib Thursday through Saturday. The adjacent casino features a card room with eight table games. Murals by artist Jack Fordyce take you back to the Old West. Folks from the community could tell you what a good neighbor Nob Hill Bowl is, lending its support to organizations such the Police Athletic League and local charities. When it's time to knock some pins, head to Nob Hill Bowl.

3807 W Nob Hill Boulevard, Yakima WA
(509) 966-1070

Yakima Athletic Club

As the demand for fitness options grows, the Yakima Athletic Club grows right along with it. Back in 1978, when the club first opened its doors, tennis and racquetball were the rage. The Yakima Athletic Club obliged with eight racquetball courts and four tennis courts. Today, people who like to stay fit require much more. They enjoy working out on weights, swimming laps and practicing yoga. The Yakima Athletic Club offers the fitness equipment and services to meet these needs, and you can still play racquetball and tennis. What's more, you can soak afterwards in a hot tub, sit in a sauna and make a tanning appointment. Offering world class group fitness to water fitness classes to youth programs, the calendar at the Yakima Athletic Club is always full. To accomplish its mission of getting more people, more active, more often, the same folks who make the club such a premier establishment also run a second fitness facility in Terrace Heights called YAC Fitness. For a world of fitness options, consider becoming a member of the Yakima Athletic Club and YAC Fitness.

2501 Racquet Lane, Yakima WA
(Yakima Athletic Club) (509) 453-6521
2500 Business Lane, Yakima WA
(YAC Fitness) (509) 574-0711
www.yakimaathletic.com

EASTERN WASHINGTON

Automotive

Prosser Auto Mall

Selling used cars might not sound like a dream come true but that's exactly what it is for Rick Shafer, co-owner and founder of Prosser Auto Mall. Shafer began washing cars at his father's Spokane lot when he was only nine years old and sold his first car when he was just 17. Phil Davidson, Rick's partner, entered the picture after he purchased a car from Rick. The duo became fast friends and discovered, one evening over dinner, that they shared common goals of business ownership and that they both yearned to spend more time with their families. After investing a lot of sweat equity and gaining a small business loan from the Benton-Franklin Council of Governments, Rick and Phil opened their business in 2003. Prosser Auto Mall sells only certified used cars that undergo a 40-point safety inspection from Les Schwab. During inspection, the tires are rotated or replaced, all fluids are drained and replaced, and the automobile is given a thorough detailing inside and out. Rick, Phil and their family members, many of whom you can meet at the lot, are dedicated to bringing quality transportation that is both affordable and dependable to the Prosser area and maintain a low pressure sales strategy geared toward customer satisfaction. They additionally give back to the area by contributing to numerous local events and causes. Find a previously owned car you can depend on at Prosser Auto Mall.

355 Wine Country Road, Prosser WA
(509) 786-3315
www.prosserautomall.com

McIntyre Auto Repair

As a mechanic who can fix whatever is ailing your car, Dale McIntyre is worth his weight in gold. As someone who is not only a competent repairman but a straight-shooting, honest businessman, he deserves sainthood. McIntyre Auto Repair enjoys a stellar reputation around Prosser. Many customers know Dale from when he did repairs at a new car dealership in town. He spent a total of 16 years there practicing his trade. Leaving to pursue other options, Dale found a customer base that appreciated his no-nonsense approach. McIntyre Auto Repair has built its reputation upon fast and thorough diagnostics combined with honesty and integrity. Dale credits his grandfather and high school automotive instructor for inspiring him to choose auto repair as a career. Even now he participates in continuing education to keep up with innovations in engine design and the latest repair technology. The recipient of so much community support, he enjoys giving back by sponsoring high school sports teams and charities devoted to cancer research. When your car isn't running right, let the saint at McIntyre Auto Repair fix it for you.

1207 Sheridan Avenue, Prosser WA
(509) 786-1980

Photo by Jennifer Gifford

EASTERN WASHINGTON

Bakeries, Markets, Coffee & Tea

L-R: Kathleen Young, Production Manager; Pam Montgomery, Founder;
JT Montgomery, CFO

Chukar Cherries

Pam and JT Montgomery, Kathleen Young and the Chukar
Team are pleased to introduce to you what they feel captures the
best of the Pacific Northwest in naturally dried and chocolate-
covered cherry, berry and nut treats. Most days they're busy in
the Chukar kitchen creating a sleighful of luscious new sweets
such as Pinot Noir Chocolate Cherries and Dark Chocolate Cocoa
Pecans. They create high-protein snacks like Triple Cherry Nut
Mix, flavorful savories such as Peach Cherry Salsa and a wide
variety of beautifully packaged, delicious gifts. All are 100 percent
natural, of course. As always, their approach is pretty simple.
Use only the finest ingredients. Combine them in delicious and
creative ways. Listen to their customers and employees. And have
fun. It's a recipe they have strictly followed, from the first dried
cherries developed on the family farm to the sumptuous array of
pure fruit preserves and fillings, sauces and confections, fruits
and nuts. They invite you to visit Chukar Cherries throughout the
year for your personal and business gifts, and promise outstanding
quality, flavor and value for every season, reason and occasion.
One taste and you'll know that Chukar is synonymous with the
Best of Nature and Best of Chocolate. Visit the website or stop by
a Chukar Retail Outlet and taste for yourself. Cherry Cheers!

320 Wine Country Road, Prosser WA
(509) 786-2055 or (800) 624-9544
www.chukar.com

All Photos © 2006 Chukar Cherry Company Inc.

Taste of Heaven

The thick, fluffy, cookies made by Taste of Heaven are quickly becoming a favorite at coffee shops, espresso stands and flower stores around Washington and Oregon. *Custom Cookie Review* says these are "not your average cookie." Taste of Heaven makes its signature flower-shaped cookies with real butter and all-natural ingredients. Partners Glenna Dragoo and Chris Flodin handcraft well over 1,000 cookies per week and many more during the holidays. Glenna's passion for the cookies developed when she was a child. Taste of Heaven's cookies are prepared with "a recipe my mom used during the holidays. We'd spend a couple of days making cookies and spread dozens and dozens all over the house while the frosting was drying." Taste of Heaven also makes seasonal shaped cookies and frosting, and it fills custom orders for weddings, graduations, baby showers and other special occasions. The cookies-on-a-stick are popular for flower arrangements and gift baskets. All of the cookies have a shelf life of seven to ten days and you can preserve them for up to three months in the freezer. Taste of Heaven is involved in the community by supporting the Sunnyside, Prosser and Paterson school districts. The cookies are a hit whether you are buying them for a business or to complement your morning cup of coffee. Call Taste of Heaven and order these delicious cookies today.

1604 Mead Avenue, Prosser WA
(509) 786-3657

Griffin's Bakery & Café

Owner Ingrid Griffin, the baker at Griffin's Bakery & Café, serves some of the tastiest pastries, breads, cookies and cakes you'll find in this side of the state. All of the baked goods are made fresh daily. Walnut blue cheese, sourdough, ciabatta and rosemary semolina are just a few of the bakery's fragrant breads. The café serves a variety of breakfast and lunch sandwiches in addition to breads paired with daily soup specials. The sandwich and soup menu varies by season. Tuesday is vegan soup day, with delicious choices you needn't be a vegan to enjoy. The shop has a selection of egg-based breakfast sandwiches and a host of both vegetarian and meat-eater's lunch choices. Want a dozen cookies? You'll get the old-fashioned baker's dozen—13. The whole Griffin family is involved in the bakery's success. That includes Ingrid's husband, Chuck, as well as the two children, who pitch in after school. The bakery is committed to community support and donates to local food banks and school events. Be sure to stop at Griffin's Bakery & Café, known for friendly service and scrumptuous breads and food.

101 E Broadway Avenue, Moses Lake WA
(509) 765-2832
www.griffinsbakeryandcafe.com

EASTERN WASHINGTON

Fashion
& Accessories

Slam Dunk Athletics

The right shoe can make all the difference, not only in sports but in all of life's many activities. Slam Dunk Athletics provides the necessary equipment so you can forget about your feet and concentrate on your backhand, your stride or anything else. The variety of shoes, apparel and accessories paired with great customer service keeps customers coming back. From trendy to classic, this shop in the Mid-Valley Mall has the goods. You'll find Nike, Adidas and other name-brand apparel for the whole family—Slam Dunk has many second-generation customers. The store has shoes for every foot, from adult to infant and toddler. Hot name brands such as DC, Baby Phat and Etnies deliver fashion along with the quality demanded by today's savvy consumers. Owner Ken Winters attributes the stores' success to its impressive selection and to the capable staff, which includes his daughter, Manager Heather Berg. He also credits a general increase in health awareness. Runners, skateboarders and bicyclists have one thing in common: they can find the shoes they need at Slam Dunk. Whether you're looking for a shoe tailored to a specific sport or just want comfortable feet, Slam Dunk Athletics will come through for you.

2010 Yakima Valley Highway Unit 39, Sunnyside WA (509) 839-3822

Brothers Jewelers

Personalized service, as well as fine quality custom designed jewelry and jewelry repair are what keep customers coming back to Brothers Jewelers in Richland. Brothers Mark and Scott Smith are Certified Senior Bench Jewelers, and are the only two in the state to have achieved this certification. Mark's wife, Pamela, also works at the store and is a GIA Graduate Gemologist. The two brothers started their business together 26 years ago after attending diamond setting school in Portland, Oregon. Their abilities as designers and accomplished goldsmiths allows them to do everything from ring sizing to very detailed custom designed pieces in their workshop. All work is done on-site. Mark and Scott take pleasure in creating one-of-a-kind pieces or restyling an existing piece of jewelry. They encourage customers to have a part in the design process, thus giving more of a special touch to their finished piece of jewelry. Brothers Jewelers also offer designer lines such as S&R Designs, Chad Allison, Color Story, Strellmans and fine Swiss watches from Roven Dino. For service you can depend on, and jewelry worthy of passing down to future generations, come to Brothers Jewelers, where you can talk to the jewelers doing the work.

430 George Washington Way, Suite 102, Richland WA (509) 946-7989

EASTERN WASHINGTON

Galleries
& Fine Art

Shopkeeper

When Joe Simon began working part-time at the Shopkeeper in 1982, he never imagined that eight years later he would own it. In 1990, Joe and his business partner purchased Yakima's premier gift and floral shop, expanding its already impressive vendor list. They continued to build upon a reputation of providing excellent customer service, award winning floral designs and showrooms that spark the imagination. The Shopkeeper and the new Shopkeeper Downtown provide the most discerning buyer with unique, one-of-a-kind gift items and each of the 10 showrooms provides a stunning display of the finest home furnishings, from leather sofas to mahogany dining tables set with Baccarat crystal water and wine glasses and the finest imported china. Customer service, unique gifts, award-winning fresh floral and timeless silk arrangements have all helped to make the Shopkeeper a unique shopping experience, but the talk of the town and perhaps the Pacific Northwest, is the Shopkeeper Christmas Open House that happens each year on the last Sunday in October. The Shopkeeper's main Christmas showroom, secreted behind draped windows for weeks, is unveiled on Saturday evening and each year the Christmas Showroom is better than the year before. The Open House draws customers from all over the northwest for the spectacular viewing of more than 40 Christmas trees, each with a different holiday theme, from traditional to contemporary. Shopkeeper and Shopkeeper Downtown, located on Yakima Avenue next to the new Hilton Garden, are a must see for anyone visiting the Yakima Valley.

3105 Summitview Avenue, Yakima WA (509) 452-6646
Shopkeeper Downtown: 399 E Yakima Avenue, Suite 180, Yakima WA
(509) 457-8500
www.shopkpr.com

Photo by Irene Pearcy

Simon Edwards Gallery

Simon Edwards Gallery opened in May of 1997, in a modest location on Yakima Avenue. As the brainchild of owner Joe Simon and his former business partner, Ed Maske, the gallery's intent was to provide the Yakima Valley with an upscale art gallery that brought local, national and internationally renowned artists together in one location. In November of 2003, Simon Edwards Gallery opened in its current location, adjacent to the Shopkeeper—Yakima's premier home interior design shop owned and operated by Mr. Simon. Simon Edwards Gallery brings museum quality art to the Yakima Valley on a six-week exhibit schedule. The gallery features Pacific Northwest glass artists Jenny Pohlman, Sabrina Knowles, Benjamin Moore and Diane Hansen to name a few, bronze sculpture by John Sisko, wood carvings, oil paintings and sculpture by Steve Jensen, and encaustic works by Mark Rediske, Susan Sweetwater and David Price. Off-hand sculpted glass, ceramic earthenware, bronze sculpture, wood carvings, oil, acrylic and pastel paintings are all part of the gallery offerings. No matter the time of year, Simon Edwards Gallery is a satisfying stop for the art aficionado or the casual viewer.

3105 Summitview Avenue, Suite 101, Yakima WA (509) 248-6886
www.simonedwardsgallery.com

Photo by Irene Pearcy

Handblown art Glass by Dan Bergsma

Lakewood Gallery & Framing Company

The artwork you create or own, the memorabilia you collect and the photographs you exhibit all reflect your spirit. Grandly displayed in frames and settings, they express your taste and personality. At Lakewood Gallery & Framing Company, staff members work closely with you to ensure you get the frame and look that you desire. You may consult with master framer and artist Dave Craig, or with owners Jan Giroux and Bob Farrelly, who formerly owned the Pacific Rim Wildlife Art Show. Lakewood Gallery & Framing uses museum-quality materials on every project. It helps develop the next generation of artists and artisans by donating recyclable materials to area schools. In addition to providing exceptional framing services, the shop displays a large collection of powerful work by local artists. Lakewood Gallery offers original paintings, prints, posters and giclees, along with stone, wood and bronze sculpture. The gallery exhibits hand-thrown pottery and stunning glass art by Jeau Bishop and Dan Bergsma. Lakewood Gallery & Framing opened in 1959. Ever since, it has been a popular gathering spot for the art community thanks to its welcoming, family-like atmosphere and flawless service. Find remarkable new artwork or ensure that your special treasures are properly displayed by visiting the Lakewood Gallery & Framing Company. It is an incredible opportunity to shop for original artwork, and handcrafted, one-of-a-kind gifts.

11004 Gravelly Lake Drive SW, Lakewood WA
(253) 584-1774 or (800) 648-0772
www.lakewoodgallery.com

Sunburst Gallery

You've probably never been to a gallery where you could bring the kids and, moreover, where you and the kids were encouraged to touch the merchandise. Sunburst Gallery wants you to touch and view art as well as hear the story behind each piece. With so many ways to experience the gallery's offerings, you can be sure your visit here will enrich your life. Owner Pamela Toey and her staff appreciate art and dedicate themselves to supporting local artists. Work here is varied and includes pottery, three-dimensional sculptures and Italian glass art. Look for original paintings and etchings of Lake Chelan. Pamela promotes Northwest artists, such as Russian born Simon Kogon, who created the World War II memorial and several other famous U.S. statues. Other artists featured in the gallery include Canadian born sculptor Bernard Hosey, U.S. born naturalist sculptor and painter Leo Osborne, and Italian glass artist Pino Cherchi. Look for stone faceting by Dale and Karen Snyder as well as jewelry, metal knotting and glass beads. A nonprofit section of the gallery contains works from Third World countries. Sales go directly to devastated communities, a concern that is close to Pamela's heart since she went on a mission trip to Guatemala. For a family-friendly art gallery experience, visit Sunburst Gallery, dedicated to making art accessible to everyone.

201 E Woodin Avenue, Chelan WA
(509) 682-8708

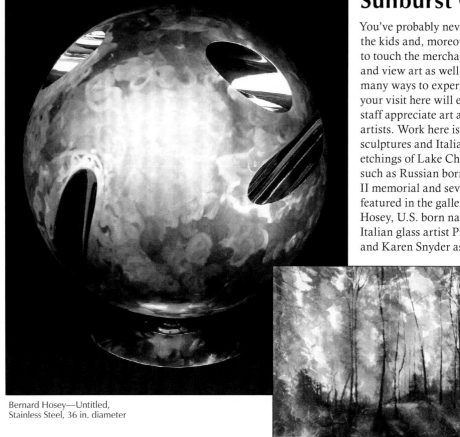

Bernard Hosey—Untitled,
Stainless Steel, 36 in. diameter

Barbara Nickerson—*Autumn Walk*

Tom McClelland—*The News*,
bronze, 53 x 16 x 11 in.

Tom McClelland—*Still Dancin'*,
bronze, 63 x 8 x 12 in.

Tom McClelland—*Icarus*,
bronze, 29 x 12 x 8 in.

Tom McClelland working on *Juggling Act*,
bronze, 114 x 32 x 28 in.
Photos by Dan McCool

Tom McClelland

Tom McClelland has an amazing, diverse portfolio of sculpture. "Art-making is a life-long process." he says, "I have made art ever since I can remember. No matter what other skills I develop along the way, my art thinking insists that I approach all endeavors with a creative spirit." Tom's sculptures have a bright pop of color, ideas and humor. His original use of color makes his work sought after by collectors. "These colors, as well as the textures, are largely inspired by those I have found while exploring eastern Washington: sage, dry grasses, basalt and lichens," Tom says. He strongly believes in the connection between humanity and nature. Tom, an eastern Washington native, was sculptor-in-residence at Mount Rushmore after earning his MFA. He later taught at Mesa State College and Columbia Basin College. You can find Tom's sculpture all over Washington, in Pasco, Seattle and Bellingham and other cities, and on college campuses as well. He has recently created major installations for clients such as the Washington State Arts Commission and the Richland Arts Commission. His pieces are also on display at the Tri-Art Gallery in Richland. Perhaps Tom's most famous piece is his reconstruction of the head of Kennewick Man, created with Dr. James Chatters. You can see it at the Kennewick Public Library's Union Street branch. Come view the work of Tom McClelland at Tri-Art Gallery or another site. You may want to make some of his creations your own.

Visit Tom's studio at the base of Red Mountain
Open by appointment (509) 967-5088
www.tom-mcclelland.com
www.triartgallery.com

Health
& Beauty

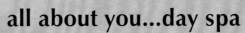

all about you...day spa

Balance is a hard quality to find in this hurried age,
yet our minds and bodies cry out for harmony and a
center amid the seasons. Think of the team at all about
you...day spa in Yakima as your partners ready to aide
you in achieving and maintaining this balance. Meet
esthetician Molly Callahan, nail technician Bonnie
Detrick, massage practitioner Lisa Stevens and spa
coordinator Vickie Shroyer. They describe all about you...
day spa as a place where you can experience a refuge
from every day life in a private, serene environment and
escape from the ordinary. They offer services designed
to reduce stress levels, promote healthy skin and elevate
your overall sense of well-being. Your visit to all about
you...day spa may consist of an appointment with
one of these professionals or an all-inclusive package
lasting a half or a full day. For relaxation, good health
and radiant beauty, visit all about you...day spa.

614 N 16th Avenue, Yakima WA
(509) 575-4555
www.theallaboutyoudayspa.com

Revitalize! Health Spa & Organic Store
—Modalities from Around the World

Whether you're looking to balance your mind, body or spirit, Revitalize! Health Spa & Organic Store has what you need. This shop in the recharged historical district of downtown Kennewick is a center for modalities from around the world. Customers enjoy shopping from one of the widest selections of gluten-free and sugar-free products around. To help you with your health concerns, browse through a diverse number of self-help books on topics that range from cooking, diet and wellbeing to taking control of and managing your finances. Owner Erickson is a living testament to the effectiveness of the therapies and techniques offered at her shop. Before opening the spa, Erickson, a 14-year mail carrier, faced debilitating asthma. Her use of healing modalities from across the globe has transformed her life and she now prides herself on helping others to discover the techniques that helped her. People from around the world and professionals from many fields have come to Erickson and her knowledgeable staff for help. Revitalize offers a variety of therapeutic options. While listening to tranquil music in the Infrared Sauna, you can lose weight, burning up to 900 calories in a 30 minute session. Experience a reduction of cellulite, muscle soreness and pain relief. Another favorite is the Australian Energy Spa, a detoxifying foot bath. The Solo System uses far infrared, the healing rays from the sun, for everything from skin conditions and stiff joints to strengthening cardiovascular. Revitalize yourself with a trip to Revitalize! Health Spa & Organic Store.

Photos By Barrett Brown Photograhy

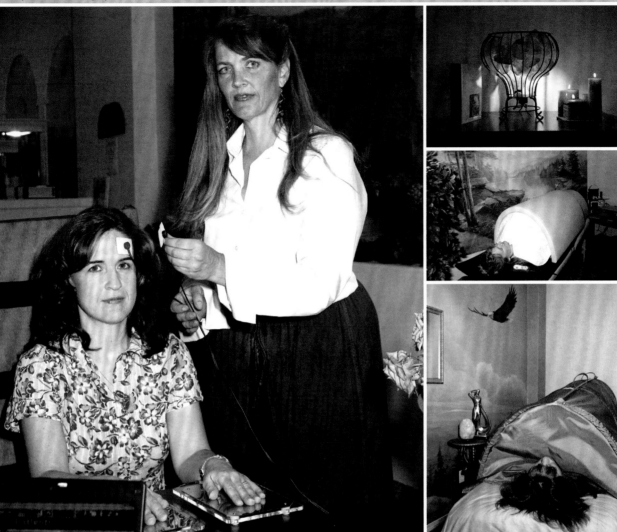

Photos By Barrett Brown Photograhy

Revitalize! Health Spa & Organic Store boasts a number of licensed and certified biofeedback therapists and specialists. Having such, it is well-suited to sell to health professionals, offer therapy and provide training on a number of bioenergetic and biofeedback devices from around the world. Biofeedback refers to techniques in which people receive feedback on the state of their body, allowing them to alter their own bodily state through conscious or unconscious responses. Two biofeedback systems offered are the LIFE system and the EPFX/QXCI/SCIO. These noninvasive devices screen for organ weaknesses and check toxicity, pH balance and hormone imbalances. They are useful in leveling out stress and releasing emotional traumas on a cellular level. Erickson has been awarded exclusivity in sales of the Electro Interstitial Scanner (EIS) in the state of Washington. The EIS is capable of scanning the body for 69 parameters in two minutes, with 87-percent repeatable accuracy. Revitalize's top seller, the SCENAR, a therapeutic device small enough to fit in your pocket, generates electrical signals that feed information back to the brain and body. Therapy with the SCENAR can greatly reduce or even eliminate pain in just minutes. Revitalize! has a hard time keeping this product in stock. If you or someone you know is in need of relief, come in and visit the Little Shop with Big Variety. Revitalize your health and your life by experiencing this unique gem in Washington's treasures.

311 W Kennewick Avenue, Kennewick WA
(509) 586-6574
www.BiofeedbackPlus1.com

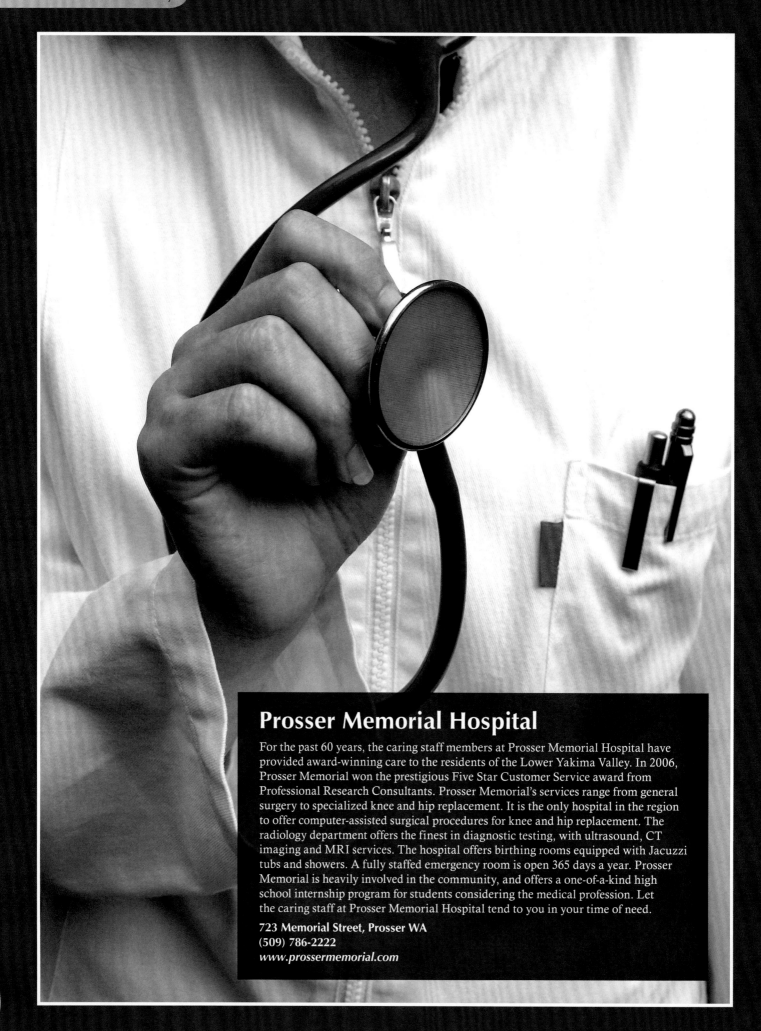

Prosser Memorial Hospital

For the past 60 years, the caring staff members at Prosser Memorial Hospital have provided award-winning care to the residents of the Lower Yakima Valley. In 2006, Prosser Memorial won the prestigious Five Star Customer Service award from Professional Research Consultants. Prosser Memorial's services range from general surgery to specialized knee and hip replacement. It is the only hospital in the region to offer computer-assisted surgical procedures for knee and hip replacement. The radiology department offers the finest in diagnostic testing, with ultrasound, CT imaging and MRI services. The hospital offers birthing rooms equipped with Jacuzzi tubs and showers. A fully staffed emergency room is open 365 days a year. Prosser Memorial is heavily involved in the community, and offers a one-of-a-kind high school internship program for students considering the medical profession. Let the caring staff at Prosser Memorial Hospital tend to you in your time of need.

723 Memorial Street, Prosser WA
(509) 786-2222
www.prossermemorial.com

Catalina's Hair Care

When the folks who live around Sunnyside need a makeover or a new hair style, they go to Catalina's Hair Care. Since 1994, Catalina Espindola and her team have been building a reputation as the friendliest, most dependable stylists and cosmetologists in the area. They've garnered an Award of Distinction for their community service, and draw people from miles around for their high-quality work. Catalina's is a comfortable, upscale salon where you'll get quality foils and up-to-the-minute cuts from Catalina, Ricardo, Dee, Kendra, Sue Ellen and Juanita. They specialize in coloring, spiral perms and makeup, but there's not much they can't do when it comes to making people look their best. They do complete makeovers, and they're especially good at getting people ready for big events, such as weddings. The salon is enjoyable, with a flat-screen television, a big leather wrap-around couch and a gift shop. Catalina is a very enthusiastic person who has inspired others to start their own salons. The next time you're in Sunnyside and feel the need for a little cut-and-buff, call Catalina's. You'll walk out looking as special as they'll make you feel.

436 S 6ᵗʰ Street, Sunnyside WA
(509) 837-5413

City Slickers Salon & Spa

City Slickers Salon & Spa is honored that they have been chosen to represent Aveda, including the complete product line, hair care, color and retexturing services. These all-natural, plant-based products provide some of the most beautiful colors in the world. Setting the standard for beauty and environmental leadership, Aveda Salons make up a worldwide network. Every season Aveda stylists rock the runways during Fashion Week in New York, London and Milan. City Slickers owner Sandra LeFore and the staff at City Slickers Salon & Spa engage in advanced training to introduce and support cutting edge trends in hairstyling, cut and color, as well as innovative new products and concepts in botanical science and aroma therapy. The staff of City Slickers takes joy in providing customers with personalized attention and products that they will love and this is, simply put, what they're all about. The stylists will enhance your well-being from roots-to-ends. The colorists are artists who can make your color truly yours. They take special care of the fried and the flipped, the over-dyed and the dull, as they inspire the uninspired. City Slickers does it all with the purest flower and plant ingredients, allowing nature's beauty to naturally enhance yours. Make time to free your hair, your body and your mind with Aveda. City Slickers now offers a customized build-your-own-spa package. Feel the difference at City Slickers Salon & Spa.

14 W Main Street, Walla Walla WA
(509) 529-2108
www.cityslickerssalon.com

Pampered Day Spa

It took a car crash to divert Joy Maiers from construction work to becoming the owner of a day spa. In hindsight, she says it was "the best thing that ever happened." Guided by her guardian angels and encouraged by her family, Joy created a rejuvenating spa that would offer the kind of therapeutic treatments she had come to rely on. In addition to massage, you'll find pampering esthetic treatments such as waxing, microdermabrasion and eyebrow shaping at Pampered Day Spa. Men are not overlooked, with back, ear and nose waxing available. Joy is an estheticican herself, with an unfailing intuition for what works. Bring your bridal party or a group of friends to Joy and she'll create a package deal just for you. Gift certificates are available for friends and family members with difficult schedules. The spa is also the exclusive distributor of Seda France candles, hand soap and room mist. Take a break from the regular grind and step into the tranquility of Pampered Day Spa. One visit will inspire you to come back for more.

821 E Broadway Avenue #7,
Moses Lake WA
(509) 766-7779

Electric Beach

If you don't live in Sunnyside, you may be quicker to hear the appeal to a sunny vacation embedded in the name. Seven years ago, John and Joyce Dalrymple were the first local entrepreneurs to take the idea and run with it. The result was Electric Beach, a tanning, toning and styling salon dedicated to providing the props and services of beach culture to Sunnyside. With state-of-the-art tanning beds in both standup and laydown options, you can start by getting your sunny side golden at Electric Beach. Then head for the exercise room, where experienced trainers will help you tone your body to beach-ready condition. Now you're ready to try on the swimsuits at the Electric Beach gift shop, where you can admire your new look in a parade of suiting styles. While you're there, you can also browse children's clothing, local products and wine accessories. Of course, no trendy shopping place would be complete without an espresso bar. Electric Beach makes a latte so coveted that patrons ask to have it delivered to their homes—that's complimentary, of course. Finally, you can polish your look by visiting the in-house stylists, who'll have your hair looking great in no time. Whether it's primping, shopping or just a cup o' Joe you're looking for, check out Electric Beach, where you'll find it all in one spot.

318 S Seventh Street, Sunnyside WA
(509) 839-2226

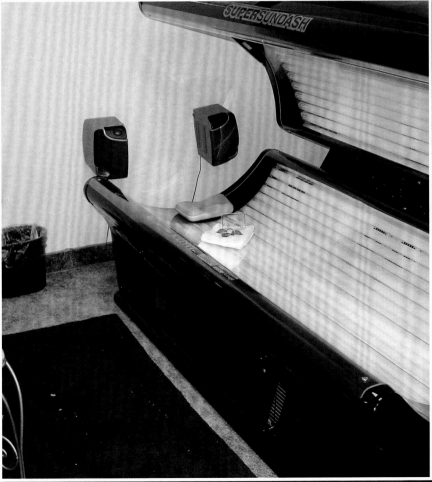

Sunnyside Physical Therapy Services

Sunnyside is located in the middle of the Yakima Valley, a paradise of agricultural enterprise, multiple cultures and broad vistas. Its locale provides access to mountain, water and outdoor western recreation opportunities during all four seasons. Additionally, it lies in the center of world-class wineries, orchards and dairies, which provide superior products to the world. For over 30 years, Sunnyside Physical Therapy Services and Dyke Dickie, PT, has been proud to assist the surrounding population with quality physical therapy service to help friends and neighbors live full and productive lives. Locally owned and operated, Sunnyside Physical Therapy is a cutting edge facility attuned to the rehabilitative needs of its clients. Combined with the top-notch staff of office manager Mary Caballero, licensed massage practitioners Tiffanie Hester and Jessica Morrow, Gloria Dickie, IT, and Mary Ramirez, a therapy aide, clients receive personalized care that is second to none. As a long time member of the American Physical Therapy Association and its state chapter of the Physical Therapy Association of Washington, Sunnyside Physical Therapy adheres to and promotes the use of the Guide for Ethical Conduct for physical therapists. Feel free to stop by, say hello and see what a extraordinary therapy clinic looks like.

841 E Lincoln Avenue, Sunnyside WA (509) 839-0414

Meadowlark Centre

Toni (Antoinette) Harris of Meadowlark Centre has a lifetime's experience in making people feel better. Since she received her first formal massage training in 1977, Toni's need to knead has led her around the world in an ongoing quest for continuing education in many modalities of bodywork and massage. Toni opened her first massage practice in Tacoma in 1985 and was very successful, numbering several movie stars among her roster of clients. In 1991, she moved the business to Prosser and renamed it Meadowlark Centre after listening to the chirping of meadowlarks. Their symphony was so tranquil, peaceful and cheerful, she thought to herself, "That's it and that is how I want people to feel after a massage." Since then, Toni has continued to expand her knowledge and techniques, in addition to earning a diploma in spa therapy. In 1998, hot rock massage became popular and she thought it was brilliant. This led her to the development of the Medistone. The semi-precious agate Medistones are designed for therapeutic massage, relaxation and much more. In 2007, the Medistone evolved into the Medistone Meditation Stone, which focuses the mind on self awareness in order to construct positive attitudes and emotions while the body relaxes with a Medistone massage. This transforming experience establishes a new attitude and a new you. Please visit the beautiful Meadowlark Centre to view the beautiful Medistone merchandise.

611 6th Street, Prosser WA
(509) 786-7001
www.medistone.com

Wear Red Day is an annual event to focus on the issue of heart disease in women

Dr. April Biggs with one of the more than 660 newborns who started life at the hospital in 2006

Sunnyside Community Hospital

Expectant mothers judge a hospital by one critical question: "Would I want to have my baby here?" Around 600 mothers a year say yes to Sunnyside Community Hospital and its beautiful Family Birth Center. As you approach the main area, you will see the lovely waiting room, which features a fireplace and large windows facing the east. The center offers five spacious delivery suites, each containing a Jacuzzi tub and everything needed for labor, delivery and post partum care of mothers and their babies. Overall, Sunnyside Community Hospital is large enough to offer a wide range of services, though small enough that you won't feel like a number. Whatever your needs may be, the staff is committed to providing you with individualized quality care. The hospital has a 24-hour emergency room and a four-bed intensive care unit in addition to a surgical floor, operating rooms and a laboratory. Its diagnostic imaging center provides everything from x-rays for common sports injuries to CT and MRI scans, ultrasounds and bone density scans. This nonprofit facility has been a vital part of the community since 1984. Jon Smiley has been Chief Executive Officer since 1991. The doctors and supporting staff at Sunnyside live and work by the motto Whatever You Do, Do It Well. When you need a wellness ally, consider Sunnyside Community Hospital.

1016 Tacoma Avenue, Sunnyside WA
(509) 837-1500
www.sunnysidehospital.com

EASTERN WASHINGTON

Home
& Garden

Cliff's Septic Tank and Sewer Services

Septic tanks and holiday cheer don't often go together—unless you're Cliff's Septic Tank and Sewer Services owner John Dalrymple, that is. Every Christmas, John and the crew at Cliff's tape more than 23,000 lights to one of their pumper trucks and enter it in local parades, where it often wins awards. There are so many lights on the truck that you'll find it towing a fully decorated trailer with a generator on board. John and the

staff at Cliff's bring the same in-it-to-win-it attitude to work with them every day. For more than 58 years, Cliff's Septic Tank and Sewer Services have been seeing to the needs of the people of the Yakima Valley when it comes to septic tank sales, installation and maintenance. Cliff's offers a full range of septic pumping and sewer drain services, in addition to a full line of portable chemical toilets. When it comes to septic and sewer services, there's no acceptable margin of error. Trust Cliff's to make every day a holiday from septic and sewer concerns.

1536 Mabton Road, Sunnyside WA
(509) 837-4060

Marchant Home Furnishings

Fine furniture is the family business at Marchant Home Furnishings. Originally founded in the mid-1950s, the store came into the Marchant family in 1961 when Lonnie Marchant took it over from his father-in-law. Today, Lonnie's daughter Mandy Hoffard and her husband, Ty, are upholding the family tradition of beautiful furniture at affordable prices. Ty and Mandy pride themselves on providing big city selection with small town attention. You'll be amazed at the variety of furniture you'll find in this 20,000 square-foot space. From La-Z-Boy recliners to elegant Charles Schneider or Flexsteel sofas, you'll find it here. Whether you're looking for something in soft leather or an ornate fabric, Marchant Home Furnishings can help you find just the right piece for your price range. You'll find beds, family-room pieces and home accents such as lamps and paintings that can beautify any room. The store also carries a selection of gift items from around the world. If you can't find it in the showroom, the staff is happy to special order a piece for you. Marchant Home Furnishings offers free delivery to most parts of the state. Ty, Mandy and their staff keep current by attending markets throughout the region. If you're looking to furnish your home or office, come take advantage of the family tradition of friendly service at Marchant Home Furnishings. Just minutes from anywhere.

1017 W Wine Country Road, Grandview WA
(509) 882-1247 or (800) 525-4467
www.marchanthomefurnishings.com

Co2 Furniture Gallery

In 1999, Matt and Patti Murphy joined their passions for fun furniture and started their first small store. They boldly painted the building a bright orange color to let customers know this was not another boring furniture store. Today, the Co2 Furniture Gallery occupies 18,000 square feet at Broadmoor Square Mall. The store is distinguished by quality stock from around the world and superlative consulting services. Talented decorating consultants can make over any room in your home or business in a way that's truly marvelous. Viewing its portfolio of makeovers provides the proof. Co2 consultants can turn a plain-Jane room into a warm, inviting haven you'll absolutely love. Co2 provides complimentary in-home decorating services with a minimum $500 purchase that can include determining your long-term decorating plans and coordinating accessories and furniture, plus savvy advice on purchasing. The gallery will even re-arrange your existing furniture. Co2 carries an extensive line of home and office furniture, featuring famous names such as Lexington, Hickory Hill and Stone Country, to name just a few. Styles run the gamut. From children's furnishings through to environmentally-friendly paints, you'll find what you need at Co2 Furniture Gallery.

5202 Outlet Drive, Pasco WA
(509) 544-0818
www.co2furnituregallery.com

Elements Inside & Out

Filled with an eclectic and interesting mix of high-quality furniture, gifts, home décor items and jewelry, Elements Inside & Out is a treat to browse and shop. This home décor and accessory shop has furniture from around the world, including antiques. There's a large inventory of jewelry, including Robin Fode pieces and handmade jewelry from Peru. You'll see home décor items, accent pieces, candles and unusual lamp shades. The shop also carries the popular Lynette Pierce scarves. During the third week of October, the shop has a spectacular Christmas celebration, with a dazzling display of ornaments and trees. Owner Krista Hamilton opened the shop to provide the community with quality items for the home decorator, outside of the usual fare. Krista tirelessly searches the world for new and exciting items, so the shop's stock is ever-changing, and each repeat visit is a new experience. What stays the same is the quality of the goods and the friendly service. The shop also has a bridal registry. Krista believes in giving back to the community and supports local youth education programs as well as the local cancer walk. For a fun and fruitful shopping experience, be sure to visit Elements Inside & Out.

922 W Broadway Avenue, Moses Lake WA
(509) 765-0738

Green Door

For more than 30 years, Barbara and Gene Campbell have never needed to advertise. Good old fashion word of mouth is all the publicity they've used. Known for great bargains on quality pre-owned furnishings, you will now find the Green Door at its new location in Sunnyside. When asked about their website, the Campbells response was, "Why bother with a website when we can't keep items on the floor long enough to post them?" People travel from miles away to comb through the patio furniture or bedroom sets (sometimes new), quality tables, toys and baby furniture. Here, professionals, migrant workers and farmers shop for some of the best deals you'll find in Eastern Washington. You'll even find the occasional entertainment system, major appliances, televisions and stereos. Barbara and Gene attend auctions on the weekends to keep the store well-stocked with bargains on quality pieces that their customers have come to expect to find at the Green Door. Shiela oversees the showroom on the weekends and keeps the customers entertained. During the week Gene helps with delivery and installations. There is always something new waiting for you at the Green Door. Don't miss some of the best bargains you'll ever see in pre-owned home furnishings.

1610 Mabton-Sunnyside Road, Sunnyside WA
(509) 840-1785

Van Wingerden Landscaping

Van Wingerden Landscaping has been making its community prettier since 1950, when Dutch immigrant John Van Wingerden started the business with $100. Rolling green lawns and dazzling flower beds throughout Sunnyside owe their origin to the hardworking team at this full-service landscape business. Backyards have been transformed into sanctuaries with water features, retaining walls and intricate stone pavers. Van Wingerden Landscaping specializes in automatic irrigation systems that discreetly keep your landscape green. The business is now in the hands of John's sons, John and Bill. As the longest-running family business in the Lower Yakima Valley, Van Wingerden Landscaping has a tradition of excellence to uphold with every job. Its reputation remains impeccable. "Our work speaks for itself," say Bill and John, who are happy to donate flowers and maintenance to Sunnyside's Centennial Square. Enjoy a beautiful landscape from the community-enhancement experts at Van Wingerden Landscaping.

1291 Cemetery Road, Sunnyside WA
(509) 837-5593

Photo by Jennifer Gifford

EASTERN WASHINGTON

Lifestyle
Destinations

Himsl Real Estate Company

Moving into a new community can be exciting and nerve-wracking unless you have a friend in the area to help ease the transition. If you're considering a move to the Lower Yakima Valley—or from one area location to another—you can find that friend in Douglas Himsl of Himsl Real Estate Company. Doug and his staff assist clients not only in Prosser, but in the Tri-Cities, Grandview and Sunnyside. Doug has been a licensed and practicing realtor since 1983, and is dedicated to delivering the highest degree of customer service to all of his clients. Many of Doug's customers have relied on him before and are now moving again locally. Some are even the children and grandchildren of his earliest clients. Most of his other referrals are based on word of mouth. The faith-based company holds a subcontract to market government-owned housing, a sign of confidence in the company's experience and ethics. Doug has much experience with Veterans Administration loans and military family relocations. Himsl Real Estate can also aid sellers of both residential and commercial property. Doug and his professional team happily go the extra mile to give you all the information needed so that you can choose the right home for your family. Himsl Real Estate Company further shows community spirit by supporting the Prosser School District, Boy Scouts of America and other worthy area organizations. Take the worry out of your real estate adventure with a call to Himsl Real Estate Company.

702 6th Street, Prosser WA (509) 786-1234
www.himsl.com

Sun Terrace–Prosser

Sun Terrace Retirement and Assisted Living Community offers independence with the convenience of personal, tailored plans of assistance. Residents can fashion their personal lifestyle from the abundant choices that come with living in Sun Terrace. Three balanced meals and snacks throughout the day offers convenient access to an excellent diet, and Sun Terrace provides housekeeping, a weekly laundry service and daily trash removal that contribute to keeping the living quarters sparkling. Community members occupy attractive apartments, each with a full bath. Every resident can easily choose a comfortable level of social life close to home. Community areas include a living room area for socializing and library and activity rooms open for the use of all residents. Daily physical fitness programs, activities and services are available to contribute to fun and good health. Residents can also choose to take advantage of a number of daily creative and educational programs. Group trips and resident-sponsored clubs foster many enjoyable interactions with friends. The prime location and proximity to local attractions make it easy to find stimulating activities to attend. It's a complete package of delight living at Sun Terrace in Prosser.

2131 Wine Country Road, Prosser WA (509) 839-0579
www.regencysunterrace.com

Sun Terrace–Sunnyside

The Sun Terrace assisted living community lets its residents enjoy the highest level of independence possible. Its personalized plans are tailored to each person's needs to help maintain good health and a satisfying quality of life. Sun Terrace's dedicated professional staff gives residents the attention they deserve. Residents can choose from a variety of apartment floor plans. The community's private dining room serves seasonal specials and a wide variety of fresh recipes. Sun Terrace provides exercise and wellness programs, housekeeping services, transportation and an activity center. Onsite beauty and barber shops make it easy to look your best. The community is located in the Yakima Valley, famous for their apples, wine and the beautiful Yakima River. A full schedule of activities is available to anyone who wants to participate, including shopping excursions and group trips. An example is the tour of a Sunnyside cheese plant, tasting room and deli. Golfers enjoy games at the scenic Blackrock Creek golf course in Sunnyside, a professional 18-hole course. Sunnyside is the location for Washington's largest Cinco de Mayo celebration, a chili pepper festival and a nationally famous lighted farm-implement parade at Christmastime. Sun Terrace is conveniently located for visitors from Sunnyside, Yakima, Toppenish or Grandview. Experience assisted living at its best in Sun Terrace.

907 Ida Belle Road, Sunnyside WA (509) 839-0579
www.regencysunterrace.com

EASTERN WASHINGTON

Restaurants
& Cafés

Bern's Tavern

Planet Prosser Pale Ale can be found at just one place, Bern's Tavern in Prosser. It is a perfect stop when traveling along I-82, about midway between Yakima and Tri-Cities. The original antique back bar is housed in a building dating back to the early 1900s. Bern's, owned by Darren and Carla Dodgson, is a landmark, one of the few remaining taverns in the State. Of nearly a dozen saloons from the past, it is the only one left in Prosser. Bern's is famous for its Bern's burger and other great pub foods, music and comedy. The museum-like décor represents 100 years of town history. Musical instruments are used as decorations, and many world-class entertainers pop in for the occasional hideaway gig. The environment is laid back, a place where everyone seems to know each other, but where visitors feel welcomed. Calling Bern's a sports bar would be an understatement. There is a television in each booth and many more placed throughout. You can have your privacy or socialize away. In true pub fashion there are pool tables, music, video games and the great fun of gambling pull-tabs. Bern's sells many microbrews and all your old favorites, as well as Washington Wines. Stop in, relax and be entertained, especially if Darren is there. Darren has beaten those drums professionally for 25 years. Bern's was his first gig, at the age of 14, in the late 1970s. Darren and Carla purchased the business from Carla's parents a decade ago, but her father, Carl Grimes, can still be seen helping out. Patrons insist old ghosts still roam the city from the real Underground that once existed and partially remains. In Bern's Tavern, a persistent lone cowboy and a frequent sailor in an old uniform, are often seen as quickly as they disappear. Stop in for some fun and great food at Bern's Tavern. See all there is to see, and maybe more.

618 6th Street, Prosser WA
(509) 786-1422

Backstage Bistro

Backstage Bistro in Walla Walla's historic downtown, focuses on simple food prepared to perfection. The nationally acclaimed restaurant combines fine foods, friendly service and one of the largest wine selections in the Pacific Northwest for a lunch and dinner destination that suits just about any occasion. Backstage Bistro offers a choice of 250 to 300 wines, and an espresso bar provides still more engaging beverage options. Start with an appetizer of baked portobello mushrooms or spicy tiger prawns while looking over the menu. Barbecue at Backstage is a masterful combination of carefully timed cooking and a signature barbecue sauce. The popular barbecue chicken is slow-cooked over hickory, while the wild Alaskan salmon is roasted on a cedar plank. The grilled ahi tuna gets a drizzling of lime-ginger teriyaki sauce. The bistro has earned accolades in national publications on both coasts, from Sunset magazine to the New York Times. The indoor dining area reflects the building's past as an art gallery with rich colors, gleaming wood floors and fine architectural detailing. Outdoor dining is popular in fine weather. On weekends, local and nationally known jazz musicians perform, and if you are lucky, owner Bob Parrish might entertain you with one of his dazzling magic tricks. Whether you are young or old, wear jeans and t-shirts or business suits, you are sure to feel right at home at the bistro. Visit Backstage Bistro for a satisfying fine dining experience.

230 E Main Street, Walla Walla WA
(509) 526-0690
www.backstage-bistro.com

The Emerald of Siam

After 25 years of family ownership, the first Thai restaurant in the Tri-Cities continues to earn rave reviews as one of the Northwest's best Thai restaurants. Sisters Ravadi Quinn and Sunanta Kulthol opened the Emerald of Siam in 1983 and grew it from a tiny café to the well known restaurant it is today with seating for 100. Sunanta has retired in Thailand, and three of Ravadi's children, Dara, Bill and Suzanne, have joined the staff. The Emerald serves entrées family style and offers an inviting array of seafood dishes, curries, rice and noodle dishes, as well as many specialty dishes featuring chicken, duck, beef and pork. "I believe that a family gathering with a variety of foods representing each individual's interest will bring the most fun and joy to our inner beings," says Ravadi. Dishes are made to order, and substitutions are welcome. You will find many vegetarian and vegan selections as well as gluten-free, lactose-free and low carb choices. Ravadi encourages artistry in all its forms and explores that artistry in two books, *The Wings of My Soul* and *The Joy of Thai Cooking*. The restaurant showcases her artistic, individual approach to cooking as well as the artwork of her son Bill and piano performances by Dara. The Emerald of Siam participates in the Prosser Wine & Food Fair and the Tumbleweed Music Festival. For a taste of Thailand in a restaurant known for its culinary artistry, visit the Emerald of Siam.

1314 Jadwin Avenue, Richland WA
(509) 946-9328
www.emeraldofsiam.com

Classic Events Catering

Did the bride's mother forget to thaw the rolls? Donna Menard, owner of Classic Events Catering, has a solution. Donna understands that people hire catering services so the caterer can do the worrying and the client can enjoy the event. At a wedding, for example, the caterer should do the work, not the bride. Donna has been catering for more than 20 years and has handled events for up to 500 people. At first, it was a part-time job, but now business is booming. Today, Donna and general manager Lori Devitt sometimes handle three to four events in a weekend using multiple crews. Donna has an album of thank-you cards and long letters from grateful brides and their families. She earns this praise by doing everything possible to understand the needs and tastes of her customer well in advance of the event. On the day itself, "there's no situation I can't handle," says Donna. Classic Events can accommodate almost any menu request, but Donna has recipes of her own that are much in demand. These include her signature Wine Country Salmon and Baron of Beef. Donna has handled events at most of the local wineries, as well as fundraisers for Heritage University and the Yakima Symphony. She was vice president of the Washington Bridal Show for more than 15 years and has hosted a local public television show called *Best of Yakima Valley Cooking*. You can rely on Classic Events Catering for your next celebration. Don't just hope for the best, let Donna create it for you.

5453 Ashue Road, Wapato WA
(509) 961-7525

Snipes Mountain Microbrewery & Restaurant

Every good restaurant has one or two specialties, but at Snipes Mountain Microbrewery & Restaurant nearly everything touched becomes a specialty. Take a tour of the microbrewery and meet the man behind the award-winning brews, Terry Butler, whose passion for the craft shines through in every batch. The Sunnyside Pale Ale is a four-time award winner in the Best Bitter category, including a gold medal at the World Beer Cup, and the Coyote Moon dark brown ale took a bronze medal at the North American Brewers Awards. Crazy Ivans was awarded first place in the People's Choice award at the 2004 Washington Cask Beer Festival's afternoon session. The restaurant accommodates groups of friends, families or romantic dinner dates with equal aplomb, and patrons can be comfortable dressed casually or formally. From five-course meals with wine to a pizza fresh from a wood-fired oven, the menu covers your every craving. Try the fish and chips battered in Snipes ale, the Greek pizza, pork medallions with apple Dijon sauce and smoked salmon fettuccine. There are entrées designed for children and teens, pub plates, gourmet burgers and expertly executed highbrow fare. Lush decór includes a high log ceiling, rock wall and fireplace, and etched glass doors. The banquet rooms can be dressed up or down to fit any occasion and options for on-site events include a built-in stage on the outdoor covered patio. Just as it was in the 1800s when Ben Snipes, the Northwest Cattle King, welcomed travelers and neighbors to his cabin to enjoy a fine meal, Snipes Mountain Microbrewery & Restaurant still offers some of the best cuisine in the region.

905 Yakima Valley Highway, Sunnyside WA (509) 837-2739
www.snipesmountain.com

Sweet Basil Pizzeria

It's no wonder the Sweet Basil Pizzeria enjoys a huge local following. The pizzeria is a casual, fun place to come and enjoy one of 16 delicious pizzas, prepared in the simple and authentic Italian tradition. The shop is known for its signature 18-inch pizzas and its five types of calzones. You're assured of quick and friendly service, either in the dining room or out on the patio. The hand-tossed pizza dough and sauces are freshly made on-site. Sweet Basil always has New York pizza by the slice, a major hit. Accompany your meal with a fresh garden salad, or make a light meal from the slice-and-salad menu. The most popular whole pizza in the lineup is the Margherita pizza with garlic, basil and tomatoes. Another delectable choice is the Pesto, topped with garlic, mushrooms, olives and artichoke hearts. The restaurant serves local micro-brewery beers and Washington wines by the glass. Sweet Basil is a family business, owned by Dorene and Steve Brooks and Steve's parents. The Brooks family generously contributes to local charities, churches and school groups and also provides food for various local events. For great pizza in convivial surroundings, visit the Sweet Basil Pizzeria.

5 S 1st Avenue, Walla Walla WA
(509) 529-1950
www.sweetbasilpizzeria.com

Michael's on the Lake

Michael's on the Lake is a steak and seafood restaurant that offers more than great food and quality service. The restaurant's dining room features a sun room overlooking the lovely lake. You can also enjoy your meal, along with a beautiful sunset, on the lighted deck. Michael's on the Lake provides fine dining at reasonable prices in a casual, pleasant atmosphere. The restaurant's signature dish is its slow-roasted prime rib of Angus beef. All of the beef served here is Angus, a serious taste treat. Other tempting entrées include the Dungeness chicken breast filled with a crab-cheese mixture and topped with hollandaise sauce, as well as the Alaskan Amber tempura halibut. Appetizers include wild mushroom ravioli and deep-fried zucchini. Pizza and pasta dishes are available as well as a kid's menu. The wine list offers fine wines, many from Washington and California. You may also buy wine by the glass. Michael's on the Lake is well-known for its catering services, which offer a host of menu options, including customized menus for parties both on and off site. The restaurant has banquet facilities that accommodate groups as large as 100. When in Moses Lake, bring your family and friends for a fine dining experience you won't soon forget.

910 W Broadway Avenue, Moses Lake WA
(509) 765-1611
www.michaelsonthelake.com

Lakefront Bar & Grill

After five years in a corporate cubicle, owner Mike Wilcox decided to follow his dream and open the Lakefront Bar & Grill. This restaurant provides family dining at reasonable prices and also has a full bar. Indoor and outdoor seating provide terrific views of the lake—the main dining room and the bar both look out over the water. The Lakefront is clean and modern, with friendly service and substantial portions of food. It's also a convivial happening spot, where friends meet friends and make new friends. Mike's specialties include his famous all-beef, broiled-to-perfection double burger and the Hot Chick to Go, a flame-broiled chicken sandwich with all the extras. The restaurant has a sports bar atmosphere, and motorcycle enthusiasts enjoy the biker theme. A disc jockey works the bar every Friday and Saturday, and there are occasional live entertainment dates. The Lakefront features micro-brewery beers as well as fine wines from across Washington State. Five flat-screen televisions keep you entertained. Mike is a generous sponsor of local baseball teams and community events. When in Moses Lake, treat yourself to an afternoon or evening on the lake at the Lakefront Bar & Grill.

302 W Broadway Avenue, Moses Lake WA
(509) 764-5535

Bon Vino's Bistro & Bakery

"I needed to do this," says Roger Hazzard, "it's been a dream of mine forever." Judging by how the people of Sunnyside have responded to Bon Vino's Bistro & Bakery, it seems that having such a stylish eatery in their community has likewise been a dream of theirs. Even before its official opening in December 2006, Bon Vino's was booked through the month for private dinner parties. When Roger and his partner, Joreen Mensonides, aren't catering such events, you will find them preparing breakfast and lunch. Belgian waffles, pancakes and French toast are popular with the morning crowd. The lunch menu includes several hot sandwiches, such as the Reuben, patty melt and Philly cheese steak, along with salads and pasta dishes. Panini is popular, too. Chef Roger's catering specialty is Italian food, particularly fettuccine Alfredo. Joreen is the pastry chef here. She interned at bakeries in Ontario, Canada, and Koudum, a village in Friesland, the Netherlands, to learn the secrets of making Dutch pastries. Her muffins, scones and cinnamon rolls disappear quickly every day. The atmosphere at Bon Vino's is cheerfully European. Sconces grace the walls, and Joreen's Dutch morsels seem to smile in their display case. The bistro tables and chairs await your arrival, so why not plan on eating at Bon Vino's soon?

122 N 16th Street, Sunnyside WA
(509) 837-3936

El Valle Family Mexican Restaurant

At the El Valley Family Mexican Restaurant, friendly staff members warmly greet customers. Delve into one of the restaurant's signature dishes, such as Gabriel's Platter, sautéed shrimp with mushrooms, skirt steak and a Guadalajara-style enchilada. Jose's Special is chicken and steak served with rice, beans, *pico de gallo*, guacamole, sour cream and tortillas. Head out for an evening of dancing on Friday and Saturday at the restaurant's sports bar, where a disc jockey spins everyone's favorite tunes. El Valle offers catering for your special occasions, as well as take-out service. Gabriel Garcia long dreamed of two things—playing professional soccer and opening his own restaurant. For more than 25 years, he served as head chef in a Mexican restaurant and trained many people. Six years ago, he opened El Valle. Despite a busy schedule operating a successful restaurant, Gabriel still makes time to play soccer, and stays involved in the community by sponsoring local sports teams and providing them with new uniforms. Come to El Valley Family Mexican Restaurant to experience delicious food and a realization of Gabriel's dream.

410 Yakima Valley Highway, Sunnyside WA
(509) 837-7222

Photo by Jennifer Gifford

Jack-Sons Restaurant and Sports Bar

When was the last time you left a sports bar raving about the food? If you are having trouble answering the question, then it's time you treated yourself by visiting Jack-Sons Restaurant and Sports Bar in Terrace Heights. A good game and good companionship are usually the best that you can hope for, but sports fans at Jack-Sons have come to expect more. Feasting on hand-battered halibut and chips, crab-melt sandwiches or coconut prawns makes a winning touchdown feel that much better—and that's just the seafood part of the menu. Look for prime rib on Friday nights, hand-cut steaks any day of the week, and chicken wings available with nine homemade sauces. Local produce is prominent on the menu. When asparagus is in season, the kitchen comes up with creative dishes that sell out quickly. In summer, onion rings made with sweet Walla Walla onions are a big hit, as are the daiquiris and desserts made with local peaches. Jack-Sons always features an outstanding selection of Northwest wines and beers. Eat and follow the sports action on the large screen in the bar, or bring the whole family and enjoy lunch or dinner in the restaurant. It's the same great food no matter where you are sitting. Find yourself cheering for more than just your team at Jack-Sons Restaurant and Sports Bar.

2710 Terrace Heights, Yakima WA
(509) 248-5911

Café Azure

Azure Goltz had always dreamed of running her own business. A mother of four, she knew how to prepare fresh, healthful and delicious family foods and plenty of vegetarian alternatives. In 2006, with a little help from family and friends, the Café Azure opened its doors with fresh salads, sandwiches and homemade soups, including a soupe du jour. Azure built her business on personalized service, offering customized meals made to-order. To back up her menu, she installed a full espresso bar and soft-serve yogurt machine for anytime treats, offering non-dairy ice cream for vegans. For the kids in all of us, she added homemade soft pretzels, served with cheese sauce or filled with sweet cream cheese. Azure built a café after her own heart and home, offering a casual, indoor-outdoor atmosphere like coming home to mom's kitchen, but with a lot more choices. Her children are proud that she fulfilled her dream. Although Azure decided to retire her café to offer better support to her family, she offers this story for the memory of her children and as an inspiration to other aspiring small business owners: "It's never too late to follow your dreams."

110 E 5th Avenue, Moses Lake WA
(509) 766-2233

The Blue Goose Restaurant

When Carlos León took over the Blue Goose Restaurant, he found his calling. The Blue Goose serves the kind of food that keeps people coming back. It also has the lower Yakima Valley's most extensive local wine list. Carlos believes that restaurant reputations are built from the quality of the food, as revealed in presentation and taste. All of his specialties start from scratch, including the fresh oysters and fragrant French onion soup. For prime rib, steaks and seafood, you've come to the expert. Also on the menu are flavorful Italian recipes and divine desserts. The Blue Goose serves traditional Oktoberfest grog in the fall. If the weather is fine, you can choose to dine in the outside seating area. In any case, the atmosphere in the restaurant is always relaxed and friendly. You might even see one of Carlos' five children (nine thru 18 years) here from time to time learning the business. Carlos dedicates to you the spirit of his family along with the tradition of good food and hospitality taught to him by his grandparents and parents. The Blue Goose Restaurant has prospered in its location for many years, and its tradition is still going strong. Come in and be a part of it.

306 7th Street, Prosser WA
(509) 786-1774

Photo by Jennifer Gifford

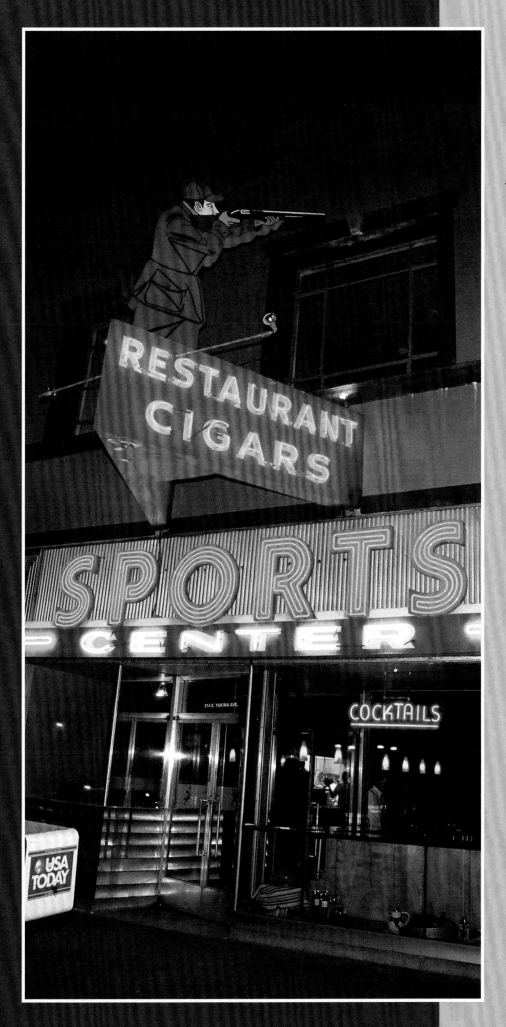

Yakima Sports Center Restaurant and Lounge

For a one-stop cultural indoctrination to Central Washington, drop by Yakima Sports Center Restaurant and Lounge. Whether it's the season for Mariners, Seahawks or Supersonics, sports have been woven into the daily fabric of life here for four generations. Catch televised games among fans on high-definition screens or peruse the historic memorabilia of local legends, such as boxing champ Pete Rademacher. The Northwest is synonymous with micro-brewed beers, and Yakima Sports Center keeps an impressive selection in the bottle or on tap. Pair one of the restaurant's featured entrées with valley wines from the neighboring wine country. The restaurant is open for lunch, dinner and late night seven days a week with breakfast served on Sundays. Calamari, pork chops and burgers served with hand-cut fries are just a few of the menu favorites. The Sports Center does its part to support local artists, whose work you can view throughout the premises. The Center stage is a hub for the music scene, too, with live performances every week. Musicians from the Northwest and beyond perform everything from bluegrass and folk to rock and reggae, and the bar stays open until the crowds fade away. Yes, Yakima Sports Center is a second home for many sports enthusiasts, but it is not a sports bar. For a seat right in the thick of Northwest culture, head to Yakima Sports Center Restaurant and Lounge in the heart of downtown Yakima.

214 E Yakima Avenue, Yakima WA
(509) 453-4647
www.yakimasportscenter.com

Shy's Pizza Connection

Often times, it seems that the smaller the town is the bigger its heart is. In Prosser, Shy's Pizza Connection enriches the area with great food, amazing service and community involvement. Shy's is a popular local hangout for students and families and creates a feeling of kinship over homemade pizza and entertainment. Stop in for Monday night football on the big screen and a tasty slice of pepperoni. Bring the kids in for an evening of arcade games and Shy's famous chicken and jojos. For informal business lunches, don't miss the daily lunch specials, usually including salad bar, pizza and drinks. All food is made-to-order, and customers are welcome to experiment with different toppings to create their own pizzas. The pizza sauce is an original recipe, and blended fresh with quality ingredients. Savor the taste of a real homemade pizza with crispy crusts and a wide selection of toppings. Shy's meeting and party room allows large groups to celebrate and meet in their own private area. In addition, many local high school students frequent the restaurant after games for what they call Pack the Place Night. A fired-up sports team and 80 to 90 students and faculty come to Shy's for hot pizza, cold drinks and down-home rowdy fun. Owner Sheryl Roberts revels in this lively environment and welcomes anyone who wants to join in the celebration. Find yourself in pizza ecstasy at Shy's Pizza Connection and become a part of this fun-filled caring family.

1306 Meade Avenue, Prosser WA
(509) 786-4095

EASTERN WASHINGTON

Shopping
& Gifts

Hopfengarten

A one-of-a-kind gallery, shop and interior design studio, Hopfengarten is an artist's haven. Owner Beki Anderson uses her artist's eye and interior design degree to create the perfect blend of merchandise and atmosphere. Beki features her own oil paintings in the gallery along with works of her family and community. Her daughter, Roz Anderson, contributes jewelry and mixed-media art, while her husband, Gary, adds tables and yard art made of scrap metal. From international craftspeople, Beki gathers home décor and attractive gifts. These elements combine to form artful and constantly-transforming displays. "I wanted to bring a different kind of store to Prosser," says Beki. Daughter Roz adds, "We try to carry things that you would normally have to travel to Seattle to find." As the gallery grows, Beki envisions it as a gathering place for wine-tasting and show openings. Meet one of Prosser's most creative people in the beautiful environment of Hopfengarten.

10 Merlot Drive, Prosser WA
(509) 786-9900

Revitalize! Health Spa & Organic Store

Shopping for someone with diabetes, high blood pressure, gluten or lactose sensitivities? Feel it's a monumental undertaking to find great taste and still make that lifestyle change? Revitalize! Health Spa & Organic Store offers a wider variety for people with special dietary needs than any other store in the entire Columbia Basin. Revitalize stocks the most popular, and tasty, gluten-free baking mixes and pastas by brands such as Bob's Red Mill, Gluten Free Pantry, Pamela's, Arrowhead Mills, Gifts of Nature, Tinkyada and Namaste. To start the morning out right, try gluten-free cereals from Erewhon, Enjoy Life and Glutino. For those who enjoy hot dog and hamburger buns, toast or sandwiches, there is an entire line of Ener-G baked goods that are wheat, dairy and gluten free. Indulge yourself with a bowl of the highly sought after certified Gluten-Free Oats. For those who are watching their glycemic index and for no diabetic spiking, Revitalize carries Xylitol, which is highly recommended by dentists, plus fructose, agave nectar and kurlu for baking. Sugar-free cereals, snacks and chocolate bars are also on-hand. Just in, try adding flavored Stevia to your favorite beverage, or make your own soda from seltzer water. Eco Friendly and Mrs. Meyers, which are environmentally friendly, toxin-free household cleaning and pet care products, line the shelves. To help you with your health concerns, browse through a diverse number of self-help books on topics that range from cooking, diet and wellbeing to taking control of and managing your finances. The Little Shop with Big Variety is ready to serve you.

Photos By Barrett Brown Photograhy

Photos By Barrett Brown Photograhy

If your partner's snoring raises the roof and keeps you awake, then step into Revitalize! Health Spa and Organic Store, the little shop in friendly downtown Kennewick where you can purchase Himalayan Crystal Salt Lamps. Not only are these lamps beautiful, but the negative ions they emit kill bacteria, purify the air, increase well being and soothe the mind, body and soul. Negative ions are abundant where nature is unspoiled, such as waterfalls, caves, mountains and the air following a thunderstorm. Customers swear by the salt crystals' therapeutic abilities, and they love the good night sleep they get when the effects of the crystals' negative ions quiet or even eliminate their partner's snoring. Some clients have reported that even their dogs have stopped snoring. However, snoring reduction isn't the only benefit people realize from the lamps: allergies, the common cold, sinus conditions, anxiety, fatigue, insomnia, migraines, depression, headaches and more have been relieved. The lamps can also protect you from harmful electrical magnetic frequencies, such as are emitted from computers, televisions and other electrical devices. Himalayan Crystal Salt Lamps are one of the shop's most popular items and Revitalize is noted for having the largest selection of these lamps for miles around, priding themselves on having the shapes and sizes to fit every décor and budget. Let the helpful staff assist in selecting a lamp that is right for you.

311 W Kennewick Avenue, Kennewick WA
(509) 586-6574
www.BiofeedbackPlus1.com

The Funny Farm

A man walks into a card shop and asks the person at the counter how to make a mojito. No, this isn't the opening line of a joke. Actually, it describes a fairly typical scene at the Funny Farm, one of the more unusual stores that you are likely to visit in Sunnyside. Part light-hearted gift shop and part state liquor store, the Funny Farm has got you covered when you need a card for that friend who just turned 30 and a bottle of spirits for the party. You're likely to find a suitable gag gift as well. Owners Loran and Theresa Hancock say that their selection of cards is the largest of any independent store in the Lower Yakima Valley. From a little naughty to very nice, there's a card expressing just the tone that will cause your friend to break out in a smile. The Funny Farm has been making people laugh and keeping spirits high since 1991. Its owners won the Manager of the Year Award for 2003, placing at the top of the state's more than 200 liquor stores. The business is active in the Chamber of Commerce and sponsors many local events. Plain and simple, it's just a fun place to visit. Drop by soon.

416 E Edison Avenue, Sunnyside WA
(509) 837-5445

Perfect Printing & Signs

After 35 years of old-fashioned service to its clients and the community, a highly respected business deserves to be acknowledged as a true community treasure. Perfect Printing & Signs continues to thrive and contribute to the city of Prosser. Eric and Donna Barnard started Perfect Printing in a tiny downtown shop in 1972. In 1976, they purchased a larger building on Sixth Street. Since then, they have expanded their services to include affordable full-color printing, outstanding graphic design, bulk mailing capabilities, continuous multiple part forms and computer generated signs, banners and vinyl lettering. Their ever-expanding services and their reputation for excellence bring customers from all over the northwest. One of their many contributions to Prosser was to spearhead the acquisition and renovation of the old train depot, which the city dedicated to Eric. The Eric Barnard Depot Square houses both the chamber of commerce and the economic development offices. The Barnards have received many awards as a result of their commitment to their business and to the community. Two of their grandchildren, Jenni and Andy Watson, carry on the family tradition. Their mother, Kari, and their grandfather, Eric, both passed away in 2006; however, Donna and her dedicated staff continue to serve the needs of Prosser and beyond. When you're ready for quality and old-fashioned customer service, Perfect Printing & Signs is where you want to be.

708 Sixth Street, Prosser WA
(509) 786-3811 or (800) 572-9660

Romanza Gifts (Walla Walla)

John Sterlin and Vince Harris, the owners of Romanza Gifts, often find nose prints on the windows of their Walla Walla store, located in the historic heart of town. Romanza's windows contain gift items that fulfill longings you didn't even know you had. John and Vince own Romanza stores in Walla Walla and Seattle, plus a thriving e-commerce business. John's mother, Judy Rostollan, was a great inspiration to the two young businessmen and operates the Walla Walla store as if it were her own. Come see the original restored tin ceiling installed in 1896. Both the Walla Walla and Seattle shops offer remarkable fragrances, accent pieces, wine and chocolate. You'll find candles that ignite the imagination. The bath and body products invite you to bring spa luxury into the lives of you and your loved ones. Many of the shop's colors and products evoke Tuscany, but you'll find influences from France and England, too. Currently, Romanza prepares the gifts for every celebrity guest on the *Ellen Degeneres Show*. John and Vince opened Romanza in 1999 and used their natural sense of style to guide their initial efforts. "Vince and I love boutiques," says John, "and this gave us the chance to bring all the things that we love together in one place." *Romanza* is Italian for romance, and visitors experience that giddy otherworldly feeling that accompanies amour. A combination of intriguing offerings, a peaceful interior and a friendly staff account for the store's loyal following. Next time you need a gift or just inspiring surroundings, visit Romanza Gifts.

12 E Main Street, Walla Walla WA
(509) 525-9731 or (800) 608-5489
www.romanzagifts.com

Woven Threads Quilt Store

Woven Threads Quilt Store is doing its part to keep a centuries-old tradition alive and well in this age of modern technology. After quilting for years, owner Rose Buhl jumped at the opportunity to own her own store and opened her quilt shop in 1995. Inspired by her grandmothers who were both seamstresses, Rose delights in building relationships with others who share her passion. On Wednesdays she opens her back room to community women and tourists who come together to quilt and inspire one another. Woven Threads Quilt Store features an extensive selection of colorful fabrics and fabric books as well as yarns and gift items. It also offers numerous quilting classes for beginning to advanced quilters. In 2002, *Quilt Sampler*, a *Better Homes and Gardens* magazine, chose Woven Threads Quilt Store as one of the top 10 quilt companies in the United States. Rose gives plenty of credit to her wonderfully knowledgeable staff members, all of whom have a passion for knitting and sewing themselves and love helping others find their creative flair. Whether you're looking for beautiful fabrics, colorful yarns, a special gift or simply the camaraderie that quilting offers, you'll find it at Woven Threads Quilt Store.

136 E Woodin Avenue, Chelan WA
(509) 682-7714

Photo by Jennifer Gifford

Photos by Dan McCool

Roxy Theatre Antiques & Gifts

Historic buildings have a special charm of their own. They carry memories from the past that seem to settle in the walls. Roxy Theatre Antiques & Gifts in Historic Downtown Kennewick, resides in just such a building. First built in the 1920s as a theatre, the building has won numerous awards for its reconstruction and current use. Roxy Theatre Antiques & Gifts includes a full-service espresso bar and a café that features baked goods, gourmet teas and a home-like setting. Visitors can relax and enjoy a book, talk with friends or browse through 3,200 square feet of 18th and 19th century antiques offered by numerous dealers. The antiques have been tastefully set in decorative arrangements, so you can picture how they will fit in your home. Ann Steiger, owner of the Roxy, takes an active interest in downtown revitalization efforts through membership in the Historic Downtown Kennewick Foundation. Her husband Tom McClelland, an artist, supports the effort as well. Whether passing through the area or staying for a while, plan on spending time relaxing and browsing at Roxy Theatre Antiques & Gifts.

101 W Kennewick Avenue, Kennewick WA
(509) 585-2301

EASTERN WASHINGTON

Weddings & Events

Cozy Rose Inn Bed and Breakfast

Mark and Jennie Jackson go the extra mile to ensure that you will truly experience the luxury and privacy you are looking for in this beautiful country setting. After all, they are experts when it comes to knowing how travelers like to be treated. They have traveled around the world and have visited more than 400 inns and bed-and-breakfasts. From the moment you enter one of the five suites, you will feel like you have stepped into another country, perhaps France or Italy. The rooms catch the sunlight, while providing views of waterfalls and other lovely vistas. An air of freshness rises from the garden, where the Jacksons grow fruits and herbs for the inn's gourmet, intimate dinners in the beautiful new Tuscan-style dining room. The grounds are dotted with fruit trees and two acres of a lush green oasis of yards, flowers and gazebos. Stroll through the family vineyards and enjoy sweeping views of both grapes and hops. Modern amenities complement the Old World charm. Each room is very large with a private entry, large jetted or two-person soaking tub and shower. All suites host king-size beds, fireplaces, wireless Internet and satellite television. A candlelight breakfast can be delivered to your suite. An 18-hole golf course is located just five minutes away. With 50 wineries and breweries within 30 minutes of your door, the inn is perfectly located for tasting tours. *Bed and Breakfasts in the Northwest & California* awarded the Cozy Rose Inn its highest five-star rating. It is the perfect balance of pampering and privacy. If you are ready to be pampered, let the Jacksons be your hosts. Wine and roses are available upon request.

1220 Forsell Road, Grandview WA
(509) 882-4669 or (800) 575-8381
www.cozyroseinn.com

Redneck Limo Service

Comedian Jeff Foxworthy may have saluted the redneck, but it is partners Frank Pullum and Cyn Davis that give him the celebrity treatment he deserves. In 2006, this dynamic duo founded Redneck Limo Service, a car-and-driver-enterprise designed for the workingman. Frank had always wanted his own business and was able to buy a used limousine from a friend. He and Cyn started out by offering rides to friends and family who were out for the night at local bars and taverns. Word of mouth took off. The business quickly blossomed into a full-service limousine company known for exceptional service and affordable pricing. In addition to offering standard driving services, Redneck Limo Service can also provide custom packages for weddings, wine tours and other special events. Packages designed to suit the clients' budget can include everything from decorating the limo for a wedding party to adding a gift basket of gourmet treats for a celebratory night out. Experience the champagne and caviar lifestyle on a burger and beer budget with the gang at Redneck Limo Service.

P.O. Box 416, Benton City WA
(509) 528-2185

EASTERN WASHINGTON

Wineries

Alexandria Nicole Cellars/Destiny Ridge Vineyard

High on the bluffs above the Columbia River, the 243 acres of the Destiny Ridge Vineyard roll out under the majestic sky. The sandy soils, low rainfall, intense heat and rugged winds of the Horse Heaven Hills provide the perfect ingredients for Alexandria Nicole Cellars' (ANC) intensely flavored and beautifully structured wines. Founders Jarrod and Ali (Alexandria Nicole) Boyle firmly believe that the secret to quality wines lies in the soil. Jarrod's farming experience began in childhood and the passion pursued him after college. While as a viticulturalist for Hogue Cellars, Jarrod was doing a routine vineyard inspection in the spring of 1998 when he spotted the lovely slope of land in the Horse Heaven Hills that would become Destiny Ridge, estate vineyard for ANC. The first vines were planted in fall 1998, and today Destiny Ridge grows 17 varietals. The choicest seven-percent of the fruit is reserved for the estate wines and the remainder is sold to other wineries under contract. Through attentive viticulture management, balanced crop levels, gentle processing of grapes and passionate winemaking, ANC produces consistent quality in every bottle. In addition to its delicious wines, ANC delivers fun and inspiring wine events to wine club members and guests at its beautiful tasting room and banquet facilities in Prosser, 45 minutes north of Destiny Ridge. Tours of the wine production facility and estate vineyard are offered by appointment. Come experience the majesty of Destiny Ridge, captured in every bottle from Alexandria Nicole Cellars.

2880 Lee Road, Suite C, Prosser WA (509) 786-3497
19501 144th Avenue NE, Suite E-700, Woodinville WA (425) 293-2220
www.alexandrianicolecellars.com

Kestrel Vintners

Kestrel Vintners is a shining example of what can be achieved when a talented and deeply passionate group of individuals come together to explore new frontiers in their chosen career. This remarkable Prosser winery opened in early 1999, and is owned and operated by John and Helen Walker, who are dedicated to crafting superior wines at an affordable price. The duo began their mission by hand selecting an outstanding staff and then encouraging them to be creative. This genius staff includes General Manager Mike Birdlebough and Winemaker Flint Nelson, who joined the team in 2003. Flint had dreamt of being a winemaker since an early age and spent his life in pursuit of that dream. He is a graduate of Washington State University and has honed his skills at several notable wineries. Since joining the team, Flint has crafted a new series of select wines, including a German-style off-dry wine, Pure Platinum, for the winery's Leavenworth Tasting Room. In 2006, Kestrel Vintners earned a place in the spotlight by having seven different wines rank in the top 25 at the 2006 *Washington CEO* magazine Best of Washington Wines competition. Two of these, the 2002 Estate Old Vine Cabernet Sauvignon, and the 2004 Chardonnay Ice Wine, ranked as number one in their categories. Learn more about the winery's innovative growing process and meet the creative minds behind the vines at Kestrel Vintners, where creating the perfect wine isn't just a focus, it's an obsession.

2890 Lee Road, Prosser WA
(509) 786-CORK (2675) or (888) 343-2675
843B Front Street, Leavenworth WA
(509) 548-7348
www.kestrelwines.com

Hedges Family Estate

Hedges Family Estate brings the European experience of a family-operated vineyard and winery to North America. Tom and Anne-Marie Hedges' involvement in the wine industry began in 1986 when they sold their Cabernet/Merlot blend to Sweden from their virtual winery, Hedges Cellars. They were still without their own winery when they began selling their wine to North American markets. In 1989, the Hedges took a chance and purchased acreage in the Red Mountain American Viticultural Area, the state's smallest federally designated grape growing area. Tom is a Washington native; Anne-Marie spent her childhood in Champagne, France, and her grandfather was a Knight of the Vine, so the Old World concept of producing wines from one's own grapes suited her. The estate's French-style chateau reminds the visitor of the Bordeaux region of France. The lower level houses a fully operational winery and tasting room, and the upper level serves as the owners' private residence. Concentrating on Merlot and Cabernet Sauvignon, the Hedges embrace the concept of *terroir*, a French term that refers to the special characteristics of geography that influence a wine's character. Tom's brother, Pete, is the head winemaker here. The couple's two children, Christophe and Sarah, also work in the family business. Come taste the distinct wines from Red Mountain at Hedges Family Estate.

53511 N Sunset Road, Benton City WA
(509) 588-3155
www.hedgesfamilyestate.com

Photo by Mark Roberts Photography

Yakima River Winery

When a winery excels at making full-bodied red wines, such as Cabernet Sauvignon, Merlot, Lemberger and Port, the world's wine experts pay attention. Husband and wife team John and Louise Rauner have been earning that kind of attention since they first started making wines under the Yakima River Winery label in 1977. John studied winemaking at Columbia Basin College and the University of California at Davis. He also spent six years training in the Yakima Valley under Germany's renowned Helmut Becker, credited as the father of the Washington wine industry. Yakima River was one of the first five wineries in Washington, and John served as one of the first commissioners of the Washington Wine Commission and won the first gold medal awarded at a Washington State competition. Louise started the Yakima Valley Growers Association in 1982, helping many top wineries get their start. On the way to perfecting concentrated, long-lived red wines, the Rauners have piled up more regional, national and international awards than most winemakers ever see. World travelers pay special visits to the only winery in the United States that has its name on a permanent trophy in France listing the best reds in the world since the year 1600. All grapes used by the winery are Yakima Valley grown. All grapes are controlled by the winery—John supervises the vineyards carefully. For wines that demand attention, visit Yakima River Winery.

143302 W North River Road, Prosser WA (509) 786-2805
www.yakimariverwinery.com

Bookwalter Winery & Bistro

Owners Jerry and Jean Bookwalter founded Bookwalter Winery in 1983, and their son, John Bookwalter, joined the team in 1997 as a co-owner and winemaker. The Bookwalter Winery & Bistro offers an intriguing twist on the tasting room concept. John converted his conventional tasting room into a wine and cheese lounge with a sophisticated bistro atmosphere. When you come for a tasting, you're greeted, seated and presented a menu of available wines for tasting, all free of charge. Samples of regional artisan cheeses, as well as a full glass of the wine of your choice are available at a nominal cost. After tasting hours, the lounge opens in bistro mode, with live music Wednesday through Saturday. Locals enjoy sharing a bottle of wine and fine cheeses with friends. It's a cool place to hang out. In 2000, John teamed up with Zelma Long, a world-class winemaking and vineyard consultant. They decided to reorient the mix of wine production between red and white wines to about 90 percent red and 10 percent white. This strategy proved an immediate success. Both the 2000 vintages of Merlot and Cabernet Sauvignon garnered outstanding reviews. The Spring 2005 edition of *Wine Press Northwest* awarded this winery its Washington Winery of the Year award. In 2006, *Wine Enthusiast* magazine ranked the Bookwalter 2005 Riesling as 22nd in a group of 9,000 wines reviewed for its Top 100 Wines of 2006. John sagely remarks that wine making is a perfect blend of science and art. He loves being involved with every step of the vine to wine effort. The Bookwalter Winery and Bistro is one you won't want to miss.

894 Tulip Lane, Richland WA
(509) 627-5000
www.bookwalterwines.com

OREGON

OREGON

Accommodations
& Resorts

Mt. Hood Inn

Guest rooms at Mt. Hood Inn come with satellite television, but most guests prefer the window, with views of majestic Mt. Hood and the surrounding wilderness. You'll enjoy authentic mountain atmosphere at the 18-year-old inn, located in the village of Government Camp, just six miles from Timberline Ski Area, 12 miles from Mt. Hood Meadows and across the street from SkiBowl Summer and Winter Recreation Area. The inn makes it easy for you to tackle winter challenges with indoor parking, ski lockers and ski tuning facilities. In summer, you'll enjoy the nearby hiking and biking trails as well as ski opportunities through Labor Day on the mountain's perpetual snowfield. Whether you seek kayaking adventures, fly fishing opportunities or climbing guides, Mt. Hood Inn can put you in touch with the area's professionals to help make the most of your visit. Guests enjoy gathering at the main lobby's fireplace for video and board games or easing tired muscles in a large indoor whirlpool. Some suites feature private hot tubs. You will awake each morning to a free copy of the *Oregonian* and a complimentary Continental breakfast. When you return from your day's adventures, you'll find excellent restaurants and a local brewpub close at hand. An exploration of the inn's website often reveals special deals as well as secure online reservations. For fun on the massive Mt. Hood, stay at Mt. Hood Inn.

87450 E Government Camp Loop, Government Camp OR (503) 272-3205 or (800) 443-7777
www.mthoodinn.com

Ashland Springs Hotel

Ashland Springs Hotel, nestled in the beautiful Rogue River Valley of Southern Oregon, harkens back to a simpler time. This beautifully restored landmark hotel is on the National Register of Historic Places and is located in downtown Ashland, just steps from the renowned Oregon Shakespeare Festival. Other attractions include the Oregon Cabaret Theatre, Lithia Park, wine tasting and gallery tours. Enjoy skiing, golfing, fishing and river-rafting. Take advantage of tax-free shopping, dining and pampering at the nearby spa. A two-year restoration project has transformed this historic beauty into a haven of taste and elegance reminiscent of small European hotels. Today this nine-story boutique hotel offers first-class hospitality to those who are drawn by business, the arts or the area's natural beauty. This lovely hotel offers 70 tastefully appointed, non-smoking guest rooms in an oasis of gentility and charm. Guests are pampered with superb service and luxurious surroundings. Amenities are many and include spa services, high-speed wireless Internet connection, a complimentary light breakfast served on the mezzanine, and free parking. For celebrations, weddings and corporate functions, the Grand Ballroom with an adjoining conservatory and adjacent English garden is an ideal location. The hotel's restaurant marries the magic of Ashland's natural surroundings with the food and wines of the northwest, creating dishes from the freshest local ingredients that are sure to seduce your palate. For more information, photos and a downloadable brochure, visit the Ashland Springs Hotel website.

212 E Main Street, Ashland, OR   (541) 488-1700 or (888) 795-4545
www.ashlandspringshotel.com

Lake of the Woods Resort

Deep in the Southern Oregon Cascade mountain range lies the enchanting Lake of the Woods Resort. In 1870, Captain Applegate came across the lake while camping nearby with a band of natives and decided to name the stunning waterway Lake o' the Woods. Soon people began building forest camps and summer homes along the shore, and the area became a popular fishing retreat. Today, Lake of the Woods Resort is owned and operated by Doug and Becky Neuman, who purchased it in the fall of 1998. With a good deal of research under their belts, the Neumans began an intensive restoration process that required a full team of decorators, craftsmen and dedicated employees. Today this resort is more popular than ever and features 26 cabins, multiple RV sites and a completely rebuilt marina with over 4,000 square feet of docks, room to moor up to 25 boats and a dockside tackle shop. The Summer Lodge Restaurant and Bar, which overlooks the lake, is the resort's central hub and the ideal place to enjoy a relaxed meal with family and friends. Lunch and dinner are served Wednesday through Sunday, with country breakfasts available on the weekends. The Marina Grill, which offers dockside dining and takeout, remains open Thursday through Sunday during the winter season. Beyond the many water-based activities, such as waterskiing, sailing and fishing, visitors also enjoy hiking, picnicking, snowmobiling and cross-country skiing. Visit Lake of the Woods year-round for all your favorite outdoor activities, on land and water.

950 Harriman Route, Klamath Falls OR
(541) 949-8300 or (866) 201-4194
www.lakeofthewoodsresort.com

Rivershore Hotel

You'll be 11 miles from the Portland International Airport and just yards from Willamette Falls when you choose one of 120 rooms at Rivershore Hotel in Oregon City. Whether you've come for business or pleasure, you are sure to appreciate Rivershore's panoramic views of the historic Willamette River from your balcony. The hotel, which sits at the actual end of the Oregon Trail, offers a second floor conducive to families with extra seating and easy access to fitness, laundry, spa and pool facilities. The third floor caters to executives with wireless Internet, corporate meeting rooms and desks with ergonomic chairs. Everyone appreciates the refrigerators and microwaves that make it easy to keep snacks on hand. The outdoor pool is heated for seasonal comfort. Satellite television and videos promise entertainment when you are not engaged with such activities as fishing for Chinook or taking an excursion on a jet boat or sternwheeler. Rivershore places you close to skiing, rafting and golfing. Shopping is also nearby, along with museums, art galleries and historic homes to browse. The hotel is a favorite location for weddings, reunions and meetings with full catering facilities on-site. The Rivershore Bar and Grill offers a restaurant, lounge and deck for breakfast, lunch, dinner or a refreshing cocktail or microbrew. The grill makes its own clam chowder and serves up steaks, seafood, salads and burgers. Put the beauty of the Mt. Hood region at your disposal with a stay at Rivershore Hotel.

1900 Clackamette Drive, Oregon City OR
(503) 655-7141
www.rivershorehotel.com

Rogue Regency Inn & Suites

The Rogue Regency Inn & Suites is the place to stay in Medford. Whether you're just visiting or are here on business, this full-service hotel has everything to make your stay comfortable and enjoyable. The beautiful two-story lobby reflects Rogue Regency's reputation for service and hospitality. Fully remodeled in 2005, you can expect the best room service or you can enjoy a meal at Chadwicks, the Regency's own pub and state-of-the-art sports bar. Check the website for more information about Comedy Night at Chadwicks. If you choose to stay for the night, you may want to reserve a suite with a hot tub so you can truly relax and unwind, or you can sleep in one of the 203 beautiful rooms. Conveniently located in the heart of the Rogue Valley, the Rogue Regency Inn & Suites is just off Interstate 5 near the Jackson County Airport, giving you perfect access to rivers, mountains, forests and all of the recreational and cultural attractions found nearby.

2300 Biddle Road, Medford OR
(541) 770-1234 or (800) 535-5805
www.rogueregency.com

Photo by Jeannie Savage

Mr. Thom's Salon & Resort

Getting their hair done by Thom Martin was a must for many celebrities who stayed and performed at Caesar's Palace in Las Vegas. Mr. Thom had a salon at the famous hotel, though he always kept a place in his heart for his native Medford. Mr. Thom's Salon & Resort marks his triumphant return to southern Oregon. Photographs of many instantly recognizable stars decorate the walls, mementos of the glamorous days he has left behind to bring some pizzazz to his hometown. The salon is just part of an exciting destination business that includes a bed-and-breakfast with such resort amenities as a saltwater pool. Take a dip by the waterfall and then enjoy a leisurely glass of wine while gazing upon Mr. Thom's vineyard. The décor throughout the salon and inn reflects the owner's fondness for the tastefully outrageous. Mr. Thom makes the main house and beautifully landscaped grounds available for weddings, anniversaries and other special events. Take a tip from the stars and get your hair styled by Thom Martin while relaxing at Mr. Thom's Salon & Resort.

59 S Stage Road, Medford OR
(541) 535-8406

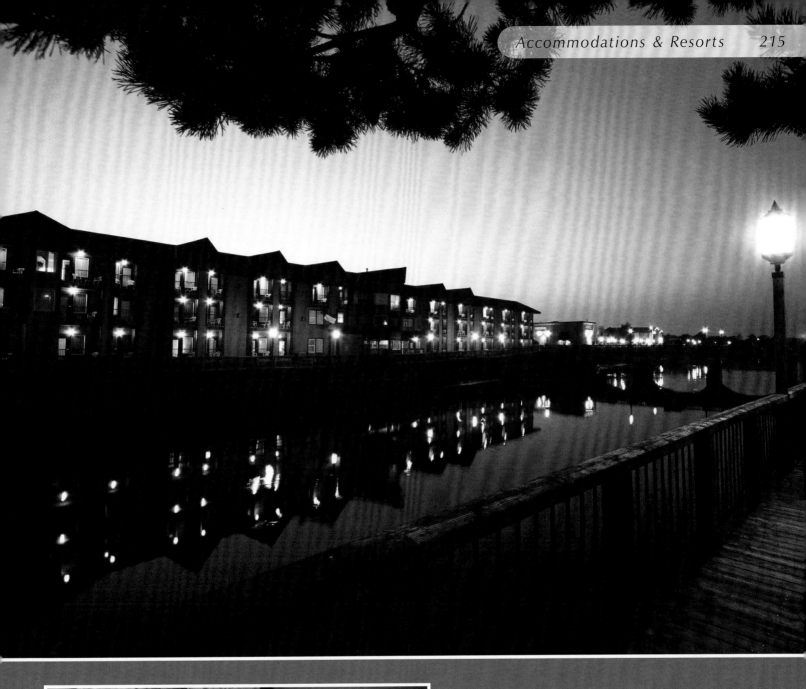

Comfort Inn & Suites

The majority of rooms at the Comfort Inn & Suites in Seaside have private balconies overlooking the peaceful Necanicum River. That's just one reason why this hotel is such a favorite for travelers along the Pacific coast. The deluxe breakfast buffet in the Riverview Suite is another. The Pacific Ocean is just moments away, and after walking the beach or flying a kite, guests love to come back to the hotel to splash in the indoor pool or soak in the hot tub. Amenities in the bright and spacious rooms include microwave, coffee maker and iron/ironing board. Comfort Inn & Suites has just the thing if you are considering a romantic weekend at the coast: beautifully appointed spa suites featuring a two-person spa and a fireplace in addition to the balcony. Freshly baked cookies are available every afternoon in the lobby. This hotel follows the Comfort Inn & Suites rule of offering boutique style and distinction at a price that even families can afford. Cap off a delightful day at the coast by watching the stars come out from your balcony at this Seaside charmer.

545 Broadway, Seaside OR
(503) 738-3011
www.comfortinnseaside.com

Seaside Oceanfront Inn

The Seaside Oceanfront Inn delights visitors with uniquely themed rooms, first-class customer service and spectacular views of the Pacific Ocean. John Gibson opened the boutique hotel on Seaside's promenade in 2006. The inn's shingled clock tower rises tall, making a striking landmark on the boardwalk. Inside, innkeeper Nancy Hillis creates an inviting atmosphere combining the personal service of a bed-and-breakfast with the amenities of a luxury hotel. Each of the 14 rooms embraces a distinctly different feeling. Some travelers enjoy discovering a new room on each visit, while others have favorites they request over and over. The blue hues and gauzy canopy over the queen bed of the Library room lend a relaxing air, while the vibrant greens and animal prints in the King's Jungle Retreat make you want to have some fun. Perched high over the ocean, the romantic Clock Tower Suite offers a round king-sized bed, cathedral ceilings, a Jacuzzi tub and stunning sunset views. A newly added restaurant and lounge offer fresh seafood, salads and other Northwest specials and a full spirits and wine bar. Visit the Seaside Oceanfront Inn to enjoy beautiful scenery both indoors and out.

581 S Promenade, Seaside OR
(503) 738-6403
www.theseasideinn.com

Photo by Jennifer Gifford

All Seasons Property Management

The staff at All Seasons Property Management feels fortunate to live in the paradise known as Mt. Hood, Oregon and to be able to share the majestic beauty with you. Mt. Hood offers year-round skiing and snowboarding. There are streams and rivers cascading all through the villages of Mt. Hood and pristine lakes waiting for you to come and enjoy. It also offers golf, hiking, bird watching, mountain biking and white water rafting, to name a few of the activities in the area. All Seasons Property Management's vacation rentals are meticulously maintained and include fully equipped kitchens, linens and many other amenities. There are hot tubs, riverfront, cozy woodstoves and fireplaces, vintage cabins and elegant lodges. It offers discounted lift tickets in the winter season and has a staff with vast knowledge of the area, including the best places to dine or picnic. All Seasons Property Management welcomes family reunions and corporate retreats as well as intimate getaways and relaxing vacations. Give the office a call, and let the staff fit you with the perfect match for your needs and price range.

23804 E Greenwood Avenue, Welches OR
(503) 622-1142
www.mthoodrent.com

The Stage Lodge

Jacksonville's only motel makes an excellent home base for an exploration of this historic Gold Rush town. The Stage Lodge mimics the historic stage stops along the stage route that ran from Sacramento to Portland. You'll be nestled in the foothills of the Siskiyou Mountains just half a mile from a downtown that is so authentic that it is listed in entirety on the National Historic Register. The spacious grounds feature a 120-year-old walnut tree. The rooms are nicely furnished with ceiling fans and armoires. Two suites offer gas fireplaces, wet bars and private spas. Guests appreciate such complimentary extras as wireless Internet access and a Continental breakfast. Owners John and Nancy Van Dyke are your hosts at the 27-room motel, built in 1991. Everything this National Historic Landmark Community offers will be close at hand, from mountain views and hiking paths to wineries, museums, restaurants and shopping. The city holds festivals throughout the year. The summer Britt Festival brings renowned performing artists to perform under the stars. Enjoy the natural beauty and historic charms of Jacksonville from a room at the Stage Lodge.

830 N 5th Street, Jacksonville OR (541) 899-3953 or (800) 253-8254
www.stagelodge.com

Bybee's Historic Inn

Judging by his home, William Bybee, a horse breeder who once owned more than 5,000 acres in Jackson County, preferred not to flaunt his wealth but to understate it with modest elegance. All who stay at Bybee's Historic Inn agree that the home, which exemplifies the Classic Revival style of architecture, is a neatly proportioned model of good taste. Built in 1857 and listed on the National Historic Register, it offers six beautifully furnished and air-conditioned rooms. Some rooms offer additional amenities, such as a two-person Jacuzzi, fireplace or sofa sleeper. The two cousins who own the inn, Tina Marie Flaherty and Vikki Lynn Maddock, invite guests to enjoy the serene country elegance while relaxing on the covered porch, listening to the gentle waterfall in the koi pond or reading in the secluded gazebo. Jacksonville's historic downtown and Britt Festivals are a mile from the front door. Other popular Rogue Valley attractions, including Medford's Craterian Theatre and Ashland's Shakespeare Festival, are just a short drive away. Guests start the day with a full gourmet breakfast that may include lemon ricotta crêpes topped with fresh rasberre sauce, almond peach French toast garnished with maple marzipan, fresh vegetable fatatas, fresh-baked seasonal scones and quiche. Snacks are served throughout the day, and the grounds include a large building for events and weddings. For a place where tranquility and quiet elegance abound, consider staying at Bybee's Historic Inn.

883 Old Stage Road, Jacksonville OR
(541) 899-0106 or (877) BYBEESINN (292-3374)
www.bybeeshistoricinn.com

Hotel Elliott

The view from the rooftop garden at Hotel Elliott is grand. Look one way and watch big ships ply the waters of the Columbia River. Look the other way and admire the lovely Victorian homes that dot the hillside. Originally built in 1924, Hotel Elliot is the only hotel in downtown Astoria's historic district. The hotel underwent a $4 million renovation to become the majestic boutique hotel it is today. Its 32 rooms and suites feature such luxuries as 440-count Egyptian cotton sheets, goose down pillows and featherbeds. Additional touches include mantled fireplaces, marble vanities and spun glass wet bar sinks. Heated stone floors in each bath add to the sense of supreme comfort. The six-room Presidential Suite on the top floor exemplifies sophistication and elegance. Beneath the main level, Hotel Elliot brings the classic film Casablanca to life. The Crabernet Room, a cozy wine bar with banana-leaf fans, offers a wide selection of wines, Champagnes and ports. The Havana Room, an enclosed cigar lounge, stocks the kind of fine cigars that readers of *Cigar Aficionado* fantasize about. Both spaces are available for special events. An adjacent conference room can accommodate up to 100 people for banquets or meetings. Make your stay in Astoria a luxurious one by choosing Hotel Elliot.

357 12th Street, Astoria OR
(503) 325-2222
www.hotelelliott.com

Applegate River Lodge

The Applegate River Lodge and Restaurant is the perfect place for a romantic getaway or family event in Southern Oregon. With its spectacular view of the Applegate River, this is truly an Oregon treasure. The Applegate River Lodge consists of seven large rooms. Themes range from a rustic gold miner's cabin to an elegant honeymoon suite. All rooms have Jacuzzi tubs for two and private decks overlooking the majestic Applegate River. The lodge has no telephones or televisions so guests can relax and enjoy the beautiful setting and impeccable service. The focal point of the lodge's great room is a beautiful river rock fireplace. The sitting area is a wonderful spot to relax with a great book or play a board game. Continental breakfast is also served here. The Applegate Restaurant is located next to the Lodge. This casual yet elegant restaurant offers unforgettable gourmet dinners. Guests can sit on the deck during the summer and listen to the rushing water and sip wine from one of the local wineries. Listen to live music on the deck on Wednesday and Sunday evenings during the summer months and on Wednesdays during the winter. The Applegate River Lodge and Restaurant is a popular wedding destination where couples can rent the entire lodge. The beautiful grounds and stunning river backdrop coupled with delicious food and service make for an ideal setting. Owners Joanna and Richard Davis opened the restaurant in 1992. The lodge was completed in 1997 and is located between Medford and Grants Pass on highway 238. The lodge is open year-round and the restaurant is open Wednesday through Sunday.

15100 Highway 238, Applegate OR
(541) 846-6690
www.applegateriverlodge.com

Cannery Pier Hotel

The Cannery Pier Hotel offers luxury boutique accommodations with unparalleled views of the Columbia River. Built on the pilings of the 1897 Union Fish Cannery, the new hotel juts 600 feet out into the Columbia, allowing for an up-close view of the ships and barges passing by on the working river. Relax by the fireplace in your well-appointed room, soak in the claw foot tub or admire the views from your private balcony, including the Washington State coast line. Enjoy a Continental breakfast each morning, as well as complimentary wine and smoked salmon in the early evening. You could easily spend a vacation within the hotel, taking advantage of the Cannery Day Spa, authentic Finnish sauna, fitness room and cozy library. When you decide to venture out, reserve the hotel's chauffeured 1939 Buick Special to do your sightseeing in style, or borrow a bicycle and pedal along the riverfront. Come to the Cannery Pier Hotel to get away from it all on the Columbia River.

N 10 Basin Street, Astoria OR
(503) 325-4996
www.cannerypierhotel.com

The Old Welches Inn Bed & Breakfast

For more than 18 years, Judith and Ted Mondun have been welcoming guests to the beauty of their home and the surrounding countryside at the Old Welches Inn Bed & Breakfast. Ted and Judith discovered the beauty of the region during a ski trip in the late 1987s, ultimately purchasing this Mt. Hood retreat. When they learned of its history as very first hotel on Mt. Hood, they couldn't resist opening a new bed and breakfast there. Guests will get an idea of the inn's historic elegance as they enter through the marble tiled foyer. The accommodations here are luxurious, with four differently decorated bedrooms, including an attic suite ideal for honeymooners. There's also a cottage, with two bedrooms, two bathrooms and a fully equipped kitchen. Guests in the main house will enjoy a delicious breakfast buffet with a main entrée, biscuits, coffee cakes and fruit dishes. The living room and sun room offer comfortable places to sit, socialize and enjoy the view. There's plenty of beautiful countryside to see, and good fishing to be had in the Salmon River, which runs through the back yard. If you're looking for a picturesque, romantic place to stay, try the Old Welches Inn Bed & Breakfast.

26401 E Welches Road, Welches OR
(503) 622-3754
www.mthoodlodging.com

Squaw Mountain Ranch

You can enjoy the foothills of Oregon's Cascade Mountains in the buff at the cooperatively owned Squaw Mountain Ranch. The nudist club owns 19 acres of secluded woodland near Estacada. The club was founded in 1933, making it the oldest nudist club west of the Mississippi. You'll be next to Mt. Hood National Forest with a private lake, hiking trails and lodge with three guest rooms and a community kitchen at your disposal. Visitors can reserve tent or RV sites with hookups for water and electricity. In summer, you can rent an Indian teepee. Co-op members stay in old loggers' cabins and RV sites. You can gather around the fire pit, relax in the wood-burning sauna or in one of two hot tubs. A clubhouse offers indoor games, billiards and television. Outdoor activities include volleyball, shuffleboard, horseshoes, miniature golf and an annual music festival. A playground captivates the kids. The club is a member of the American Association of Nude Recreation and offers a safe and pleasant retreat for anyone who enjoys a nudist lifestyle. You'll need to bring food and towels for your stay, but you can reserve the clothes for trips to town. Call ahead for reservations and the combination to the gate at Squaw Mountain Ranch.

48176 SE Squaw Mountain Road, Estacada OR   (503) 630-6136
www.squawmt.com

Cedarplace Inn

Knowing how to relax is every bit
as important as knowing where to
relax. You will be well on your way to
gaining relaxation know-how when
you choose the Cedarplace Inn, just
half an hour from downtown Portland,
10 minutes from Multnomah Falls and
a mile from the Old Gorge Highway.
Trish Perrin and Dennis Langston
purchased the bed-and-breakfast two
and a half years ago and celebrated the
building's 100th anniversary in 2007.
The farm house, previously home
to Fujii Berry Farms, features four
second-floor guest rooms accessed
off a central sitting area. All rooms
provide televisions and VCRs, and
some come with private whirlpool tubs.
Guests have free run of a downstairs
living room with a fireplace, not to
mention a billiard room and a patio
with a whirlpool tub. Even on a misty
morning, the large windows and
covered wrap-around porch offer views
of extensive gardens, showcasing
rhododendrons, roses and Douglas firs.
You can snuggle up in the terry slippers
and robe provided with your room to
enjoy a book from your hosts' diverse
library. Soft rugs, hardwood floors
and antiques set the tone for your
stay. Following a hearty Northwest
breakfast featuring fresh fruit,
homemade bread and such specialties
as frittatas with fresh vegetables,
you'll be ready for a one mile walk
to the specialty shops, restaurants
and museums of historic downtown
Troutdale. Take time to appreciate
your serene setting and develop your
ability to relax at Cedarplace Inn.

2611 S Troutdale Road, Troutdale OR
(503) 491-1900 or (877) 491-1907
www.cedarplcinn.com

Photo by Gregory Bertolini

Timberline Lodge

Timberline Lodge sits in a fairy tale setting at the 6,000-foot-level of Mount Hood. Completed in 1937, the historic landmark was crafted entirely by hand, inside and out, by workers of the WPA. While the architectural masterpiece weathered difficult times, it has since been impeccably restored. In large part, thanks go to Linny Adamson, since 1978 curator of the non-profit Friends of Timberline. Wall paintings, carvings, weaving, stonework and architectural elements come together to reflect the structure's original glory. Guest rooms feature hand-made, appliquéd bedspreads and draperies, hand-hooked rugs, original watercolor paintings, hand-carved furniture and hand-forged lamps. Timberline offers snow lovers the longest possible skiing and snowboarding season—every month of the year, weather permitting. Ski and snowboarding lessons are offered. Non-skiers can still take the Magic Mile Sky Ride, which reaches a breathtaking 7,000 feet. Amenities include a year-round outdoor heated swimming pool, a whirlpool and several restaurants. The magnificent lobby fireplace offers visitors a warm welcome. Revel in the wonder of Timberline Lodge, a true American treasure.

Timberline Lodge OR
(503) 622-7979
www.timberlinelodge.com

Summit Meadows Cabins

As the seasons change, so do the large number of outdoor recreation possibilities you'll find in the Cascade Mountains. Summit Meadows Cabins accommodate every season and interest. Husband-and-wife team Dave and Wendy own the cabins just outside Government Camp, where they have been instrumental in keeping a network of trails groomed for XC skiers and snowshoers. The five cabins range from chalets and A-frames to a small cottage. Each one is fully equipped with a kitchen, bedding and phones. Guests will find books, puzzles and games to play in the evenings. During the winter, guests park at nearby SnoParks and XC ski or snowshoe the one and a half miles to the cabins, bringing their food and clothes over the snow in a sled provided with each cabin rental. Imagine snowshoeing or cross-country skiing right out your front door. In the summer, spring and fall, guests can enjoy easy access to many trails suitable for hiking and mountain biking, and the Oregon Cascades Birding Trail. Surrounded by national forest, Summit Meadows Cabins are located just one and a half miles from Trillium Lake and six miles from Timberline Lodge. If you're looking for a cozy, private place from which to discover the Cascades, try Summit Meadows Cabins.

Government Camp, OR
(503) 272-3494
www.summitmeadow.com

Mt. McLoughlin from Lake of the Woods
Photo by Jennifer Gifford

Malarkey Ranch Inn

Although the city of Portland is just 25 miles away, the setting is tranquil and rustic at the Malarkey Ranch Inn. This bed and breakfast is situated on a working horse ranch, but horses aren't the only animals you'll see here. Peacocks and pot-bellied pigs wander the grounds, and deer frequently graze in the fields. With the Columbia River nearby, birds are quite abundant. Depending on the season, you are likely to see ducks, geese and swans, as well as herons and sandhill cranes. Listen to the yipping of coyotes at night, and wake to a delicious breakfast, which is just the fuel you'll need to enjoy one of the many recreational opportunities that the ranch offers. These include biking, walking and horseback riding on the property's many trails. Bicycles and horses are available for a small rental charge. Guests stay in one of the three bedrooms, each with its own bath, located inside the contemporary home. Outside the main house, a wooden deck overlooks Scappoose Bay. A large heated pool, just across the road, keeps guests cool in the summer. The staff at the inn specializes in catering elegant weddings and large company picnics. Children and pets are always welcome. Close to the city, yet seemingly a world away, the Malarkey Ranch Inn awaits your visit.

55948 Columbia River Highway, Scappoose OR (503) 543-7316

The Resort at The Mountain

The luxuriously appointed Resort at The Mountain, located in the western Highlands of Mt. Hood, is just an hour east of Portland. Here, you will find a wealth of gorgeous rooms and stunning views. Centrally located within a few minutes of the Mount Hood National Forest, Resort at The Mountain offers a multitude of outdoor activities including downhill skiing and snowboarding, cross-country skiing, wildlife viewing, hiking, mountain biking and fly fishing. Within The Resort you will enjoy some of the finest golfing Oregon has to offer. Understanding that golf was created in Scotland, The Resort has worked hard to present tastes of Scotland in everything they do. From Scottish-style bunkers and Scottie dog tees to the Tartans Pub & Steakhouse and Highlands Restaurant. Further outdoor offerings include a heated pool and Jacuzzi, four tennis courts, two full-sized croquet courts and lawn bowling greens. The Resort provides equipment rentals for tennis, biking, volleyball, badminton, croquet and lawn bowling. They can help organize group recreation activities or help you find local excursions. Each year The Resort at The Mountain presents several events including the International Croquet Invitational and the Wine & Art Festival. With so much to do and see it is a great getaway for families and companies. The Resort at The Mountain

OREGON

Attractions
& Recreation

Hellgate Jetboat Excursions, Northwest River Lodge and ShopRiverRock

It is widely recognized that a Hellgate Jetboat Excursion is more exciting than an average outdoor escapade. To complement the hydro-jet powered whitewater adventure, complete with famous boat spins and a narrated scenic tour, Hellgate owners offer the new log-framed Northwest River Lodge, located at the OK Corral, and 4,000 square feet of exquisite gifts and home décor at ShopRiverRock gift center. The Northwest River Lodge is reserved exclusively for Hellgate guests who are treated to brunch, lunch or dinner as part of the adventure package. The 12,000-square-foot facility is a short wagon ride from the river up a grassy slope. Hungry boaters arrive at an open-air deck with willow wood lodge-style tables and chairs that accommodate up to 350 people at a time. The OK Corral is located on a 13-acre homestead with uninterrupted views of the Rogue River below and decorated with waterfall features and an expansive river rock fireplace. Guests can relax and revive in between excursions, enjoying a country-style meal that includes beer, wine or soft drinks. For those preparing for, or returning from, the jetboat ride from Grants Pass to Hellgate Canyon or Grave Greek, ShopRiverRock carries one-of-a-kind gifts for lifetime memories. The gift shop includes a wine bar and is one of the largest home décor stores in Southern Oregon. The boutique-style shop highlights the talents of Bend artist and angler Annie O'Mohondro, whose canvas painting of Chinook salmon and other species hangs from the top floor ceiling. Her gyotaku work is backlit and surrounded by a waterfall, beautifully handmade railing and river rock features. Hellgate Jetboat Excursions, the Northwest River Lodge and ShopRiverRock create an adventure for guests from around the world.

966 SW 6th Street, Grants Pass OR (541) 956-5260 or (800) 648-4874
www.hellgate.com www.shopriverrock.com

Centennial Golf Club

Named after the hundred-year-old pear orchard that once stood on the site, the spectacular Centennial Golf Club sits on 400 acres graced with four lakes, oak trees and stunningly beautiful 360-degree views of the surrounding mountains. The 18-hole course plays to a par of 72 and 7,309 yards, with five different tee boxes to accommodate all skill levels. Two-time PGA Tour winner and 1977 U.S. Amateur Champion John Fought, who designed the course, was inspired by the Golden Age of golf course architecture when geniuses such as Donald Ross, Alistair Mackenzie and A.W. Tillinghast were creating their masterworks. The club opened in 2006 to rave reviews and has been the talk of the town ever since. Golfers who want to make Centennial their home course can purchase the Centennial Card through an annual membership fee. Or, they can join the Presidents Club to receive unlimited green fees for a year and host of other benefits. Players can bring along their children or polish their own swing with private lessons, including a special Ladies Only Clinic series. The Centennial Pavilion features its own restaurant and a complete golf shop offering quality apparel and accessories not found anywhere else in the valley. Centennial Grille offers breakfast and lunch seven days a week in a casual, friendly atmosphere. The menu offers something for every taste, from omelettes, salads, sandwiches and wraps to tacos, chicken entrées and what may be the best burger in the Rogue Valley. The Grille also offers a full bar where patrons can enjoy a cocktail or two. You owe it to yourself to stop by Centennial Golf Club. Play a round, have some lunch, play some more, then relax with a cold one. Golf doesn't get any better than this. Managed by OB Sports.

1900 N Phoenix Road, Medford OR
(541) 773-GOLF (4653) or (877) 893-GOLF (4653)
www.centennialgolfclub.com

Gold Hill, 1901

Gold Hill Historical Society

About three miles as the crow flies from the Lucky Bart Gold Mine, you'll find the home of Josiah Beeman. His gold mine was so profitable in its day that in 1901, Josiah built a rambling, two-story home for his wife and young family. A devastating fire gutted part of the meticulously built house, and afterward repairs were never completed. Josiah and descendents of the family lived in the house until 1993, when members of the Gold Hill Historical Society purchased it as a permanent home for their museum. That same group of volunteers lovingly restored the home to its former glory, making it the hub for all things historical in the city of Gold Hill. A warm, comfortable atmosphere is evident the moment you walk through the front door. Volunteers can give you an interesting tour, help you research information or even locate photographs of long lost family members. The Gold Hill Historical Society actively provides educational activities for local schools, participates in annual community events and creates the ever-popular haunted house for Halloween. Its volunteer members give countless hours of their time and share a collective love for things of historical interest. Local families have donated most of the Gold Hill Historical Society collection with the confidence that their precious heirlooms will always be cared for with respect and admiration. The society is dedicated to its motto: Recording the Past for the Future. Josiah Beeman would have surely given his nod of approval.

504 First Avenue, Gold Hill OR
(541) 855-1182

Noah's Ark

To find Noah's Ark, just follow the signs for Wildlife Safari. Look for the 60-foot rainbow and the line of animals waiting to get up the gangway of a colossal land-locked boat. Noah's Ark features the only full-size Biblical tabernacle and sanctuary on the West Coast, a replica of the tabernacle that was revealed to Moses in the wilderness. The attraction unlocks the mystery of the Ark of the Covenant with an astounding ancient temple tour. New exhibits include the Holy Land Miniature Room, which depicts Judea in the time of Jesus; the Jerusalem Room, with an eight-foot-square model of Ezekiel's Temple; and the Noah's Ark Room, where an animated Noah talks about the flood. Enjoy a snack or meal in Noah's Galley, where you'll be served healthy home cooking by characters in period attire. If you have small children, watch them play in Noah's Playhouse, a miniature ark, while you enjoy the live animals and the pastoral view of rolling hills beyond the bow. You'll definitely want to visit the gift shop, which has been called the best Bible bookstore anywhere by many visitors. For a theme park you won't forget, come to Noah's Ark.

411 NW Safari Road, Winston OR
(541) 784-1261
www.noahsarkwinstoncom

Three Hats Farm

If Michael Wakefield had been born in the Old West, he probably would have driven a stagecoach for a living. With his partners, Adrian Navarro and John Wakefield, he runs the equestrian training and breeding facility in Scappoose called Three Hats Farm. Maybe you've seen him driving the Wells Fargo Bank's stagecoach in The Rose Festival Parade or one of the thirty or so events all over the Northwest each year. Training a horse for driving is just one of the many pursuits that bring students to Three Hats Farm. Adults and children as young as five come here to learn the basics of riding. In hand showing of sport horses, dressage, equitation, and jumping are also offered. Once a month, Michelle Binder of Spokane conducts advanced clinics for the farm's more serious dressage students. You will also find riding and driving horses as well as carts for sale, and lessons for driving single and multiple hitches. Michael's passion for carriage driving shows off in the farm's carriage service. They hire out the horse and carriage in full livery for weddings and special occasions in the Portland Metro Area. Sure, limousines are chic, but imagine the romance of being driven to and from your wedding in the elegant style of yesteryear. The relationship between people and horses is the focus at Three Hats Farm, where motivated students are always welcome. Come by and see the new crop of sport horse foals sired by the legendary American Warmblood Stallion, Flight Time Gold and discover what Three Hats Farm can offer you.

33075 SW Dutch Canyon Road, Scappoose OR
(503) 349-9606
www.threehatsfarm.com

Oregon Chocolate Festival

What could be a more fabulous theme for a festival than chocolate? The landmark Ashland Springs Hotel in Ashland hosts the Oregon Chocolate Festival in March. Chocolate lovers of all ages can spend a weekend reveling in their favorite treat. Events are scheduled throughout Ashland. Naturally, you have ample opportunities for chocolate tasting. Oregon chocolatiers provide bars, truffles and toffees, not to mention fudge and sauce. Other vendors offer chocolate-covered Oregon pears, hazelnuts and berries. Rogue Creamery presents a delightful chocolate infused cheddar cheese and Rogue Ales pours astonishing chocolate stout. Have you ever considered getting your daily ration of antioxidants with a glass of red wine and a piece of dark chocolate? The festival offers chocolate and wine pairing events both in-house and at local wineries. The festival is educational as well as tasty. Seminars at the hotel have covered the health benefits of chocolate, chocolate history and chocolate varietals. Chocolate cooking classes are also available. Local entertainment venues put on chocolate-themed entertainments. The vast local art gallery scene gets into the chocolate spirit, as well. The Oregon

Bridal Veil Lakes

Bridal Veil Lakes is the perfect setting for your wedding or other special event. The site is nestled in the heart of the scenic Columbia River Gorge 30 minutes east of Portland. Beautiful wildflowers and 100-year-old forests fill the 40 acres of lush greenery. Wildlife abounds. "Bridal Veil Lakes is truly one of the most beautiful places in the world," commented one client. "Every one of our guests was stricken with awe over the majesty of your property." The Miller family is your host. Bridal Veil Lakes offers a covered pavilion, covered outdoor patio and a custom barbecue grill, plus opportunities for hiking, catch-and-release fishing and canoeing. More than one newlywed couple has glided away in a canoe at the finale. The pavilion and patio are protected from the wind. The parking lot can hold 150 vehicles and the grounds up to 1,000 people, though 300 is a more comfortable maximum and groups of 200 are common. Your rental lasts all day—you can come in the morning and leave at midnight. Rehearsal times are provided. Bridal Veil Lakes is open May through October. Whether you are the star of the show or a guest, you will never forget your visit to Bridal Veil Lakes.

3255 NE Henderson Road, Corbett OR
(503) 695-2312
www.bridalveillakes.com

Charlton Deep Sea Charters

The Charlton family knows the waters around Oregon's northernmost point well, as they have been fishing the area for more than 60 years. Bud Charlton started Charlton Deep Sea Charters, the first charter business in the area, in 1948, and now Mark Charlton owns and operates the family business. From May through September, Mark spends long days on the water captaining the 50-foot Ruby Sea, a Coast Guard-inspected and approved vessel. Group trips accommodate up to 20 people with bait, tackle and fishing equipment provided. You can even purchase a one-day fishing license right at the charter office. Captain Mark takes the boat into the Pacific and the lower Columbia River for Chinook and Coho salmon and into the Columbia River for sturgeon and Dungeness crab. In the recent past, charter guests have landed halibuts weighing in at 70 to 80 pounds. The company offers private charters, as well, perfect for corporate groups and large families. Be sure to call ahead to verify the seasons and times for excursions. Come catch your limit with Charlton Deep Sea Charters.

470 NE Skipanon Drive, Warrenton OR
(503) 861-2429
www.charltoncharters.com

Forests Forever—Hopkins Demonstration Forest

Hopkins Demonstration Forest, owned and managed by Forests Forever, provides a valuable learning experience for professionals, students and all those who love the beauty of Oregon's woodlands. This forest, located near Oregon City, is open to the public for tours, self-guided exploration, workshops and educational programs. It also helps the owners of small woodlands improve their sustainable forestry management skills. Howard Hopkins, a professional forester, bought his 120-acre Grouse Hollow Tree Farm in 1962 and spent the next three decades clearing brush, planting seedlings and transforming the cutover slopes into a productive forest. Following his death in 1989, his family's desire to see their family tree farm managed as a productive forest in perpetuity led them to Forests Forever, and in 1990, with the help of tree farmers and forestry professionals, the demonstration forest opened. Three miles of roads and trails lead hikers to a variety of habitats and forestry demonstrations. The tree farm hosts educational activities throughout the year for school and youth groups as well as monthly community workdays, where adult and youth volunteers learn about forest stewardship by working together. Come hike along Little Buckner Creek and enjoy the forest while learning how to conserve it for generations to come at Hopkins Demonstration Forest, Where Learning and Growing Go Hand in Hand.

16750 S Brockway Road, Oregon City OR
(503) 632-2150
www.demonstrationforest.org

Mount Hood Skibowl

Seasons change and so do the activities at Mount Hood Skibowl. Known internationally, this picturesque alpine village is open all year round. Winter brings unequalled downhill skiing and snowboarding. Discover America's Largest Night Ski Area as you wind your way down beginning, intermediate or advanced slopes. Lessons are available to everyone from snow bunnies to advanced mogul busters. No matter which run beckons, you're never far from a cozy lodge complete with a warm fire, hot drinks and enticing snacks. The Historic Warming Hut, built in 1935, offers a quick beer and a bowl of traditional goulash. The Outback Café & Espresso features fresh sandwiches, soups and hot coffee. In spring, the Skibowl reopens as Mount Hood Adventure Park. Ride the wild alpine slide, mountain bike through the glorious landscape or play a round of miniature golf. Volleyball, badminton, batting cages and horseshoes lure sports buffs. If you're nuts, there's always the seven-story bungee tower. For over-the-top escape, the Rapid Riser Reverse Bungee launches you 80 feet in the air. For serenity, try a ride aboard the sky chair and get a breathtaking view of Mount Hood and the Cascade range. The SuperPlay Zone, a 2,400 square-foot, two-story zone encourages tiny tots to indulge in the wild world of imagination. No matter what time of the year you visit Mount Hood Skibowl, fun and excitement await.

87000 E Highway 26, Government Camp OR
(503) 222-BOWL (2695) or (800) SKIBOWL (754-2695)
www.skibowl.com

Old McDonald's Farm, Inc.

Old McDonald's Farm is a great way for you to see what life on a farm is all about. This 68-acre farm serves fun and education on the same plate to kids and adults alike. Learn how to ride a horse. Learn to work with all kinds of animals—the farm has more than 30, from chickens, ducks and geese through cows, goats and sheep. The farm is a non-profit organization that offers hands-on, structured day camp programs, including week-long summer sessions and one-day field trips. The six summer sessions are geared to kids entering the 2nd through 6th grades. For 5th through 10th graders who want to learn to care for horses or are interested in the veterinary field, the Junior Vet. Equine Camp is perfect. Customized programs are designed to nurture healthy social and emotional development through classes that use animals, agriculture, gardens and natural resources. Be a farmer for a day or just take a hay ride beneath the stars. You can arrange for your whole family to come learn the chores and work of a farmer. A family can spend the night or hold a family reunion. Old McDonald's Farm also offers boarding for horses. Enjoy an enriching day or week, learning and having fun at Old McDonald's Farm.

1001 SE Evans Road, Corbett OR
(503) 695-3316
www.oldmcdonaldsfarm.org

Krayon Kids Musical Theatre Company

Krayon Kids Musical Theatre Company has a 14-year history of entertaining young audiences with original musicals. The all-kids, all-volunteer company, which performs at the Barclay Theater in Oregon City, has a reputation for exquisite costuming and spectacular dance productions. Singing, gymnastics and plenty of comedy are also part of the Krayon Kids experience. The movers and shakers behind the self-sufficient company are directors Dianne Kohlmeier, Vicki Mills and Yvonne Peebles. Dianne was a performer and figure skating champion in her youth and went on to create, write and direct her own work. She's the company's artistic director, and the costume, set

and music designer. Vicki is a choreographer, and Yvonne is the vocal director. The women's duties include directing all phases of Krayon Kids and management of the Elite Travel Troupe. The troupe comprises the some of the most talented members of the Krayon Kids cast. It won gold in 2004 at the Asia-Pacific Festival of Children's Theater in Japan and was the only U.S. troupe invited to attend the World Festival of Children's Theatre in Germany. For performance art that engages children and their parents, contact Krayon Kids Musical Theatre Company. Original musical productions perform through the month of November.

1404 7th Street, Eastham School, Oregon City OR
(503) 656-6099
www.krayonkids.org

ScienceWorks Hands-On Museum

With a mission to inspire wonder and stimulate creative exploration through interactive science and art, ScienceWorks Hands-On Museum knows how to make education fun. Whether they're petting lizards on reptile day or enjoying one of the museum's many mind-boggling exhibits, kids come from miles around to get in on the action. Be sure to check out the Bubble-ology Room, where you can build a wall of bubbles or enclose yourself in a giant bubble. The Hall of Illusions offers an eye-catching treat for visual learners, where visitors can try and decipher the hidden messages underneath colorful artwork. Kids with a creative eye are sure to delight in Einstein's Art Studio, where they can make 3-D art or experiment with fun tools, such as the spinning blackboard and the sand pendulum. Even parents might find themselves joining in on the fun when they see the pulley chairs, cannonball blaster and the dark science tunnel. In addition, the museum hosts Be a Kid Again events with live music and appetizers. Each season boasts new themes and demonstrations, so a season pass is your best bet. Make your next family trip to ScienceWorks Hands-On Museum and experience the fun of science.

1500 E Main, Ashland OR
(541) 482-6767
www.scienceworksmuseum.org

City of St. Helens

Natural beauty and an artistic environment make the city of St. Helens one of the best kept secrets of Oregon tourism. Named for its striking view of Mount St. Helens across the Columbia River, the city grew up on the riverfront, where the 10 blocks of Olde Towne are a nationally registered Historic District. You can pick up a walking map of the city's historic buildings at the Chamber of Commerce Visitors Center. Alternatively, just enjoy the atmosphere while browsing Olde Towne's charming shops. The riverfront is the heart of the community with parks and trails, fishing, and art and music festivals throughout the year. St. Helens is the place to be on the 4th of July—it has the biggest fireworks show on the Oregon side of the river. The river itself is a magnet for those who love recreational boating, kayaking in Scappoose Bay and bird watching on Sauvie Island. Visitors to the island can see bald eagles, sandhill cranes and tundra swans in season as well as Oregon's only lighthouse that's not on the Pacific Ocean. St. Helens is home to several nationally celebrated artists and many local artists whose works grace street corners, parks and restaurant walls. In 2006, the National Endowment for the Arts awarded the city $5,500 to sponsor new works for the city's public art collection. The Columbia County Event Complex hosts performing arts and annual events, including the County Fair and Oktoberfest. With so much to enjoy, you should make plans to visit the city of St. Helens.

2194 Columbia Boulevard, St. Helens OR
(Chamber of Commerce)
(503) 397-0685

Quail Point Golf Course

The 9-hole Quail Point Golf Course is known throughout the Rogue Valley as the friendliest course in Medford. It is a favorite for golfers of all ages and all skill levels because the Quail Point staff is so helpful and attentive. Its central location also makes it a favorite for people who want to get a round in after a long day at the office. Quail Point features 75 acres of lush fairways and manicured greens, along with five ponds, two lakes, a natural running stream and tremendous views of the surrounding valley. Golfers can play unlimited golf seven days a week and book tee times up to 14 days in advance. There's also a golf shop and snack bar at the clubhouse and plenty of room on the covered outdoor patio to relax after your game. Quail Point hosts a number of special events, clubs and leagues throughout the year, so there's always something fun to be a part of. You can even sponsor your own private tournament. Everyday at Quail Point, children under 18 play for free (children must be accompanied by an adult). So, whether you're looking for equipment to improve your game, looking for a few tips to help hone your skills or just looking for a great time, you'll find what you're looking for at Quail Point Golf Course.

1200 Mira Mar Avenue, Medford OR
(541) 857-7000
www.quailpointgolf.com

Rogue Rock Gym

Matt Lambert got his first taste of rock climbing when he was a 10-year-old Boy Scout working toward a merit badge. As he grew older, he became more serious about the sport and honed his skills. In 2005, Matt and his wife Chrysten opened Rogue Rock Gym, a vast indoor rock climbing facility. With more than 6,000 square feet of climbing surfaces rising up to 30 feet, there is a challenge for every skill level. The gym offers classes ranging from introductory techniques to advanced skills that will prepare you for climbing outdoors. The instructors have more than 30 years of combined experience, ensuring that you'll stay safe and learn proper technique. There's even a fitness area with weights and cardiovascular machines to help get you in shape for your climbing adventures. Let the kids burn off energy at the Rogue Rock Gym with activities geared toward the younger crowd. Start with one-on-one instruction in Climb Time or enroll the kids in the Junior Program, which trains three times per week. During summer vacation, a day camp keeps boredom at bay. Birthday parties at the gym are sure to be a hit, with plenty of time for scaling rocks and a cake break. Discover the fun of rock-climbing in an ideal learning environment at the Rogue Rock Gym.

3001 Samike Drive #104, Medford OR
(541) 245-2665
www.roguerockgym.com

Anderson's Outdoors

Whether you're looking to hook the big one or just to enjoy the beauty of Oregon's sparkling rivers and lush, green shorelines, Anderson's Outdoors has the trip for you. For the past nine years, Kent Anderson and his staff have offered travelers the chance to experience the rivers of Oregon and Alaska through their Welches business. Anderson is an expert outdoorsman, having earned a degree in fisheries and served eight years with the Oregon Department of Fish and Wildlife. Fishermen will enjoy the Spring Combo and Oregon Steelhead packages, which offer three full days of guided fishing for steelhead and spring chinook salmon on three different rivers. All fishing equipment is provided. The Spring Combo package includes a one-day tour of Mount Hood and the Columbia Gorge, while the Oregon Steelhead package takes passengers on a tour of the scenic Northern Oregon Coast. Anderson's Outdoors also books trips into Alaska. Sightseers will thrill to the scenic float trips offered here, in McKenzie style drift boats with propane heaters and comfortable seats. Let Anderson's Outdoors take you on a journey through the scenic rivers of Oregon.

25069 E Tillicum Street, Welches OR
(503) 550-6303
www.andersonsoutdoors.com

Black Butte Ranch

Outdoor recreation and excitement are not hard to find in Oregon. Each river, mountain and trail offers new and wonderful things to explore. The Black Butte Ranch, located just eight miles west of Sisters on Highway 20, has everything your family needs to enjoy the splendor of this lovely state. Black Butte features two championship golf courses and scenic views of seven of the peaks of the Cascade Mountains. Black Butte Ranch is a serene luxury resort offering myriad ways to enjoy nature, including hiking, biking, fishing, rafting, canoeing, tennis, trail rides and more. Black Butte Ranch offers dining at The Lodge, the Big Meadow Clubhouse, or Lakes de Bistro. No matter which you choose, the cuisine will be as magnificent as the views. The Ranch offers a Recreation Center that includes a playground, rock wall, video arcade, sports equipment and games. During summer, the Ranch Days Kids Camp is open Monday through Friday. Guests of the Ranch have several accommodation options available ranging from smaller hotel-style rooms to full vacation homes. The Black Butte Ranch has several packages available, such as golf packages and holiday getaways. Head to either of the Ranch's two sport shops for equipment or great souvenirs. You can even make reservations for a facial or massage. Black Butte has more than 30 years of experience in welcoming people and helping them make the most of their Oregon vacation. Treat yourself and your family to the trip of a lifetime at the Black Butte Ranch.

Highway 20, 8 miles West of Sisters OR
(541) 595-1536
www.blackbutteranch.com

Mountain Tracks

Looking to hit the slopes of Mt. Hood but don't have the necessary equipment? Make tracks for Mountain Tracks, which has everything you need to make your ski adventure one to remember. Glenn and Sara Nilsen are the owners of this Government Camp store, which has served area adventurers for more than ten years. Mountain Tracks specializes in equipment rentals ranging from skis and snowshoes to climbing equipment. You'll find top brands here, including Solomon skis, Rossignol snowboards and Atlas snowshoes. Climbers will delight in the array of supplies available, from ice axes, crampons and climbing skins to coats and gaiters. The store also offers a variety of high-quality skis and snowboards for sale. If you've got your own, Mountain Tracks can service your skis with hot wax treatments, tune ups and repairs. Ask the friendly staff about the best skiing and snowshoe opportunities around Mount Hood for your abilities. Let Mountain Tracks take care of all your skiing and outdoor equipment needs.

88661 E Government Loop Road, Government Camp OR
(503) 272-3380
www.mtntracks.com

Ryan's Float Flying-Sea Plane Rides

You can tour Portland by bus or car, but a tour by air provides the most spectacular view of all. Sea Plane Rides take off from a seaplane base near Oregon City and swoops a heart-stopping 500 feet over Willamette Falls. The Piper Super Cruiser then follows the Willamette River up to the city, past Lake Oswego and Lewis & Clark College to downtown Portland. At 1,000 feet, you're at eye level with the tallest skyscrapers. You'll bank past the Rose Gardens and return to Oregon City to splash down 30 minutes after takeoff. The seaplane is intimate—it holds two passengers plus your pilot, Ryan Smith. Ryan offers tours from late April through October. He schedules the seaplane flights around his day job, flying a chartered Citation II jet out of Salem. Ryan fell in love with seaplanes as a boy when he saw them take off from White Bear Lake in Minnesota. He comes from an interesting family. His father was a fighter pilot who later flew for Pan Am, and his grandfather Elmo, also a pilot, was a governor of Oregon in the 1950s. In addition to the standard tour, Ryan offers instruction and customized tours for private parties. The seaplane base provides lodging for those passing through, especially other seaplane pilots. For an adventure you'll remember forever, sign on with Ryan's Float Flying-Sea Plane Rides.

905 Highway 99E, Oregon City OR
(503) 657-6769
www.ryansfloatflying.com

Gimme-A-Go Fishing Adventures

After 35 years on Oregon rivers, Jon Ball knows the ways of the big fish, and he shares his expertise on guided fishing trips. Gimme-A-Go Fishing Adventures can take you and your family or business associates on the fishing trip of a lifetime, where sturgeons are more than 10 feet long. You can fish for King and Coho salmon or do battle with athletic steelheads in the kind of heart-pounding fishing adventure you've dreamed of experiencing. Interested in walleye or shad? Jon is at your service, ready to give you an honest assessment of what's happening in the river. Jon guides trips on the Columbia, Willamette, Sandy and Wilson rivers. He's been a full-time guide since 1998 and runs his company with his wife Stacy. When he's not out on the water or spending time with his wife and six kids, you might find him holding a seminar on fishing at a local sports store or participating in a sports trade show. He's been featured on several television shows, including *World Wide Fishing* and *Inside Sports Fishing*. Make the most of your fishing day with guided services from Gimme-A-Go Fishing Adventures.

18145 Bodley Court, Sandy OR
(503) 668-5697 or (877) 347-4662
www.sturgeon-salmon.com

Imperial River Company

Visitors to the Imperial River Company choose exactly how much adventure they want in their vacation, whether it's a heart-pounding rafting trip down the Deschutes River or a lazy afternoon lying on the grass with a good book. Just two hours east of Portland or two hours north of Bend, the hotel, restaurant and rafting company is tucked away in the rugged Deschutes Canyon right on the river. Owners Rob and Susie Miles purchased the inn seven years ago and recently underwent an extensive remodel and expansion of the property. Stay in one of 25 individually decorated rooms, including the Flybox, complete with a large fishing mural, and Railroad, decorated with pictures of railway history. Rafting adventures range from a short, two-hour trip to a three-day overnight voyage. The most popular is a six-hour river ride with a catered lunch. You can have a great time in the paddle-raft with one of their knowledgeable guides leading the way. The Imperial Restaurant continues the rustic décor, using natural elements from the surrounding area such as rough-hewn juniper posts and beams. The high desert cuisine includes free-range Angus beef steaks from the nearby Imperial Stock Ranch, where Susie grew up, as well as fresh seafood from Astoria and other specialties using local ingredients. Relax with a glass of wine, liquor or one of several Oregon microbrews in the Imperial Bar. Take it easy or pack in the fun and excitement at the Imperial River Company.

304 Bakeoven Road, Maupin OR
(541) 395-2404 or (800) 395-3903
www.deschutesriver.com

Slick Kart Track & Arcade

If you have ever dreamed of taking the checkered flag at Indy, then you are going to love the Slick Kart Track & Arcade. It's the place where people who share your need for speed get their kicks racing go-carts around a waxed oval track. These are high-performance machines that are designed to pitch sideways on turns and can zip along at speeds of 25 to 30 miles per hour. Eight of them are allowed on the track at the same time for a racing experience that promises plenty of competition without being crowded. A double-seated cart allows for an adult to be the driver for a small child or handicapped rider. This all-indoor facility, the only one of its kind in Oregon, is a popular spot for parties. When you book a closed party, you and your guests will have the track all to yourselves for an hour. Open parties during regular business hours are also common. A smaller version of the main track caters to children younger than 11 or shorter than 54 inches. After you have tested your racing skills, conquer the challenge of climbing the 24-foot rock wall. For some fast fun, go to the Slick Kart Track & Arcade.

1029 Narregan Street, Medford OR
(541) 608-3863
www.slickkart.com

Stone Creek Golf Club

Stone Creek Golf Club presents an enjoyable challenge to every level of golfer. "Our design philosophy is to create fun, playable courses that reward good shots," explains Peter Jacobsen, who designed the course with Jim Hardy. The two set the Oregon City course on 120 acres of land among old-growth Douglas firs, lakes, wetlands and 43 bunkers. The views of Mount Hood are spectacular. *BrainstormNW* magazine has named Stone Creek the best value in the Pacific Northwest. *Golfweek* calls it one of the six best public courses in Oregon. *Golf Digest* awards it four stars. A green facility in more ways than one, Stone Creek has received several environmental awards. The 6,000-square-yard practice area includes a full-swing area with realistic target greens of variable distances. The practice greens are ideal for putting, chipping and bunker shots. Under Ted Westling, director of instruction, the teaching program focuses on the whole game, including the full swing, the short course, course management, rules and etiquette. A premiere winter destination, Stone Creek has a firm course that drains exceptionally well. The Stone Creek Pro Shop features golf equipment and clothing lines chosen for quality and value. The Stone Creek Deli provides excellent fresh sandwiches, soups and beverages all year round. A beverage cart canvasses the course. With a large tented area for special events, Stone Creek Golf Club is a prime spot for hosting tournaments, corporate outings and other gatherings. Spend some time at Stone Creek Golf Club, and you'll soon become a regular.

14603 S Stoneridge Drive, Oregon City OR (503) 518-4653
www.stonecreekgolfclub.net

OREGON

Automotive

Rogue Automotive

Owners Buddy and Amie Pickard of Rogue Automotive have been providing outstanding automotive service for Southern Oregon and Northern California for years. Loyal customers will tell you that at Rogue Automotive you'll get immediate, fast, professional service. They are proud of their consistent attention to detail and all of their services are provided with honesty and courtesy. Rogue Automotive is a family-owned, friendly, total-service facility that is focused on satisfied customers and repeat business. All of Rogue Automotive's staff are fully trained and highly experienced. One of their missions is to provide a unique automotive experience. Customers come from many miles away because of their past successful dealings and because of Rogue's reputation. In addition to their regular fine service, Amie and Buddy provide free air-conditioning check-ups year round. Bring your automobile to Rogue Automotive and you will both leave satisfied.

940 N Central Avenue, #B, Medford OR
(541) 245-1740
www.rogueautomotive.com

River City RV

Your claim that you are just looking will be respected at River City RV, where a casual sales environment reigns. These salespeople aren't the high-pressure type. They see themselves as guides who simply enjoy helping customers determine the model and floor plan that are right for them. River City RV draws its clientele from a 100 mile radius that includes Klamath Falls and northern California. Its rows and rows of fifth wheels, motor homes and travel trailers represent such leading lines as Keystone, Itasca and Jayco. The Everest fifth wheels on the lot always attract much attention. Everybody loves peeking inside to view the interiors inspired by the absolute luxury of a premiere resort or condominium suite. Trade-ins are welcome at River City RV, which also offers a complete parts, service and repair facility. Manager Shannon Prince says that the company's top goal is to make your sales experience an enjoyable one. Count on River City RV for the service, selection and respectful attitude that have made this business a southern Oregon favorite since 1986.

5179 Crater Lake Highway, Central Point OR
(541) 779-6331
www.rivercityrv.com

Crater Lake South Rim
Photo by Jennifer Gifford

Fred's RV World

If you are thinking of a traveling second home, or want something you can use to traverse the country, all roads lead to Fred's. Fred's RV World has been the most trusted name in RVs in the Pacific Northwest since 1971. It was founded by Fred and Delores McNally with little more than three cars, borrowed money and dedicated, friendly service. Through the years they grew the company into what it is today, an enterprise with eight acres of space and a 10,000-square-foot indoor showroom. Now owned by Cory Stone, who began working for Fred and Delores as a lot boy back in 1972, the business is still family-run and continues with the same mission of dedicated service .Fred's has a huge inventory that is sure to meet any need and every expectation. They offer dozens of standard models of new 2007 RVs—class A and C motorhomes, vans, truck campers, travel trailers and fifth wheels in regular and sport models. You'll find names such as Allegro, Phaeton, Bigfoot, Forest River and Escalade, plus K-Z, Montego Bay and Pleasureway. Also find Leisure Travel, Coach House, New Vision, Road Runner trailers and Adventurer campers. Fred's can also enhance your engine performance with the Banks Power system. It also has a large selection of pre-owned stock. Fred's Service Center features 12 bays for rapid maintenance or repair of your RV, or the installation of accessories. The service center has just added a 4,000-square-foot parts and accessories department. Discover why so many customers return to Fred's again and again. When you are at Fred's RV World, you are family.

41777 SE Highway 26, Sandy OR
(503) 826-8888 or (800) 888-5083
www.fredsrvworld.com

OREGON

Bakeries, Markets
Coffee & Tea

Photo by Dominic Morel

Oregon Mountain Coffee Company

In 2006, Ryan Burke and Marleece Burke took on the ownership of the popular Oregon Mountain Coffee Company, a staple for Medford's coffee aficionados for the past 10 years. After eight years in structural engineering, Ryan was ready for a change when the original owners eyed them as the right people to continue the coffee tradition that is on its way to becoming a local legend. Owning their own hospitality business seems to appeal to Ryan and Marleece, despite the long hours they keep at a business that opens at 6 am on weekdays. They know most of their customers by name and their coffee preference to boot. They offer blends made from Columbian, Brazilian, Sumatran and Ethiopian beans. The medium roast Mt. Ashland Blend is popular with drip and espresso drinkers. For a refreshing change of pace, customers turn to the Avalanche, an intoxicating blend of espresso, white chocolate and caramel sauce. Ryan and Marleece also serve tea and many treats, including scones, muffins and bagels. The coffee shop donates products to Grace Christian School and St. Mary's High School. It also supports Christian concerts and many school church activities. Let Ryan and Marleece know your coffee preferences at Oregon Mountain Coffee Company.

**930 N Phoenix Road, Medford OR
(541) 245-4401**

Caffé Diem

Caffé Diem is the kind of place you could wile away an afternoon in, having lunch, sipping an espresso or lingering over a pastry and a good book. Owner and native Oregonian Cherish Tucker took over the café in 2007 and continues to provide the exceptional customer service and delicious food that keeps regulars coming back. Stop by for a lunch of homemade tomato bisque soup and a grilled panini. The signature sandwich, made on fresh Focaccia bread, comes in several varieties, including roast beef with sun-dried tomatoes, Gorgonzola cheese and green olives, or veggie, with roasted garlic spread, Provolone cheese, basil, tomato and onion. Catch up on email or check the weather with the café's free wireless Internet. After watching a movie at the theater next door, rehash the flick with a friend over a cup of java. Caffé Diem serves Allann Brothers coffee. Purists may insist on a straight espresso or perhaps an Americano, while those with a sweet tooth indulge in a Crème Caramel or Kahlua mocha mousse. The eatery offers smoothies, teas, Italian sodas and other refreshing drinks. Impress party guests with salads, soups and sandwiches catered from the restaurant. Come to Caffé Diem for great food and espresso in an inviting atmosphere.

675 Medford Center, Medford OR
(541) 772-1561

Josephson's Smokehouse

For generations, the Josephsons have been a family of commercial fisherman, fish buyers and fish processors. They know fish, and they know how to minimally process it to make delicious smoked seafood sought after the world over. Owned and operated by the Josephson family for 88 years, Josephson's Smokehouse continues a longstanding tradition of using only the finest #1 grade seafood, natural ingredients and natural alder wood smoke. The family has never used any preservatives, dyes or additives in its products. Gourmet food magazines including *Cuisine*, *Sunset* and *Eating Well* give Josephson's products rave reviews. The smokehouse produces both hot and cold smoked seafood as well as salmon jerky, fresh and frozen fish and canned goods. Try the flaky and moist hot smoked prawns or wine-maple salmon. Cold smoked salmon comes as lox or in the traditional Chinook style. Elegant wooden gift boxes filled with the Josephson's most popular selections make great gifts and can be shipped world-wide. Visit Josephson's Smokehouse to taste the fine flavors of specialty seafood perfected over the last eight decades.

106 Marine Drive, Astoria OR
(503) 325-2190
www.josephsons.com

Bread Barn

Introducing the Bread Barn, Klamath Falls' only from-scratch whole wheat bakery. Grace and Joy opened the bakery in February 2001, in a new rustic cedar building across from Motel 6, to produce all-natural, preservative-free bread. There is a 24-inch stone mill in the store to keep fresh-ground wheat flour on-hand at all times. You will find a wide variety of breads, yummy cookies and pies. Try the fresh deli sandwiches made-to-order and soup in a bread bowl. A line of jams, jellies, syrup and gift items are also available. The Bread Barn staff prepares dough each morning on a large maple table. They have cinnamon rolls, muffins, scones and pastries read for you at 7 am. Come visit the Bread Barn for the best bread you've ever eaten.

**5035 S 6th Street, Klamath Falls OR
(541) 273-8414**

OREGON

Galleries
& Fine Art

Photo by Robert Jaffe

The Red Vase, Watercolor by Judy Morris

Porcelain vase with ash glaze by Stephen Kirkland

Rogue Gallery & Art Center

Fostering a continuing love of self-expression in Southern Oregon, the Rogue Gallery & Art Center is the heart of the visual arts community. Founded in 1960 to promote and support the arts, this non-profit community-based center focuses on art education, exhibitions and artists' services. The gallery displays a wide-range of artistic styles not seen in most commercial galleries. From innovative displays vibrant with color and detail, to the subtle classic beauty of traditional art, this gallery has it all. It is one of the only organizations where both established community artists and up-and-coming artists are celebrated for their creative endeavors of artistic self-expression. For instance, the extravagantly painted smudge pots from local artists and the Smudge Pot Crew celebrate the rich history of orchards in Southern Oregon. The Art in Bloom Invitational exhibit is a springtime salutation to local arts and flowers, where vibrant displays of natural art line the downtown streets. The Rogue Gallery & Art Center is also a place for aspiring artists of all ages to engage in artist-led workshops and classes. Summer art day camps for children help to expose the younger community to a wide variety of artistic mediums and educate them on the importance of keeping the arts alive in the community. In addition, the gallery is a huge participant in the third Friday art walks, and artists can experience what it's like to be a part of a professional exhibition. Take a look into the soul of this beautiful valley's community when you visit Rogue Gallery & Art Center.

40 S Bartlett Street, Medford OR
(541) 772-8118
www.roguegallery.org

Clearwater Gallery & Fine Art Framing

Step through the door of the Clearwater Gallery and you will find yourself surrounded by peacefulness and the soothing sound of a waterfall. Owners Dan and Julia Rickards want your visit to be a joyful experience, so there is no sense of urgency or pressure. Julia knows her customers by name and keeps the gallery walls fresh and ever-changing. In addition to artworks by Dan Rickards, the gallery carries Bill Hamilton's acrylics, Annie Omohondros's fish on fabric, R.L. Rickard's Lewis and Clark series, and Nancy Taylor Stonington's original and limited edition prints. The gallery looks for artistic diversity and dimensional works to augment its primarily western, wildlife and angling art. You'll find handcrafted tables and lamps, bronzes, finely decorated gourds and hand-woven baskets. All of these works attract attention in a beautiful and functional way. Bold jewelry makes the statement that art is not just for your walls. Dan and Julia, along with their talented custom framers, Chris Saba and Arlene Hannah, invite you to visit their frame shop. As an oil and acrylic artist, Saba has been creatively designing and framing for over 10 years. He believes that framing is an extension of the art—the picture continues it and becomes part of the piece. Saba and talented stained glass artist Arlene Hannah will guide you to the perfect frame to preserve the past for enjoyment in the present. At Clearwater, your framing need not be pricey, just thoughtfully and joyfully chosen to bring out the art and artist's personality.

391 W Cascade Avenue, Sisters OR
(541) 549-4994 or (800) 348-9453
www.clearwaterstudio.com

Elizabeth Daggett Ganji—*Turned Out*

Dan Rickards— *Cascade Springtime Elk*

Clearwater Gallery— Dan Rickards

Gallery owners Dan and Julia Rickards would be the first to tell you to relax and enjoy the retreat experience of being in their gallery. Dan is the gallery's featured artist. His American Dream series showcases his ability to create a view for a windowless wall, or anywhere a client wants to capture a landscape the way it once was. His work helps to maintain a memory of where we have been, or at least give hope to the possibilities of where we might like to go. As a child, Dan evidenced an interest in drawing, but painting did not become his primary occupation until 1991. The springboard to his career was the watercolor titled Autumn Rise. He shifted to acrylics to create his second piece, Bare Camp. He describes his technique as painting loose, with a small brush. While his natural talent has been important, he attributes much of his success to the support of his wife and parents. Dan paints landscapes and wildlife and, on request, will customize artwork to create a one-of-a-kind painting with personal and individual details. His work reflects a strong sense of place and character. His use of color and light allows you to feel as though you are present in the place he has portrayed. Dan has received many awards and sees a future filled with creative possibilities. Believing that a balance between business and artistry is essential to success as an artist, the Rickards look forward to building relationships and enriching the lives of their customers with both Dan's artwork and the ambience of Clearwater Gallery. Visit the gallery, relax, enjoy.

391 W Cascade Avenue, Sisters OR
(541) 549-4994 or (800) 348-9453
www.clearwaterstudio.com

The Ashland Hardwood Gallery

Since 1999, the Ashland Hardwood Gallery in Ashland, Oregon, has been showcasing fine works of art by a variety of different artists, a majority of them local. Owner Aaron Diamontopoulos proudly displays finely crafted furniture and sculpture, as well as pine-crafted clothing by Livio Demarci. Woodcarvings of hats, bras and shoes are all available for purchase. The gallery features an impressive collection of wood art, including Balinese handcrafted sculptures, beautiful breadboard sets by Edward Wohl and heirloom bowls by David Lory. Local furniture makers Don DeDobbeleer and William Olson contribute exquisite pieces that combine art and function. Whether you are looking to outfit your kitchen, living or dining room, a visit to this gallery is a must. Discover a stunning selection of artistic wooden masterpieces at the Ashland Hardwood Gallery.

17 N Main Street, Ashland OR
(541) 488-6200
www.hardwoodgallery.com

Lorang Fine Art & Gorge-ous Gifts

Brad and Debora Lorang believe art is more than just an expression, it's a lifestyle. At Lorang Fine Art & Gorge-ous Gifts, this husband and wife team brings you a wide expanse of artistic styles, themes and mediums. More than 40 artists are represented in this eclectic store. Oil, acrylic, pastels and watercolor paintings add splashes of color throughout the gallery. Themes include wildlife and local landmarks, such as Mt. Hood and the Gorge, along with Asian and Native American motifs. The gift lines include cards, jewelry, glass art, wood work, baskets and pottery all made locally. New works include hand-pulled Block Prints by Michael Smith, Native American masks and jewelry by Lillian Pitt, photo-realistic acrylics by Phil Smith, and Romanian folk art by Tatiana Rogovsky. Brad himself displays distinct steel and bronze sculptures. The recently enlarged studio allows him to share his passion. "After 35 years in the art industry, educating people about sculpting, and the process of casting or fabricating metal sculptures is the most enjoyable part," Brad says. He believes that getting others excited about his craft serves to stimulate his own creativity. Stop by Lorang Fine Art & Gorge-ous Gifts to energize your own feelings for art.

96 WaNaPa Street, Cascade Locks OR
(541) 374-8007
www.lorangfineart.com

OREGON

Health
& Beauty

Waterstone Spa

Waterstone Spa is as popular with residents as it is with tourists. A membership is offered to Rogue Valley residents for discounts, and Waterstone offers comprehensive packages with the adjacent Ashland Springs Hotel. Spa guests can chose from a wide menu of treatments, from a Vichy shower to couples side-by-side treatments in the Duet Suite. Deep relaxation comes quickly when you succumb to the efforts of two massage therapists in the Twice the Bliss massage. LaStone Therapy is a treatment that involves being massaged with both hot and cold stones, creating a hydrotherapy effect and deep muscle relaxation. Waterstone's Signature Spa Treatment is an herbal skin-softening wrap that begins with a bath infused with locally made bath salts and essential oils. This treatment ends with a mini-facial. Waterstone's menu includes five incredible facials all utilizing Jurlique, an amazing organic skincare line from Australia. Co-owners Deb Cleland and Deanne Anderson are both massage therapists. They take an organic approach to spa treatments and work with a core of talented professionals who prefer conscious products. As a guest of Waterstone Spa you can restore balance in your body, mind, spirit and emotions.

236 E Main Street, Ashland OR (541) 488-0325
www.waterstonespa.com

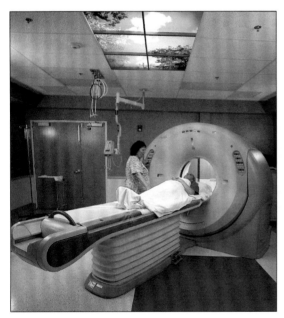

Willamette Falls Hospital

In an age of hospital mergers and large health care systems, Willamette Falls Hospital remains true to its roots. It is a proudly independent, uncommonly personal community hospital dedicated to providing high quality, compassionate care. The 100-bed hospital provides Clackamas County with a wide range of health care services. The 200 physicians and surgeons practicing in this state-of-the-art facility are committed to medical excellence. In 1954, eight physicians practicing in Oregon City founded a not-for-profit community institution named Doctors' Hospital. With community support, the hospital reopened in 1961 as Willamette Falls Community Hospital. In recent years, the hospital has seen unprecedented growth. New additions include fully renovated Surgical Services, Diagnostic Imaging and Emergency departments. Hospitals from across the country have modeled their birth units after those at Willamette Falls. Two medical office buildings on the campus house affiliated physicians. Since 1985, the hospice program has given end-of-life care to thousands. The hospital offers popular urgent care and family practice clinics in Clackamas, Oregon City, West Linn and Canby. For exceptional care, close to home, visit Willamette Falls Hospital.

1500 Division Street, Oregon City OR (503) 656-1631
www.willamettefallshospital.org

Mt. Hood

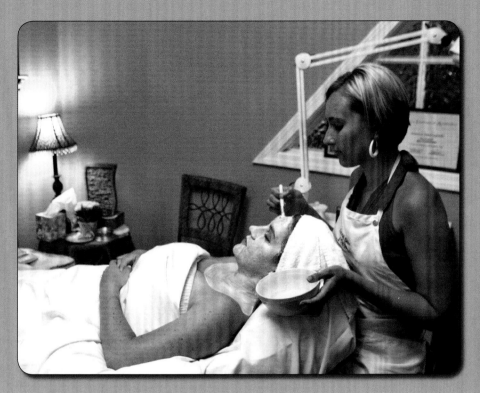

Four Oaks Salon & Day Spa

Bask in the luxurious treatment that only a day at Four Oaks Salon & Day Spa can provide. With a gifted and dedicated staff of nine stylists, two estheticians, two massage therapists and two nail technicians, Four Oaks' goal is for you to feel special from the moment you walk in the door. Each treatment and massage is geared towards relaxation, revival and rejuvenation of the body and mind. Offering a wide variety of professional spa services, including hair, nail and makeup styling, Four Oaks is devoted to meeting every beauty need. More recently added to the selection of treatments is the Synergie AMS, or aesthetic massage system. Synergie AMS is a revolutionary FDA approved system to aid in the reduction of cellulite. Also available is Four Oaks' ultimate facial. Using the synergie system, microdermabrasion and light therapy, this facial takes skincare to a new level. For special occasions, let the talented hair, airbrush eyelash extension, makeup and nail experts prepare you for your day. Waxing is also available to add a finished touch to any look. Trying to find the perfect gift for Mother's Day or the exceptional lady in your life? Gift certificates are available with a variety of different packages. Body relaxation, hair rejuvenation and the ultimate spa experience are a few of the exceptional deals that include several different types of treatments. No matter which services you choose to enjoy at Four Oaks Salon & Day Spa, know that the experience will be an unforgettable one.

411 Oak Street, Central Point OR (541) 664-3214 *www.fouroaksdayspa.com*

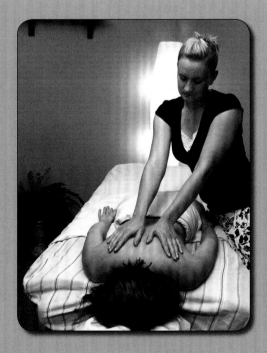

OREGON

Home
& Garden

Buda Glass and Screen

Nearly 20 years ago an impressed customer handed John Buda a ten dollar tip then made John promise to use the money to start his own business, because John went above and beyond on his job. The Budas always talked about starting their own mom and pop glass shop, so the thoughtful gift encouraged John and eventually they opened Buda Glass and Screen. John and his wife Sue still have that ten dollar bill proudly displayed in their office. It is an inspiring reminder of how they began. This energetic husband and wife team make integrity and customer service their top priorities in business. Word of mouth referrals are the basis for this wonderful team. The Budas are well known in the Rogue Valley for doing good work at a fair price. John has over 28 years of experience in the business and Sue runs the office. John is happy to work on old and new windows alike, custom mirrors, shower doors and John is willing to tackle any job, no matter how small, complex or just plain unusual. Perhaps the best part of the business is their friendly mascot, Ruby. As a rescue dog she is John's constant sidekick, and she loves to meet new friends. If you want to improve and maintain your home or business then you can't go wrong if you invite Ruby and her humans over for the day. John will do the repair work and Ruby will inspect the job for you.

Medford OR
(541) 857-8817

Jolene's

When it comes to finding a gift for that person who has everything, folks in Medford go to Jolene's to find distinctive home décor and gifts. Jolene Hedstrom is a gifted collector of artistic artifacts with an eye for that special thing you never knew you always needed. She fills her shop with a wide variety of U.S. and Oregon-made products, including the scented candles that fill the air as you browse. Her taste is backed up by some of the best—the bedroom slides adorned with beautiful hand-painted silk pansies by Spa Fluer are on Oprah's favorites list. Jolene's stocks an expanding collection of body products that will pamper you, including bath crystals, lotions, perfumes and soaps. One of the rarer finds at the shop is the collection of Sid Dickens Memory Blocks. These decorative hand-painted plaster tiles are one-of-a-kind and are created by five different artists in several stages. The plaster is molded, then finished to a porcelain-like quality and cracked for an aged Italian fresco look. Each is painted with watercolor-like pigments and gold leaf. Jolene makes it her business to seek out hard-to-find treasures such as these for her customers and bring them together in one place. Visit Jolene's to see what she's found lately.

1310 Center Drive, Medford OR
(541) 770-6804

Taylor Creek, Briggs Valley
Photo by Prairie Smallwood

Doug's Cabinets

Doug Wilkie has been designing and building custom cabinets, fireplace mantles, furniture and entertainment centers for over 34 years. He opened Doug's Cabinets after working as a foreman for a furniture factory and discovering his gift for creating quality custom cabinets. Specializing in design aspects that might test the average builder, Doug enjoys a challenging project in which he can make a difficult space shine with detail and his unmatched professional quality. Using only materials of the highest standards, he takes pride in creating lasting pieces that not only complement the home and interior design but the personality and preferences of the customer. Every project is a custom job when you're working with Doug's Cabinets. Whether it's a simple room remodel or a completely new home design, Doug is happy to personally consult with the owners to create a stunning addition to their home. Update your kitchen with many different door designs or utilize your corner spaces with a beautiful hutch. Whether you prefer a smooth, modern look or want expertly detailed cabinets to match your traditional Victorian décor, Doug guarantees you'll be ecstatic with the final product. With decades of happy customers, attention to detail and hand craftsmanship, Doug's work is a testament to the integrity and expertise he brings to each job. Call Doug's Cabinets today to schedule a free consultation, and let Doug make your home as exceptional as you are.

Grants Pass OR
(541) 660-1407

OREGON

Lifestyle
Destinations

Jennings McCall Center

"I've never felt so pampered in my life," says one resident of the Jennings McCall Center. The Jennings McCall Center offers three facilities in one: a retirement center, an assisted living center and a Progressive Care Unit. At the retirement center, the friendly and compassionate staff take care of all the clients' needs. Residents choose either a studio, a one-bedroom or a two-bedroom apartment. Each is equipped with a full kitchen, so you can either cook in your apartment or visit the restaurant-style dining room. A covered patio or private balcony is standard with each apartment, as is an outdoor storage area. The assisted living center offers a comprehensive range of care services, including 24-hour on-site nursing care. For those needing a higher level of care or a secure environment, Jennings McCall has the Progressive Care Unit, which provides more one-on-one assistance. The center's tradition of service dates back to 1922, when it opened to provide housing for elderly members of the Masonic and Eastern Star orders. Expansion in 1989 made it possible to open the center to the general public. Residents enjoy the lovely waterfall on 15 acres of park-like gardens. A paved walkway surrounds the campus for easy strolling. Favorite gathering places inside the center include the libraries with big screen televisions, the pool table room and the exercise/activity rooms. "They rolled out the red carpet, and it's been out ever since," says the daughter of one resident as she recalls her initial campus tour with her father. Contact the office and arrange to have someone show you around this outstanding facility.

2300 Masonic Way, Forest Grove OR
(503) 357-4133
www.jenningsmccall.com

Mirabella Portland

Mirabella Portland, the newest member of Pacific Retirement Services (PRS) fine family of Continuing Care Retirement Communities (CCRC), is being built in Portland's most up-and-coming area, the South Waterfront district along the Willamette River. Sitting on 1.16 acres, Mirabella Portland will be a 30-story tower offering an urban senior lifestyle that supports the findings of the MacArthur Foundation's study of successful aging. At Mirabella, PRS's goal is to help residents create a vision of their future—one that is bright, vibrant and exciting. One that is rich with friends, fun and personal fulfillment. And equally important, one that is filled with vitality and peace of mind. When complete, Mirabella Portland will be state-of-the-art in everything. From the spacious apartments to the host of outstanding services, fine amenities and on-site health care it offers, this new community will truly stand alone. Mirabella Portland will be the only CCRC that enjoys a relationship with Oregon Health and Science University (OHSU). Mirabella residents will be able to participate in wellness, clinical, and research activities sponsored by OHSU.

3030 SW Moody Avenue, Suite 107, Portland OR
(877) 254-9371 or (503) 245-4742
www.mirabellaretirement.org

Holladay Park Plaza

Another member of Pacific Retirement Services, Holladay Park Plaza has been serving seniors for more than 40 years. Located in the Lloyd District, the campus offers a wealth of fine services and amenities including a fitness center, an indoor saline pool and spa, a hair salon and a gift shop. Residents can also enjoy a deli, a bank, a library, craft and activity centers and more. Each day, residents enjoy delicious meals in the beautiful dining room and many end their evenings socializing with friends in the gorgeous Penthouse Lounge. All Plaza apartments offer lovely views and plenty of space for treasured belongings. Like all PRS communities, residents have the security of knowing Continuing Care is there if they need it. To learn more about Holladay Park Plaza, call the toll-free number today.

1300 NE 16th Avenue, Portland OR
(800) 777-5517 or (503) 280-2216
www.retirement.org/hpp

Rogue Valley Manor

As one of the top Continuing Care Retirement Communities (CCRCs) in the nation, the award-winning Rogue Valley Manor offers just about everything you can think of in terms of accommodations, services and amenities. The beautiful apartment homes in Skyline Plaza and the main Manor offer spectacular vistas of the Rogue Valley's bountiful orchards, pastures, interesting geological features and the Cascade Mountains. The spacious cottage homes overlook Centennial Golf Club and Quail Point Golf Course. The 668-acre campus offers virtually every type of daily convenience, including two banks, a travel agency, a hair salon, a boutique, a convenience store and pharmacy, a financial planner and a CPA. But that's just the beginning. There are also two fitness centers with brand-new equipment, an indoor saline pool and spa, a sauna, two steam rooms and two massage rooms. Wellness classes include yoga, tai chi, low-impact aerobics and aqua-aerobics, plus tap dancing, ballroom dancing and more. With more than 90 interest groups on campus, there's something for everyone. Discover woodworking, ceramics, musical and theatrical groups and book clubs or walking, hiking, RVing and more. Each and every day the Executive Chef and his culinary team create delicious and healthful meals with the freshest ingredients. Most importantly, what sets the Manor apart is its comprehensive Continuing Care program. This means that independent living, residential living, memory support and skilled nursing care are all here if you if you ever need them. Rogue Valley Manor has been serving residents for nearly 50 years. It is fully accredited by the prestigious Continuing Care Accreditation Commission.

1200 Mira Mar Avenue, Medford OR (541) 857-7214 or (800) 848-7868
www.retirement.org/rvm

OREGON

Restaurants
& Cafés

38 on Central Restaurant & Wine Bar

The buzz that 38 on Central created when it opened in late 2006 has yet to die down. It remains a hip choice on Medford's restaurant scene, often filling up on weekends with large parties in search of fine cuisine and a classy, open space in which to enjoy each other's company. "Like the refurbished, historic building it occupies, this establishment infuses downtown with some much-needed style," notes Sarah Lemon, food critic for the *Medford Mail Tribune,* whose enthusiasm for the atmosphere matches her appreciation for such menu stand-outs as the spinach salad with softshell crab, rack of lamb and wild mushroom pasta. Get your evening off to a scrumptious start with the pulled duck quesadilla appetizer. Owners Darrin Richards and Sam Tinsley recruited Franco Console to serve as executive chef. His culinary training with an emphasis on Italian and French cuisine results in a menu rich in creativity. With its selection of more than 200 wines, this establishment lives up to its reputation for having something to please every wine lover. Kick back in the mezzanine lounge and enjoy a glass before your meal. Such early-19th-century features as hardwood floors and exposed brick walls blend with the modern furnishings, resulting in a very tasteful hybrid style. Consider stopping by 38 on Central before or after a show at the nearby Craterian Ginger Rogers Theatre, or at any other time that your plans in Medford call for inventive cuisine in an attractive urban environment.

38 N Central Avenue, Medford OR (541) 776-0038
www.38oncentral.com

Como's Italian Eatery

When you're in the mood for classic steak or seafood with an Italian twist, head to Como's Italian Eatery, where chef and owner Budd Wolchik serves up crowd-pleasing continental cuisine. He starts with traditional Italian recipes, then pulls in the best of the West with a splash of originality to make your favorite meals exciting again. Since opening just three years ago, Como's has made a hit in Pendleton with its fun house specials featuring Budd's original sauces, sautés and seasonings. He cooks with wine, fresh herbs and spices and uses only fresh local ingredients. A community-oriented establishment, Como's sources its bread and desserts from local bakers. You'll also find a fine assortment of hand-picked microbrews and boutique wines from Oregon and around the world. The atmosphere is cozy and inviting, a great place to spend an afternoon or evening with friends and family, or with a book, watching the world go by. Enjoy a great meal, locally-made treats and a community feeling at Como's Italian Eatery.

39 SE Court Avenue, Pendleton OR (541) 278-9142

McAndrews Avenue Grill

Rene Fournet and Kathleen O'Loughlin spent nine months developing and designing McAndrews Avenue Grill. They both left long careers to open the Medford restaurant in 2006. Customers are soothed by the Italian style décor, which includes Murano glass lamps in the windows, carefully planned indirect ceiling lighting and parquet wood floors. You can choose to spend warm summer nights on the patio, starting with a choice of 100 wines and the popular Avenue Crab Dip. The prime USDA steaks come from Allen Brothers of Chicago. Customers also look forward to fork-tender barbecue ribs, pork chops and deep-fried stuffed shrimp. The grill serves fresh Alaskan fish daily, a large choice of sushi dishes and inventive salads. Let that sweet tooth loose on Bananas Foster for two or Crème Brûlée Cheesecake. Lunch favorites include burgers, pizza and tacos. When we visited, the grill was looking for sponsors for a 2008 golf tournament in support of Mobility Unlimited, an organization that helps physically disabled adults buy the equipment they need for independence. Prepare to be charmed at McAndrews Avenue Grill.

1251 E McAndrews Road, #110, Medford OR
(541) 772-5100 or (866) 876-8715
www.mcandrewsavenuegrill.com

Wild River Brewing & Pizza Company

Over the years, Jerry and Bertha Miller have expanded their Southern Oregon pizza and microbrew empire, opening the newest Wild River Brewing & Pizza Company location in Medford in 2006. The couple started out with a pizza parlor in Cave Junction in 1975 and expanded to Brookings in 1980. Their business has changed names several times, settling on the Wild River title in 1994 as a way to introduce the Grants Pass brewery. Pizzas, burgers and sandwiches are always fresh and flavorful at Wild River. The brews have been praised by readers of local publications throughout the Rogue Valley and have won many awards at the Great American Beer Festival. On tap year-round are such favorites as Harbor Lights Kolsch-style Ale, made from yeast gifted by a brewery in Koln, Germany, a traditional English-style bitter ale, a classic pilsner, a mild honey wheat and an India pale ale. Seasonal beers add to the lineup. Like the Grants Pass restaurant, the new Medford space features an open design with wood-fired ovens. Discover a classic combination of microbrews and pizza at Wild River Brewing & Pizza Company.

595 NE E Street, Grants Pass OR (541) 471-7487
2684 N Pacific Highway, Medford OR (541) 773-7487
www.wildriverbrewing.com

Elements Tapas Bar & Lounge

Owners Chris Dennett and Dani Arzner came up with the idea for Elements Tapas Bar & Lounge over a bottle of wine. There's no telling what brainstorm might strike you as your evening at their seductive restaurant unwinds. Tapas are the perfect food for socializing, and because Elements stays open at least until midnight, you are free to enjoy good conversation, creative cuisine and excellent wine well into the night. Executive Chef Chad Smith, who attended the Cascade Culinary School, prepares a tempting variety of cold and hot tapas in addition to gourmet flatbreads and desserts. The trio of lamb meatballs is a house favorite. One comes with local smoked bleu cheese, another with Spanish chorizo wrapped in Serrano ham and the third with spiced peach and a peach glaze. Other crowd pleasers include Idiazabal cheese, a semi-firm Spanish sheep's milk cheese. It tastes superb marinated in a citrus- and herb-infused olive oil and balanced with whole cloves of roasted garlic. The very lengthy wine lists reflect the Elements philosophy of supporting local industry and of being true to the gastronomic history of Spain. Southern Oregon wines dominate the Oregon list, while the Spanish list offers Montecillo Gran Reserva, a tempranillo produced by one of Spain's oldest wineries, along with a variety of other fine wines from the different wine-producing regions of that country. Plan your next grand venture during an evening at Elements.

101 E Main Street, Medford OR
(541) 779-0135
www.elementsmedford.com

Bruno's Pizza & Pasta

During the past 18 years, thousands of Medford teenagers have has their first experience in the work world at Bruno's Pizza & Pasta. That's exactly what Stan Miller had in mind when he quit his job in the real estate business 18 years ago to launch the restaurant. Stan's approach to bettering his community by providing a good place to eat and jobs for young people has been a stunning success. Since opening, he has hired more than 2,200 workers and only fired five. Young people working at Bruno's develop self-esteem, discipline and people skills. Stan puts a lot of thought into his food as well as his staff. He believes in using wholesome ingredients, including real cheese, real Canadian bacon and lean beef and sausage. You can choose from as many as 40 pizza toppings as well as pastas served with marinara, meat and Alfredo sauces. Appetizers, a salad bar, soups and sandwiches add to the variety. Son Bruce Miller shares day-to-day operations with his dad, and Bruce's son Allias helps when needed. Stan's wife, Shirley, decorated the restaurant's interior, including party rooms for special functions. The family invites you to enjoy a fun, communal experience at Bruno's Pizza & Pasta.

2105 Roberts Road, Medford OR
(541) 773-3708
www.brunospizzaandpasta.com

Bambu

Once you have tasted the Shanghai baby back ribs or the sesame and macadamia nut-encrusted mahi mahi at Bambu, you will know why the words traditional and conventional do not apply to the menu. For Executive Chef Adam Ward, cooking is a matter of interpretation. He takes the regional flavors of Asia and gives them his own twist. A meal of lemongrass soup, Thai lime salad and crispy chicken with spinach will leave your taste buds tingling. Don't overlook the appetizers either, because the rock shrimp spring rolls with lemongrass and coconut sauce are scrumptious. For dessert, try the flourless chocolate torte. All foods are prepared with the absolute freshest ingredients. The wine list includes draws from local wineries such as Roxy Ann and Foris. When the weather is pleasant, guests often ask to be seated on the patio with its garden-like setting. Adam has been cooking professionally since training at the San Francisco Culinary Academy. His tenure as executive chef of Bambu dates back to 2001, but since 2006, he and his wife, Veronica, have owned it. Adam is constantly seeking new ways to present the flavors of Japan, China and Vietnam, as well as Thailand, Indonesia and the Philippines, to his ever-growing clientele. Join Adam and Veronica for a meal of exploration and discovery at Bambu.

970 N Phoenix Road, #106, Medford OR
(541) 608-7545

Stone Cliff Inn

Nestled amid old growth and surrounded by granite spires, the majestic Stone Cliff Inn embodies the true spirit of Oregon. Guests bask in the sun on the traditional handcrafted deck, while gazing at the spectacular Clackamas River as it lazily twists its way towards civilization. Festive laughter is part of the casual, yet sumptuous atmosphere. Carver locals know the Stone Cliff Inn well and come any day of the week, whether for a quick lunch, special dinner or Sunday brunch. Executive Chef David Pruyn has designed a menu that focuses on the best the Northwest has to offer. His original recipes are prepared from scratch using fresh local ingredients. Enjoy a glass of wine from the eclectic list featuring Oregon and Washington vintages. The Stone Cliff Inn is on the site of the historic Baker's Rock Quarry in Carver, several miles east of Oregon City on the Clackamas River. Workmen rafted basalt from this quarry down the river to build many of Oregon's most famous old structures. Today, the basalt mountain is one of the most popular climbing spots in the Northwest. On a summer day it is not uncommon to see bald eagles perched in tall fir trees surveying the river below, where drift boats cast their lines for wild steelhead and Salmon, and kayakers negotiate the rapids. The deck of the Stone Cliff Inn provides a spectacular vantage point to the daily activities of the Clackamas River. Offering the perfect setting for your next private dinner party, the inn will delight you and your guests with its tantalizing cuisine and intimate, candlelight atmosphere. Catering is available. The attentive staff of the Stone Cliff Inn hopes to see you soon.

17900 S Clackamas River Drive, Oregon City OR
(503) 631-7900
www.stonecliffinn.com

Kaleidoscope Pizzeria & Pub

How has Kaleidoscope Pizzeria & Pub risen above a crowded field of contenders to snatch the title of Best Pizza in Medford? The ingredients for success start with the ingredients themselves, which are always the highest-quality, freshest-tasting ones available. The sheer inventiveness of the menu has also played a role in placing this establishment at the top of local polls every year since it opened.

Veggie lovers who return again and again still can't decide on a favorite. Is it the Wild Mushroom, featuring savory portabella and crimini mushrooms, the Popeye, boasting a load of peppers and onions to go along with the spinach, or the Margherita, with its simple yet satisfying combination of Roma tomatoes, parmesan, basil and olive oil? The choices of meat pizzas are just as tantalizing. Stick with tradition by opting for a straightforward pepperoni pie or discover a new favorite such as the Prosciutto Blue, with prosciutto ham, gorgonzola and artichoke hearts. Jake Allmaras and his wife, Kristi Haavig, and son, Ben Allmaras, brought their love for gourmet pizza to Medford from Alaska, where they lived for 25 years. They had their restaurant built for them to match their vision of a bright, contemporary space that would exhibit creativity in every detail. For pizza that sets the local standard for taste and originality, visit Kaleidoscope Pizzeria & Pub.

3084 Crater Lake Highway, Medford OR (541) 779-7787
www.kaleidoscopepizza.com

Country Cottage Café & Bakery

Dine in quaint elegance when you visit Country Cottage Café & Bakery. Set in a cozy cottage-like setting surrounded by blooming flowers, this beautiful restaurant and pastry shop is famous for folksy lunches and an all-you-can eat buffet with very fresh local ingredients. You'll love the buttery-crusted vegetarian quiche and turkey pepperoncini sandwich, each made fresh with local produce and cheeses. For dessert, try the chocolate banana cream pie, banana and chocolate ganache are swirled through this cream-filled mile-high pie in a flaky crust. The Taste the Midnight Madness chocolate cake, made with six layers of dark chocolate, chocolate butter-cream frosting and ganache. For a tasty alternative, sample a homemade melt-in-your-mouth scone. Don't forget to stop in for a traditional English high tea, which includes a selection of delectables. The interior of the restaurant has a floor-to-ceiling mural of wildflowers and rolling hills, and the ceiling is covered in life-like wisteria vines. Co-owners Dianne and David Linderman and Pam and Manuel Lawrence take pride in providing affordable country gourmet cuisine in the valley. Find out for yourself why Country Cottage Café & Bakery in the Shops at Exit 24 is truly an Oregon treasure.

205 Fern Valley Road, Phoenix OR (541) 535-5113
www.countrycottagecafe.com

Mark's on the Channel

Not many owners get to welcome guests aboard their restaurant, but such is the case at Mark's on the Channel. The restaurant floats in McCuddy's Marina on a channel of the Columbia River. From your table, you can view the many beautiful boats docked at the marina for ambience to rival anything found in the Pacific Northwest. As you would expect, the menu is loaded with fresh seafood choices, including clam chowder, scampi and grilled ahi tuna. A variety of fettuccine dishes and a juicy steak burger, featuring locally raised Highland beef, are other house favorites. Overall, balance of flavor combined with strength of seasoning defines Mark's style of cooking. Mark's on the Channel is open for lunch and dinner. A full bar serves wine, beer and spirits. Live acoustic music often adds to the atmosphere at this most unusual restaurant. Many guests, stumbling upon Mark's while passing through McCuddy's Marina, find that a meal here provides the perfect punctuation to a fine day on or near the water. Staff will be happy to offer directions, if you call ahead. For the best meal you are ever likely to enjoy afloat, eat at Mark's on the Channel.

34326 Johnson Landing Road, Scappoose OR (503) 543-8765
www.marksonthechannel.com

El Gaucho—Portland

With steaks prepared before your eyes and attentive service in a luxurious, retro-swank setting, El Gaucho is "the nation's best steakhouse." That's what *Washington CEO* magazine had to say about the restaurant. The luxury experience begins from the moment you enter the restaurant, with the scent of grilled steak and seafood comingling with the gentle sounds of live guitar music. General manager Todd Moore and his staff will see to the smallest details of your visit. You'll delight in what *Sunset* magazine called "flourishes of grand tableside service." Tableside preparation of Caesar salad, Chateaubriand and Bananas Foster give you an idea of how much the individual experience is valued here. Executive Chef Jaime Mansfield presides over the exhibition kitchen, where you can watch as your food is expertly prepared over an open bed of glowing coals. *Zagat's* called this experience "dinner as theater" in its rave review. All beef here is prime, 28-day-old, dry-aged, certified prime Angus beef. Seafood, ribs and poultry also meet strict standards for freshness and flavor. An extensive wine list contributed to an Award of Excellence from *Wine Spectator* magazine. The restaurant offers a luxury cigar lounge and two elegant rooms for private dining. For food, service and surroundings that have the critics raving, come to El Gaucho.

319 SW Broadway, Portland OR (503) 227-8794
www.elgaucho.com

Avalon Bar & Grill

The lively jazz music featured throughout the week has folks tapping their feet while they eat at the Avalon Bar & Grill. Since opening in 2005, this restaurant near the quiet town of Talent, just north of Ashland, has earned scores of loyal customers who seem determined to try everything on the menu. Whether you are in the mood for a sandwich or fine cuisine, the Avalon will appease your appetite. For something special, try the roasted duck breast. Prepared in an orange balsamic reduction, it comes with herb-roasted fingerling potatoes and a grilled vegetable brochette. If you're coming for the jazz, Saturday and Sunday afternoons are sure bets, and there's a good chance that someone will be performing in the evening during the week. "There are a ton of good jazz players in the area," says Dal Carver, who owns the Avalon with his wife, Renee. A basket of sweet potato fries, combined with a glass of wine from one of the nearby vineyards, makes for a delightful snack as you listen to the music. Sunday brunch typically features eggs Benedict, smoked salmon scramble and corned beef hash. Come enjoy the local musical talent while feasting on fresh, creative cuisine at the Avalon Bar & Grill.

105 W Valley View Road, Suite 1, Ashland OR (541) 512-8864
www.avalonbarandgrill.com

Arbor House Restaurant

Since 1979, the Arbor House Restaurant has been delighting residents and visitors in the Rogue Valley. Known for both great gourmet food and friendly service, the Arbor House takes its name from the vine-covered arbor that highlights its lovely woodland setting. Outdoor dining with views of the Japanese garden and fishpond are an added pleasure during the summer months. The Arbor House has been a family-run business since Patrick and Kitty Calhoun opened it in 1979. Now run by their youngest son, Joel, and daughter, Leah, the restaurant offers specialties such as scampi alla griglia (sautéed shrimp in garlic butter), jambalaya and a variety of curries that can be ordered mild, medium, spicy or hot. Every night features a fresh fish or seafood special. Beef lovers can choose from filet mignon, New York strip steak, T-bone or rib-eye, and there are many vegetarian entrées available as well. Fine beers and wines, including many local vintages, complement the meal. Remember, by pacing your meal properly you will leave just enough room for one of the Arbor House's wonderful dessert selections. Perhaps you will choose the mouth-watering strawberry shortcake. Reservations are recommended, so call the Arbor House Restaurant today.

103 W Wagner, Talent OR (541) 535-6817

Calamity Jane's

If you want great family dining with a Western theme, saddle up and head on over to Calamity Jane's. Owned and operated by Michael and Carole Modjeski—with co-owner Patrick Modjeski—this restaurant has become a favorite destination among the locals. Word has also gotten out to travelers and those who live out of town. The service is fast and friendly and the food is exceptional. The Modjeskis have a huge selection of hamburgers that you won't find anywhere else. For something different, try the pepperoni pizza burger, or the Black Bart, which has sausage and jalapeños. Calamity Jane's also has hot and cold sandwiches and dinners, such as pot roast, halibut or country-fried steak. For dessert you will want to try one of the many shakes and malts in flavors such as cinnamon, coconut, apple pie, peanut butter and many others. The Dundee location offers line dancing on Wednesday nights, the Blues Jam on Thursday nights or live music on Friday and Saturday nights. Round up the family and enjoy a memorable dining experience at Calamity Jane's.

42015 SE Highway 26, Sandy OR (503) 668-7817
1175 N Highway 99 W, Dundee OR (503) 538-9407

Highland Still House

Whisky is the passion of Mick and Tammy Secor, who point out that the word *whisky* is derived from the Gaelic expression for *water of life*. Mick and Tammy are the owners of the Highland Still House, a friendly Scottish pub featuring more than 100 varieties of single malt Scotch and traditional Scottish fare. There are only two places in the world where you can enjoy fabulous Grist Bronzed Salmon, and one of them is here at this gathering place in Oregon City. This signature dish is a salmon filet coated with a savory blend of seasonings. The Peated Barley Grist from Ardberg Distillery is equally rare. You would have to visit the distillery on the Isle of Islay in Scotland to find it. That's how authentic the Highland Still House is. You will find fish and chips here and such pub classics as shepherd's pie and bangers and mash. Most of the furnishings have come from Great Britain, so if you didn't know any better, you would think that you had jumped the Atlantic and landed in a neighborhood pub somewhere in the United Kingdom. Another giveaway to your location is the outdoor seating overlooking Willamette Falls. Mick and Tammy invite you in for a traditional Scottish meal, a fine ale and a dram of the water of life at the Highland Still House.

201 S 2nd Street, Oregon City OR
(503) 723-6789
www.highlandstillhouse.com

Rogue Valley in Spring
Photo by Nathan Allen

Karlsson Brewing Company

Imagine a big game on the television, classic rock on the stereo and friends teasing you about your shuffleboard skills while you enjoy one of Jeremy Carlson's microbrews—maybe Pioneer Pilsner, Sock Knocker Scotch Ale or a seasonal brew made from fresh hops. You are in the taproom at Karlsson Brewing Company, where specialty beers and a friendly brewpub atmosphere keep customers entertained seven days a week. Jeremy started making beer in his garage for his own pleasure, just 10 gallons at a time. As he shared his creations, demand for his home-brewed products grew. Three years ago, his parents Ken and Patsy Carlson purchased a brew house from Utah and helped launch Karlsson Brewing Company in Sandy. Most of the beer is sold at the taproom, with some going to keg sales. Plans are in the works for a restaurant. The Carlsons grow four acres of hops, which Jeremy uses fresh to produce seasonal brews, a practice only employed by three or four breweries in the country. Do you prefer an India pale ale, a porter or a rye? Jeremy brews them all. The taproom also serves wine by the glass and complimentary peanuts that are downright addictive. Savor good times and good brews at Karlsson Brewing Company.

35900 Industrial Way, #102, Sandy OR (503) 826-8770
www.karlssonbrewing.com

Camp 18 Restaurant

The defining theme at Camp 18 Restaurant is *big*. Owner Gordon Smith began construction of the building in the 1970s, hoping to build the largest log cabin anyone had ever seen. A massive structure with 500-pound, hand-carved doors and a 25-ton ridge pole in the main room, it likely is the largest log cabin most people have ever seen. Gordon logged the timber for the structure himself. He and his wife Roberta decorated the inside of the restaurant with old saws, photographs of lumberjacks and other logging memorabilia. The oversized theme extends to the Northwest-style fare the restaurant serves. Bring your appetite and delve into fresh seafood caught in Astoria, including halibut, salmon and razor clams, or order a plate of baby back ribs, steak or chicken. The three berry cobbler is a perennial favorite dessert and the cinnamon rolls always elicit gasps of astonishment as they make their appearance on the table, taking up an entire plate. After your meal, stretch your legs by roaming the five acres of the Old Time Logging Museum, where you can see steam shovels, cranes and other logging relics on display. Stop by Camp 18 Restaurant for hearty food and a look at the historic logging industry.

42362 Highway 26, Seaside OR (503) 755-1818

Heidi's of Gresham

It's impossible to remain hungry in Gresham since Don and Marie Eklund went into the restaurant business 40 years ago. The couple started out small with Heidi's Coffee Shop in the late 1960s, a place where Marie baked pies, Don cooked and their three children took orders, washed dishes and operated the fountain. Next came a gourmet dinner house and finally in 1980, Heidi's of Gresham. Today's 350-seat restaurant includes a gift shop, a lounge, outdoor eating facilities and rooms for private banquets. The restaurant is known for its long

breakfast menu and fresh baked goods. Daily pastry selections include bear claws and cinnamon rolls. Cakes and pies are equally memorable. Burgers, sandwiches and salads dominate the lunch menu. Aunt Mary's vegetable beef soup is a reliable favorite. Dinner gives you dozens of reasons to return to Heidi's. Perhaps it will be Heidi's signature prime rib tonight, a seafood selection next time, and Swiss cabbage rolls, German sausages or Italian pasta dishes at future visits. Today, Don and Marie spend winters in Palm Springs, and Linda Hinshaw, employed at Heidi's for 32 years and part-owner, takes charge. Bring your appetite to Heidi's of Gresham, where satisfaction is as close as your next meal.

1230 NE Cleveland Avenue, Gresham OR (503) 667-4200
www.heidisofgresham.com

Tad's Chicken 'N Dumplins

There is something about a beloved local landmark that keeps the crowds coming. The quaint, cozy building housing Tad's Chicken 'N Dumplins is home to legendary fried chicken, home-smoked salmon, fish and chips, and pesto fettuccini. Follow up your meal with bread pudding in whiskey sauce, the dessert specialty, and you've got a taste of what has kept the doors open since the 1920s. Inside, the historic restaurant features a hunting lodge atmosphere, with pine paneling, banks of windows and arching beams. The original owner, Tad Johnson, was known as a rascal and a fisherman, in that order. He served a traveling crowd beer and smoked fish under the name Tad Pot Inn. The chicken and dumplings were added to the menu in the 1940s and Tad's still uses the original recipe. The same local family has owned the restaurant since the 1950s and the local's give it a high rating. The owner's have never managed to keep all of the neon sign letter's lit. It seems the one side that reads Tad's Chic Dump is a local treasure. On the banks of the Sandy River, well away from the city and the freeway, it's worth a trip to experience the food and company at Tad's Chicken 'N Dumplins.

1325 E Historic Columbia River Highway, Troutdale OR
(503) 666-5337
www.tadschicdump.com

Brookings
Photo by Clarice Rodriguez

Mt. Hood Roasters Restaurant

Oregonians have a passion for the great outdoors and great coffee, both of which come together at Mt. Hood Roasters Restaurant. Located in the shadow of majestic Mt. Hood, this place is popular with folks heading up or coming down the slopes. Swap tales of your best run of the day while enjoying a hot mocha or latte with the snack of the house, a beer donut. The master roaster skillfully prepares each batch of coffee 10 pounds at a time, using an air-roasting process that ensures a rich gourmet flavor. In a separate division called Welches' Living Room, the coffeehouse serves a full menu of hearty fare for chilled skiers, highlighted by Angus Beef burger baskets with ale fries. The charbroiled Korean teriyaki is also very popular. Drive through and take out are available, but on Friday and Saturday nights especially, you'll want to step inside and feel the vibe when the coffeehouse features live music. Make Mt. Hood Roasters Restaurant a part of your Oregon ski package.

67441 E Highway 26, Welches OR (503) 622-1389
www.mthoodroasters.com/restauranthome.htm

Tee Time Coffee Shop

New owners David and Mihaela Tscherney don't plan on changing any of the things that Grants Pass has loved about Tee Time Coffee Shop since it opened in 1985. Such changes as breakfast all day and the addition of dinner hours will simply mean more of a good thing to Tee Time's many loyal customers. The restaurant, which has been the winner of local Best Breakfast awards many times, sets out an array of foods for creating a made-to-order breakfast. It includes eggs, pancakes, French toast, hash browns, sausage, ham and a meaty, thick-sliced bacon. Juice, cereal and bread choices abound. Omelets are custom affairs, filled with just the meats and vegetables you want. Deli-style sandwiches, burgers and a choice of soups and salads make Tee Time popular for lunch, too. Some groups come in seven days a week to enjoy the food, the golf theme and the intimate environment with its cozy log loft. David and Mihaela hail from Los Alamitos, California. After David's tour of duty in Iraq, they moved to Grants Pass in 2005 looking for a small business and a more relaxed lifestyle, eventually settling in to Tee Time in June 2007. They support many school activities as well as the Veterans Motorcycle Association. For a friendly neighborhood restaurant that puts the customer in charge of options, visit Tee Time Coffee Shop.

117 SW H Street, Grants Pass OR (541) 476-3346
www.teetimecoffeeshop.com

Sophia's Soup Factory–Medford

Conveniently located under the large green arch near the Tinseltown movie theater, Sophia's Soup Factory offers healthy, feel-good foods for visitors to the South Medford Center. Each day, the Soup Factory puts out at least 10 varieties of soups, served in an Artisan Bakery bread bowl upon request. Lighter fare includes an array of fresh green salads and a diverse selection of wraps made throughout the day. Hot and cold beverages and sweet desserts round out the selection. As a special treat for pasta lovers, Sheri Cain-Westerman and her staff make a cold pasta salad-of-the-day on weekdays in the spring and summer, using Sheri's own recipes. Sheri spent 20 years in finance and banking before becoming a café owner. Her skills in business management, attention to detail and strong customer service are evident at Sophia's Soup Factory, which makes even a first-time visitor feel welcome. The indoor seating offers respite from tougher weather conditions, but the outdoor patio makes a great place to relax April through September. Whether you call ahead to order take-out or visit to dine in, there are smiles waiting for you at Sophia's Soup Factory.

543 Medford Center, Medford OR (541) 776-6955

OREGON

Shopping
& Gifts

Holly & Ivy Gifts, Ltd.

When in search of the perfect Christmas tree ornament or gift, look no further than Holly & Ivy Gifts in Oregon City. Holly & Ivy Gifts operates out of the historic 1867 Fellows house built by ship builder and engineer E.B. Fellows. Since 1999, owners Shirley Smith and Diane Petrasso have decorated every available nook and cranny with ornaments from top brands including Old World Christmas, Annalee, Williraye, David Frykman, Department 56 Krinkles, and Heartwood Creek by Jim Shore. Perhaps even more famous than their ornament collection is their upside-down Christmas tree. Raised to the ceiling but supported from the floor, these trees are made to look as if they are hanging from the ceiling. The combination of elegance and space saving practicality make these trees a wildly popular item. In addition to the 35 to 40 decorated trees, they carry exceptional signs by Hanna's Handiworks. Open seasonally July fifth thru January fifth, come and enjoy cookies and spiced cider. During off-season they are open by appointment only for small or large groups. Whether you are gearing up to deck your halls with fantastic new ornaments or just want a dose of the holiday spirit during the off-season, visit Holly & Ivy Gifts where it's Christmas all year long.

416 S McLoughlin Boulevard, Oregon City OR (503) 723-5511
www.hollyandivygifts.com

Fish Lake
Photo by Clarice Rodriguez

Art from the Heart

Art from the Heart, a family-operated paint-your-own-ceramics studio, is owned by local artist Cindy Hashin. She began the business so that she could care for her mom and still work. "Our studio offers all the instruction that you'll need, from classes to individual assistance," Cindy says. Art from the Heart is stocked with hundreds of pieces of bisqueware for you to paint. Choose from functional and decorative kitchenware: mugs, plates, ovenware, teapots and wine caddies. Figurines include fairies, dragons and other critters. Picture frames, garden pieces and banks are available, plus candle holders, clocks, magnets, seasonal decorations and more. The purchase price of the piece you select includes the use of glazes, brushes, over 1,400 stamps, stencils, sea sponges and tools. The shop is stocked with hundreds of idea books and sample pieces. Your project is over-glazed and fired right in the studio and will be ready in five days or less. The studio is a popular place to hold birthday parties or bridal showers. There is no minimum age or group size. Art from the Heart has daily $10 project classes (cost is all inclusive) and technique classes. Friday and Saturday nights feature Date Night, Girls Night Out, Pizza Pizazz Night or Sushi Night. There are fresh flowers and a candle on every table, plus free coffee and iced tea available. This creative activity is appropriate from newborn to age 99. Infant handprints, foot prints and bottom prints are popular. High chairs, baby swings, play pens and more are available for those with little ones. "We love working with all age groups, here in our shop or at your location," Cindy says. Come on in, grab a brush or have a look around, and start having some fun at Art from the Heart, a place where you can create your own masterpiece to give as a gift, or keep for yourself.

1101 E Jackson Street, #102, Medford OR
(541) 245-6777 or (877) 245-6888
www.artfromtheheartmedford.com

All About Oregon

Even if you have been in Oregon for only a few days, that's long enough to answer the burning question: Are you a Duck or a Beaver? Once you have decided your allegiance to U of O or OSU, you will want to stop by All About Oregon in the Rogue Valley Mall to stock up on clothing and paraphernalia that bear the colors and symbols of your team. Of course, you could be diplomatic and buy a cap or sweatshirt of each. If you're looking for an introduction to everything that makes Oregon loveable, All About Oregon is the place to start. The rivalry between its colleges is just a small part of it. There's also the beauty of its Pendleton blankets and myrtlewood products. There's the taste of its wines and marionberry jams. Have you stood in awe under a towering Oregon pine? If so, you can be reminded of that feeling every time you drink from the mug that you buy at All about Oregon. The store also carries gorgeous myrtlewood bowls and pretty jewelry specific to the state. Say that you love Oregon by bringing home a few things from All About Oregon.

1600 N Riverside Avenue, #1083, Medford OR (541) 245-6801
www.oregonandmore.com

The Grange Co-op

Gone are the days when Old McDonald and his fellow farmers were the sole clientele of Grange Co-op. Although this business is still committed to serving the agricultural community with its wide selection of feeds, fertilizers and insecticides, its ever-expanding array of products attracts customers from all walks of life. Patrons drop by the location nearest their home to stock up on pet supplies, wild bird food and lawn products as well as patio furnishings, barbeques, yard and garden accessories. Depending on which of the six locations you visit, you may find additional items such as clothing, fencing and hardware, and a variety of nursery items. The Grange Co-op carries rental equipment for farm, ranch and lawn; the bulk petroleum program includes gasoline, diesel and heating fuel. A part of the Rogue Valley's agricultural history, the Grange Co-op was established in 1934 in Central Point when 99 farmers invested $10 each to purchase a truck, fuel and land. A grain elevator producing Rogue Quality Feed opened in 1947. Today, it is the only certified organic mill in Southern Oregon. Currently, The Grange Co-op currently employs a staff of nearly 200 people and boasts a voting membership of approximately 2,800. The Grange Co-op invites you to become a part of this Southern Oregon shopping tradition.

89 Alder Street, Central Point OR (main office) (541) 664-1261
www.grangecoop.com

Country Quilts

Quilting is a way of life for Marge Wall, who supports the creation of 350 quilts (with the help of many quilters) each year for her 20-year-old business. Whether you collect quilts or make quilts, you are going to love visiting Country Quilts in Jacksonville. You'll find quilts in king, queen, full and crib sizes. Marge can help in restoring old quilts or finishing projects. Marge does plenty of hand quilting, but machine quilting became a store specialty when she purchased a long-arm sewing machine in 1973. She uses the machine to complete her customer's pieced quilt tops. Marge was born and raised in neighboring Medford. She's been sewing quilts for 64 years and, in the long-standing tradition of American quilt makers, she creates many quilts for good causes. She puts together quilts for breast cancer survivors and creates more than 100 quilts each year for indigent children. You can buy quilt-themed statues from Jim Shore of North Carolina, quilt kits, embroidery kits, greeting cards and such quilt storage options as glass quilt chests and wooden quilt racks. Best of all, you can talk to people who love to quilt and take classes to increase your quilting know-how. Explore a traditional American craft enjoyed by 20 million Americans at Country Quilts.

214 E California Street, Jacksonville OR (541) 899-1972 or (877) 409-5466
www.countryquilts.com

Pacific Wine Club

Victoria and Ken Green love everything about fine wines. These two aren't just wine connoisseurs, they love all the myriad details that go into the making of a great wine, from where the grapes grow to the philosophies of winemaking that different vintners espouse. They've explored this passionate hobby since the 1970s, and finally turned it into a business in 2004—the Pacific Wine Club. Victoria and Ken decided to open the Pacific Wine Club in the Rogue Valley because of its proximity to Oregon, California and Washington wineries. They travel this tri-state area visiting small, family-owned vineyards to select what they believe are the best wines these exclusive boutique wineries have to offer. What's exciting is that they often find wines that are unavailable in stores, as well as wines of exceptional value, from only $10 a bottle to $40 library wines suitable for aging. They carry international wines as well. Victoria and Ken love introducing people to wine, and have a public tasting room where they hold wine tastings every week complete with descriptive educational notes. When you've made your selection, you can purchase wines by the bottle or the case. Every six weeks or so the Greens hold a wine and food pairing. They also have special membership options where you can receive distinguished wines on a monthly basis. Visit the website to sign up for a membership or place an order. If you love good wine, good company and people who really know how to enjoy it, then the Pacific Wine Club is the perfect way to share it.

3588 Heathrow Way, Medford OR (541) 245-3334 or (800) 792-6410
www.pacificwineclub.com

OREGON

Weddings
& Events

Ainsworth House & Gardens

Ainsworth House, a mansion built in 1851 as a wedding gift from a husband to his bride, sheds its romance upon you and your guests when you choose it as the setting for your wedding. Invite nature to your big day by holding the ceremony in the pine tree garden or in the gazebo nestled in a grove of locust trees. Many couples choose the front of the house itself as the backdrop for their nuptials. Draped with colors to match yours, the four pillars and porch express splendor and elegance. If it rains, all will sigh and then be cheered by the loveliness of the conservatory, where the ceremony can move gracefully in the event of inclement weather. For the reception, the Iris Package provides a buffet table and all other basic needs, including linens, table centers and colored napkins. You may upgrade to one of three other standard packages or personalize your reception. Able to accommodate up to 100 people, the Ainsworth House & Gardens is also a popular venue for staff meetings, conferences and retreats as well as surprise parties and company dinners. In fact, this stately mansion is right for any event where style, comfort and atmosphere matter. Say you cherish elegance and beauty by choosing the Ainsworth House & Gardens.

19130 Lot Whitcomb Drive, Oregon City OR (503) 656-1894
www.ainsworthhouse.net

Brookings
Photo by Clarice Rodriguez

Index by Treasure

Washington Index by City

University Place

Walla Walla

Wapato

Woodinville

Yakima